THE LITURGICAL YEAR

THE
LITURGICAL YEAR

Volume Two

LENT

by

Adrian Nocent, O.S.B.

translated by

Matthew J. O'Connell

THE LITURGICAL PRESS

COLLEGEVILLE   MINNESOTA

Cover design by Clement Schmidt.

Available in four volumes, THE LITURGICAL YEAR is the authorized English version of *Célébrer Jésus-Christ, L'année Liturgique*, published by Jean-Pierre Delarge, 10, rue Mayet, 75006 Paris, France.

Nihil obstat: William G. Heidt, O.S.B., S.T.D., *Censor deputatus.*
Imprimatur: ✢ George H. Speltz, D.D., Bishop of St. Cloud, October 12, 1977.

Printed in the United States of America. ISBN 0-8146-0963-5

HOLY LENT

This second volume on the liturgical year will follow the pattern adopted in the first volume. First we shall attempt to give the reader greater access to the theology of Lent by asking as honestly as we can whether that theology has anything to say to us and our contemporary concerns. Then we shall examine the texts used in the celebrations and the manner in which they complement one another. Finally, we shall point out the various ways in which Lent was celebrated by the Roman Church and other Churches in centuries past.

It hardly needs to be said that we cannot aim at completeness. Lent, after all, has five Sundays, each with a three-year cycle of readings; it also has a special celebration for each weekday. On the other hand, we think that what should be important for us is not so much the details but a mentality we ought to make our own. The purpose of acquiring this mentality is not to abandon our contemporary outlook and adopt an older one, but to enrich what we now have and to achieve a personal synthesis that can guide our lives.

It seems worth recalling here a point we made in Volume 1 with regard to the reading of Scripture in the liturgy. The liturgy must, of course, take into account the data of scientific exegesis and find support in it. At the same time, however, if we wish to grasp the message being conveyed in the liturgical proclamation of a passage from the Gospels, we must keep in mind that the liturgical vision of such a passage is not the same as the exegetical vision of the same text. One and the same text receives different emphases when it is proclaimed in different celebrations, since the other two readings provide a new context and point to the primary meaning the Gospel has in a particular liturgy. In other words, the liturgical season and the first two readings of the Mass — or at least one of these two readings — will lead us to read the Gospel from a special point of view. This does not mean that we elaborate a new exegesis each time the same passage recurs; it means simply that the Church approaches the text from a new angle of vision. This, at any rate, is the way we shall be looking at the texts in each of the celebrations we are studying.

CONTENTS

THE LENTEN SEASON

THE LENTEN SEASON

BIBLICO-LITURGICAL REFLECTIONS ON LENT

1. THE ANTHROPOLOGY OF LENT

What God creates is divine

We are so used to seeing the defects and faults of the beings and the things around us that we find it difficult to pass an accurate judgment on the value, meaning, and purpose of creation. It may also be that a certain kind of religious education and a poorly understood liturgy have contributed to our having a rather pessimistic view of the created world.

On the first Sunday of Lent, for example, the first reading (Cycle A) tells us of the Fall, and thus of the inability of the first human couple to resist temptation (Gen. 2:7-9; 3:1-7). When we hear it often enough, we end up thinking that it is describing man's natural condition. Once we acquire this mentality, life becomes difficult. Either we succumb to a kind of fatalism with regard to sin and accustom ourselves to accepting the disastrous situation of sin and its effects, or else we live with a constant sense of overwhelming anxiety and of the shadowy character of human existence.

Are such attitudes a proper response to the true meaning of creation? Certainly not. But, on the other hand, can we be surprised to find people abandoning in despair a religion that is presented to them as a kind of poultice applied to an incurable wound, a religion that looks upon man as a fallen being, a weak thing who is offered Christian morality as a crutch or a form of opium for the people?

We must admit that some presentations of Lent utterly fail to give men a proper sense of what they really are in the midst of God's creation. The formula, "Remember, man, that thou art dust, and unto dust thou shalt return," which for centuries accompanied the imposition of ashes, was not calculated to give the recipient a positive vision of Lent, any more than was the account of the Fall, read on the first Sunday of Lent. If a person has only this one-sided vision of things, he will see man and his history as a failure and will not be encouraged to try to patch up a situation so radically compromised.

If, then, we are to understand the real situation of man and of the world, we must tackle the problem afresh. We must bear in mind, however, that the Church presents her interpretation of the world's history only to believers. It is not that she refuses to speak of it to others, but rather that in her liturgy she handles these problems, not as merely intellectual challenges, but as problems whose answers are to influence the way we live. Consequently, when she describes the Fall, her concern is to make us understand our human condition, not merely or primarily as wretched, but also and above all as marked by the great certainty that has power to deliver us from our wretchedness; for she shows us that God is capable of creating only what is divine.

The liturgy, like the Bible, is therefore offering us not an explanation but a sign; it tells us that creation is a language in which God expresses himself. We might even say that creation is a process wherein God reveals himself. And often he reveals himself as a Father.

We can see immediately that the facile contrast between the distant, terrible God of the Old Testament and the God of the New Testament who is so close to us has no solid foundation. Ever since the final age, the time of salvation, began, the Church has been urging us to read the account in Genesis, even while she shows us the Father of our Lord Jesus Christ. The fact that she can do both without any sense of a tension between them shows us what she is about. She is not presenting us with a religious philosophy or a humanism or a method for developing man's powers. No, she is urging upon us a bold project legitimated by a command of Christ himself: "You, therefore, must be perfect, as your heavenly Father is perfect" (Matthew 5:48).

The account in Genesis tells us that we are made in God's image. Here, in the New Testament, we are told more specifically just what this image is. A paradox, is it not? On the one hand, a God who is the inaccessible, transcendent Creator; on the other, ever since the time of Abraham, a gracious, condescending God who draws closer and closer to us and to whom man in turn can draw ever closer, to the point where he receives the command to imitate him. But the apparent contradiction is resolved by the fact that it is Christ who gives this order. For he is our salvation, and in him we discover the humanity of God. St. John records these most meaningful words of Christ: "He who has seen me has seen the Father" (John 14:9).

Consequently, when the Church reads the account of creation to us each year during the Easter Vigil, she does not think of it as an isolated episode, but thinks rather of the culmination of the revelation begun in that account. She thinks of the Trinity, into whose life we enter by way of the humanity of the Risen Christ. Though the account in Genesis speaks only of God as Creator and Father of the universe, the Church has before her eyes the whole history of salvation. In the account of creation she contemplates the germinal presence of all the great and wonderful deeds that God will perform for the salvation of the world, especially the sending of his Son and the activity of his Spirit. This Creator-God, Father of the universe, is the God whom Jesus will show us and who is already revealing himself in the initial act of creation.

How can we belong to the people of God and become part of the "wonderful deeds" that mark this people's history if we do not believe in the fatherhood of God as revealed by his Son? The Church indicates to us how the new creation is already implied in the account of the first creation. For, in the story of Jesus' baptism, we see the Spirit descending on the waters, just as he did at the beginning of the world, except that in his descent at the Jordan he officially appoints Christ, the new Adam, to his messianic role.

The Christian has to relearn that he belongs to the family of God. A more habitual reading of Paul and John will give him a sense of his divine sonship and of his divinization by the filial Spirit of God's Son. At the same time, he will be able to understand the strength of the bonds that link him to Christ, and the transcendent unity whereby all Christians are gathered into one body so that they may share in the very life of God.

Yet, even this renewed awareness may remain abstract or be inspired simply by man's age-old yearning for immortality unless, with the help of the Old Testament, it recovers a sense of its authentic human roots. The family of God is, first of all, Israel. When the Son of God became a man, he was "born of a woman, born under the law" (Gal. 4:4), and was "descended from David according to the flesh" (Rom. 1:3). The entire people of God was of one race with its Christ, and every word in the Bible is a stammering of his Word. If, then, we are to belong to the race or family of God, we must belong by adoption to the race or family of the spiritual Israel.[1]

The inaccessible God in our midst

Such a reading of Genesis evidently looks beyond the level of mere story. It shows us what our God is like and how we are to relate to him. We glimpse the face of God, but that face, close to us though it is, is never fully unveiled.

Thus, to be aware of God's nearness and humanness does not mean that we abandon our attitude of respect, reverential fear, and adoration. We retain always a clear vision of our total dependence on him whose "thoughts are not our thoughts" and who always remains incomprehensible and inaccessible. The Church does not hesitate to remind the faithful of this again and again. "Perhaps the most difficult thing required of the Christian is to accept the inaccessibility of God. But when he does so, he will also understand the nearness and the humanness of God."[2]

Father of the universe

There is a further point that we cannot pass over in silence, for unless we grasp it, we may radically misunderstand the plan of redemption and the life of the Church. The point is this: The Church does not preach to us a God who is the Creator of the isolated individual, but a God who is also Creator of all other human beings and of the entire universe. Adam was placed in paradise as a person intimately involved with the beings that surrounded him. In fact, in the view of the Fathers, God created the whole of mankind as a single totality, and it is this unity, which extends to the uttermost depths of every being, that explains how one man's sin could implicate the whole human race. But the same unity also explains how redemption could be accomplished by the sacrifice of the new Adam: "By the sacrifice of Christ the first man was saved, that man who is in us all."[3]

The Christian cannot, therefore, have the right attitude toward his Creator unless he stands before him with a soul that is open not only to other human beings but to all created things, animate and inanimate, and indeed to the universe in its entirety. For the latter, like man himself, has been redeemed. To put it another way, it is the whole man, and not just his soul, that God has created and that Christ has redeemed; and the resurrection of the flesh implies in turn the restoration of the universe as a whole. In his Letter to the Romans, St. Paul gives us his thinking on these matters, and there is no reason to believe that he is simply indulging in metaphor.

> I consider that the sufferings of this present time are not worth comparing with the glory that is to be revealed in us. For the creation waits with eager long-

ing for the revealing of the sons of God; for the creation was subjected to futility, not of its own will but
by the will of him who subjected it in hope; because
the creation itself will be set free from its bondage to
decay and obtain the glorious liberty of the children
of God. We know that the whole creation has been
groaning in travail together until now; and not only
the creation, but we ourselves, who have the first
fruits of the Spirit, groan inwardly as we wait for
adoption as sons, the redemption of our bodies (Rom.
8:18-23).

It is important for Christians to bear in mind that salvation embraces our whole being, body no less than soul, and
also the whole of creation, including all that is subhuman in
it. In setting our sights on the definitive kingdom to come,
we must therefore not separate into watertight compart-
ments the spiritual and the fleshly, the soul and the body,
the things of the spirit and material things. The world to
come presupposes that all the various orders of being are
given their proper value and brought into perfect harmony
and balance.

Man is indeed the center of creation, and everything else
was created for his sake. This means, however, that subhuman creation has a place in an overall unity willed by God.
It means, too, that Adam was put into the world as a cosmic
personage, one linked to the rest of creation by an ontologi-
cal bond. From the very beginning of Lent, therefore, the
Church already has in mind the night of the Easter Vigil,
when she will read the opening pages of Genesis to those
who are about to be buried with Christ in death in order
that they may rise with him to new life. Then the newly
baptized will understand those pages with minds reborn.

The Fall

We must acknowledge, however, that the Fall is indeed a
central focus of the Lenten liturgy. It is not the only theme,

as we have seen, but certainly the fact of the Fall and its consequences are everywhere present in the celebrations of this season.

It is, then, the Church's wish that her faithful, present and future, should be confronted with the fact of sin. Here again, however, the Book of Genesis cannot be properly understood except in the context provided by the other books of Scripture. In point of fact, it was only through concrete experience and the enlightenment bestowed by the Spirit that Israel came to understand original sin.[4] A series of disillusionments, cataclysms, and personal and collective failures made men aware of the existence of a single, first sin in which all shared. St. Paul would later say that "both Jews and Greeks are under the power of sin" (Rom. 3:9) and that "one man's trespass led to condemnation for all men" (Rom. 5:18).

We are all prisoners of sin. The Old Testament had various descriptive words for sin, but gradually it tended toward a single, unequivocal understanding of it. Sin is an action that fails of its end. More concretely, it is an action in which we fail with regard to another person. It is "a violation of the bond which unites persons to each other, an act which, because it does not respect this organic bond, only affects the person concerned by injuring him."[5]

Yet, there is nothing pessimistic about the liturgy's very realistic vision of a world destroyed by sin. The aim is rather that the Christian should become aware of his sinful state and have a concrete grasp of the deficiencies, failures, and humiliating limitations of his wounded nature. The liturgy does not indulge in extremist presentations that provide preachers with ready-made sermons in which the period before the Fall is described in language from the *Arabian Nights*, while the ages after the Fall are uniformly black and catastrophic. The Church knows only too well, from long experience, that such contrasts arouse only a passing emotion and cannot lead to radical changes in the soul's outlook. Something more is needed for a genuine conversion.

Preoccupation with paradise

If the Church likes to tell us of the paradisal state (it is a frequent theme of the Fathers), she does not do so for the pleasure of reminding us of what we have lost, but to remind us that we must return to that paradise. If we are to properly comprehend the whole paschal liturgy and its rich typology, and if we are to understand properly the spirit in which the Church will reread the account of paradise in Genesis to those about to be baptized during the Easter Vigil, we must begin now to enter into her mentality as she proclaims the story at the moment when she wishes us to begin to live, with her, the history of salvation. Paradise, in her way of thinking, is not so much a paradise that has been lost as it is a paradise we are to regain and, in fact, have already regained. In describing to us paradise when it was first created, the Church already has in mind the words Christ will speak to the Good Thief while hanging on the Cross: "Truly, I say to you, today you will be with me in Paradise" (Luke 23:43).

This is a point we must insist on: The Church cannot read the narrative of creation and paradise to us without taking into account all that happened later on, any more than she can fail to remember at every moment what she is and where she comes from. She is herself both an image of paradise and the beginning of paradisal fulfillment. In an ancient text entitled *The Odes of Solomon*, which may have been used in liturgical celebrations, the splendor of that regained paradise, of which the Church is an image, is described in poetic terms. The text tells us that our paradise is now to be found in Christ:

> Eloquent water from the fountain of the Lord was given me to drink; I drank and was intoxicated by the living water that does not die. I abandoned the madness widespread on the earth, stripped it from me and cast it away. The Lord gave me his own new garment and clad me in his light. I drew glad breath in the pleasant breeze of the Lord. I adored the Lord be-

cause he is glorious, and I said: Happy they who have their roots in the earth and for whom there is a place in his paradise.[6]

The reader will recognize in the sentence "The Lord gave me his own new garment and clad me in his light" an allusion to the grace of baptism, which consists, according to St. Paul, in "putting on Christ." And, in fact, it is baptism into the death and resurrection of Christ that fulfills the prophecy: "Today you will be with me in Paradise." The Fathers vie with one another in developing the theme of the return to paradise through baptism. Similarly, a favorite motif in the mosaics that decorate the early baptistries is the portrayal of paradise, whose running ("living") waters symbolize baptism. The sheep drinking at the stream are the faithful who have been made one within the bosom of the Church, and among them walks Christ, the new Adam.

Everything said of Adam in the Genesis narratives must be carefully noted, since the Fathers like to compare him with the new Adam as with his infinitely superior counterpart. The parallel between the two Adams, so dear, for example, to St. Irenaeus, leads in turn to a parallel between Eve and the new Eve, Mary, and between Eve and the Church. Thus, the birth of Eve from Adam's side becomes the image of the Church's birth, as Spouse of Christ, from the side of the new Adam.

Sin in the light of redemption

Evidently the Church, in her reflection on sin, does not concentrate primarily on the Adam who fell, but sees sin rather in the light of the redemption wrought by Christ. The Church here shows a healthy realism, for though she wants us to be fully aware of all that sin implies, she refuses to make sin the center of religion. The focus of Christianity is not on sin but on Christ who conquered sin and death. Consequently, in the theology of Lent the promise of redemption is more important than sin. Christianity is not a

dualist religion that sees the good and evil spirits locked in
conflict; it is the religion of the God who overcomes all evil.

Original sin?

For quite some time now, we have been uneasy with the
concept of "original sin." Our uneasiness has two causes:
the concept of original sin seems to undermine our human
dignity, and it seems to involve a basic injustice. The first
thing the modern world does, therefore, when it turns its
attention to Christianity, is to reject the idea of original
sin. By so doing it involves itself in all sorts of misunderstandings about Christianity, but at least its attitude is
an intelligible one. For there can be no doubt that the
presentation of original sin has too often been morbid, and
that it is morbid at times even today. Few concepts have in
fact been so distorted and ruined by countless misunderstandings as has the concept of original sin.

On the other hand, in order to repress the anxiety that the
concept of original sin can arouse, people at times transform
the Genesis narrative into a bedtime story for clever or
naughty children. Once it is turned into a myth, it is much
easier to reject the reality that has thus been cleverly hidden.

We do not intend to enter here into the thicket of
theological discussion on original sin. After all, the Christian who lacks specialized training nonetheless has the
right to an intelligent grasp of the essentials of a problem
that affects him very deeply. Let us therefore leave aside
the question of what elements each of the various sources
of Genesis 2–3 has contributed to the story. We may also
leave aside the question of whether "man" who sinned was
an individual; even in the story itself, after all, two human
beings sin!

Before proceeding, however, we should advert to the fact
that the word "Adam" is not a proper name applied to a
single person but signifies "man," in the sense of mankind
or all men. The Hebrew for "Adam" occurs 539 times, and

in every case the translators are justified in translating it simply as "man." Ezekiel, for example, uses "Adam" several times, and the translation "man" is quite legitimate. Thus, Ezekiel 19:3, "he became a young lion, and he learned to catch prey; he devoured men"; a more literal translation would be: "he devoured Adam." The reader may also consult Ezekiel 20:11, 13, 21; 25:13; etc. (and see Genesis 7:21; 9:5).

To repeat, we may leave this problem aside; for even if we maintain that a couple sinned, or even a multiplicity of couples, this creates no real difficulty. The important, and the more difficult, thing is to put our finger on the essential theology of Genesis 2–3. Adequate treatment would, of course, require a whole book. We can at least give a short synthesis, a series of points that can provide food for reflection and stir our interest in pursuing the question further, while supplying in the interim a sufficient foundation for our vital experience of the liturgical season we are here endeavoring to understand.

We noted earlier that what God creates is divine. This means that when he created man, his only thought was to create a being that would eventually share in the divine nature. The only qualification to this is that God wanted this creature to share in the divine nature in a free and fully personal way. In other words, man must freely accept such a participation and attain it along the lines set down by the Creator. There was to be nothing automatic in this creation of a divinized human being; man must freely consent to his divinization, he must win through to his divinized state and cooperate fully with it.

There can be no doubt, of course, that every gift is from God and that the whole work of divinization, like that of creation itself, depends entirely on him. The point we are emphasizing here is that when God created man, he was not creating a mere thing; man must cooperate in shaping his own being and in making himself what he is meant to be in the divine plan: *the image and likeness of God.* When God created man, he set participation in the divine nature before him as a goal, but he did not simply impose it on man without man's consent. This means that the possibility of failure is inherent in the plan of creation.

At the same time, we must remember that in God's plan human beings were endowed with supernatural powers. Man then lost these powers by refusing to act as God wished. But the Lord continues to invite us to live a life like his. That life is a possibility for us; it is not forced upon us, since a being compelled to be divine would really not be divine after all! The invitation and the possibility, however, are freely given by God, just as the grace to follow the invitation and to become "divine" is likewise God's gift.

There was, then, a catastrophe at the beginning of human history. Mankind lost the gift of divinization that it had refused to accept, despite the clarity of mind and the strength of will with which men were then endowed. After that catastrophe each man born, without being radically corrupt (as Luther maintained), would be born into a world that is sick in every respect: physically, physiologically, intellectually, and spiritually. Man no longer possesses sufficient strength to confront and master the world into which he is born. He must indeed grow and gradually achieve divinization or else reject it; yet, if left to his own resources, he is incapable of entering upon the true way that leads to divinization.

Every man depends upon the human race, past and present, of which he is a part. The individual is not an isolated entity; every enrichment and every perversion of man is social in character. We do not inherit the personal guilt of our family ancestors, but we do inherit their defects. The inclination to evil is perennial; it antecedes the present state of mankind. We cannot but admit that of all the beings that make up the world, man alone has the power to destroy himself, and "evil" consists in this self-destruction. Evil is the contrary of creation; it is opposed to creation, not as one being to another, but as negation. At the same time, however, this evil flows from man's will, and man is responsible for it.

Evil today

Here we have the permanent stumbling block: How is the existence of God, who is necessarily good and just, compatible with the evil in the world? Of what value have the long centuries of Christianity been?

In earlier times men were tempted to solve the basic problem by dualism: an ultimate source of evil alongside an ultimate source of good. Our contemporaries adopt a more radical solution: atheism. The existence of evil has, of course, always been regarded as the clinching argument against Christianity, but this is only because evil has been misunderstood.

Take, for example, death. According to a pagan vision of reality, death is evil supreme and unqualified. Consequently, the opposition between paganism and Christianity emerges most clearly at this point. For the Christian, death is not an annihilation of the person, but only a stage or phase in the ongoing completion of the creation of man. Therefore, there is no contradiction between death and the goodness of God. On the contrary, we may even say that death is a manifestation of God's goodness, inasmuch as he thereby continues his work of creation despite the resistance offered by man.

The same can be said for all the failures and setbacks that mark man's life. There is genuine "failure" only when we adopt the worldly perspective that makes "success" all-important. In the Christian vision, "success" can be measured only in relation to a final, future destiny. Evil, then, can also be defined only in terms of the definitive goal to which man is called.

Sin and reparation

God is concerned about man, but if he is to divinize man, he must allow man the responsibility for his actions. Divinization is always the end that God has in view, but he gives man the means of freely attaining that end. This is the point of the Adam-Christ antithesis that is so favored a theme in the New Testament (Mark 1:13; Rom. 5:12-21; 1 Cor. 15:22, 45-49).

We shall have occasion later on, in connection with the first Sunday of Lent, to attend to Mark 1:13, the temptation of Christ by Satan. The text clearly intends to contrast Christ, as head of a new human race, with the first Adam, and to show Christ as overcoming where the first Adam succumbed. The parallelism also involves both Adam and Jesus being tempted by Satan. We may think that the Adam-Christ parallel accounts for Luke's tracing the geneaology of Jesus all the way back to Adam (Luke 3:38) and for his placing the genealogy immediately before his account of the temptation (4:1-13).[7]

We are hereby invited to read Genesis with reparation and the new creation in mind. There is an air of triumph about the way St. Paul develops the contrast between Christ and Adam. We can sense it in Romans 5:12-21, which comprises the second reading for the first Sunday of Lent (Cycle A). Where sin abounded, grace has abounded still more. Adam was a figure of him who was to come (Rom. 5:14), that is, of the Christ who has bestowed life-giving grace on all mankind (Rom. 5:15). Grace is universal in its compass, so that wherever death laid its hand, there shall be resurrection (1 Cor. 15:22); and those who rise to eternal life will have a body that is glorious and incorruptible (1 Cor. 15:44-49). At that point we will lay aside our likeness to the mortal, corruptible Adam and acquire the likeness to Christ and his spiritual body.

St. Paul here cites Genesis 2:7 in the Septuagint version: "The first man Adam became a living being," and then he draws his parallel: "the last Adam became a life-giving spirit" (1 Cor. 15:45). In our material, earthly bodies we resemble the first Adam; in our glorious, heavenly bodies we shall resemble the last Adam (see 1 Cor. 15:48).

The optimism of Lent

Lent, then, offers us an optimistic vision of the world; for though it sees the world as sinful because of mankind's beginnings, it always links sin to redemption, and the destruction of the world to its renewal.

To those not yet converted, Lent offers entry into the new creation through baptism. To those already baptized, it proposes a reformation of life and thus an advance toward the divinization that is already theirs in principle but which they must make truly their own in an ever more conscious and radical way.

Sincerity and honesty

Lent thus summons us to something more than an artificial asceticism or a set of supplementary observances. It asks of all men that they have the courage sincerely and honestly to reform their lives and to judge where they are, what they are seeking, and how much they have really understood of Christian life. These forty days lived with Israel in the desert, with Moses, with Elias, and above all with Christ are a time of deep spiritual significance.

We all know that we must face temptation. We all know, too, that we are capable of overcoming with Christ. The question is, Do we sincerely and honestly want to overcome? The fact that we are capable of overcoming does not do away with our inherent weakness or with the various physiological and psychological influences at work in us. It does mean, however, that we are not tempted beyond our strength.

There is, then, a sense of risk, but also an optimism because we are assured of victory, provided we use the means Christ offers us. For the person preparing for baptism, Lent is a time for the deliberate acquisition of these means. For those who are already Christians, it is a time for learning anew how to use the means wisely and to develop or renew them. In short, Lent is a time when man is to collaborate with God in creating something divine.

2. THE EXPERIENCE OF LENT IN THE FATHERS

It is evident that the Fathers of the Church attached great importance to Lent. In fact, we find it quite normal that they should have been preoccupied with this season of penance. After all, was it not part and parcel of the religious mentality of their times, somewhat as the camel's-hair garment and the meals of grasshoppers and wild honey were part of the religious personality of John the Baptist? The Fathers lived in an age that called for a strict and rather dour asceticism; harsh temperaments required a harsh asceticism.

Many are inclined, therefore, to let the dust of history rest undisturbed on patristic ideas and attitudes, for it is assumed that these must be irrelevant to people today. And yet, if we familiarize ourselves with some of the Fathers, we will soon find that the human and spiritual physiognomy of the Christians of that time is surprisingly similar to our own.

It is remarkable that our contemporaries almost always associate Catholicism of the early centuries with men and women of iron temperament, armor-clad souls, unremitting energy, and unimaginative minds. Fasting and mortification seem to have been so much a part of that world that we would be almost scandalized to discover any laxity in the practice of these virtures. Their absence would introduce a false shading into the picture.

But the picture is in fact one that we have simply created for ourselves with little if any foundation; it represents only our own preconceived ideas. It is an almost totally false picture, drawn in unconscious justification of our contemporary rejection of asceticism. The Christians of the patristic age were in reality very much like us and the Christians around us today. The homilies of the Fathers offer clear proof of this. Indeed, the topicality and relevance of these compositions are perhaps the most striking thing about them. We are indeed the contemporaries of the Fathers; they speak to us, and no sincere Catholic can regard himself as dispensed from heeding them.

A balanced asceticism

Our contemporaries will find the ascetic demands of the Fathers acceptable because the Fathers are very much concerned that this asceticism be both down-to-earth and utterly permeated by the authentic Christian spirit. For the Fathers, practices as such are secondary and a means to an end. Practices are valid only on certain conditions. The first condition is union with our brothers through fraternal love; this is to find concrete expression in the practice of almsgiving. The second condition is authentic union with God through prayer that is selfless and that derives its power from the dispositions created by fasting. If these two conditions are not met, the asceticism of fasting degenerates into selfishness and self-delusion; it becomes a means of turning in, unconsciously, on oneself and creates an atmosphere of spiritual inauthenticity.

Prayer and fasting

Prayer is the chief activity of Lent, and Lent is a time for renewal in the practice of prayer. The spiritual life, after all, is a coherent whole. A period of fasting requires that we give ourselves to prayer. In turn, the ascetical effort to liberate the self from the downward pull of the flesh and the effort to go out of ourselves to our neighbor in generous fraternal charity will affect the quality and power of our prayer. St. Augustine observes:

> No one can doubt, then, that fasting is profitable; for when a man imposes on himself the burden of fasting, he shows that he really wants what he is asking for.

That is why it is said that "prayer is good when accompanied by fasting" (Tob. 12:8). Therefore, prayer
seeks fasting for a companion so that it may be heard.[8]

In a Lenten sermon St. Augustine told his hearers:

By almsgiving and fasting we add wings of fervor to
our prayers so that they may more easily fly up and
reach God. . . . Through humility and charity, fasting
and almsgiving, abstaining and forgiving, avoiding
evil and doing good, our prayer seeks peace and
achieves it. For such prayer takes its flight on the
wings lent it by these virtues and easily reaches
heaven, where Christ our Peace has gone on ahead.[9]

The same image occurs in another Lenten sermon: "During
these days our prayer rises aloft because it is borne up by
pious almsgiving and austere fasting."[10]

It is clear that St. Augustine closely associates fasting
with prayer and almsgiving. In his view, Lent is to be
chiefly a time for prayer, but also a period in which prayer
is greatly enriched and refined because it receives the
"food" it needs if it is to rise up to God: "Prayer has a food
of its own which it is bidden to take without interruption.
Therefore, let it always fast from hatred and feed on
love."[11]

Brotherly love

While St. Augustine, in his Lenten asceticism, insists
very much on the quality of prayer during this season, St.
Leo the Great concentrates more on the brotherly love that
is given concrete expression in almsgiving. Almost all of St.
Leo's twelve sermons on Lent that have come down to us
speak of love, the forgiveness of offenses, and almsgiving.

Therefore, beloved, mindful of our weakness that
makes us readily fall into all kinds of sins, let us not
neglect this powerful remedy and most efficacious
means of healing our wounds. Let us forgive so that

we may be forgiven; let us grant others the pardon we seek for ourselves. We pray for forgiveness; let us not seek revenge.[12]

The Saint reminds his hearers of the custom by which emperors released prisoners in honor of the Passion and resurrection of the Lord:

> Therefore let the Christian peoples imitate their princes and be spurred by the royal example to a domestic clemency. The laws that govern private life should not be more severe than those that govern public life. Forgive sins, break fetters, wipe out offenses, and eliminate vengefulness so that the sacred feast may be marked by pardon human and divine, and thus find everyone joyous and beyond reproach.[13]

> Beloved, remove the causes of discord and the thorns of enmity. Let hatred cease and rivalries disappear, and let all the members of Christ meet in loving unity.[14]

The concluding theme in most of St. Leo's Lenten sermons is that we should forgive the offenses done us by others so that we may ourselves win pardon from God. This great Pope constantly urges his hearers to pray the Our Father and emphasizes the fact that what we say in that prayer imposes an obligation on us, for it sets a condition for the forgiveness we ask of God. "If we say, 'Forgive us our debts as we forgive our debtors,' but do not act according to our words, we fasten heavy chains upon ourselves."[15]

Our forgiveness must be given not only to our peers but to our subordinates: "Beyond any doubt, you may promise yourselves God's sure mercy if, in dealing with those subject to you, you make every offense an occasion for pardon."[16]

St. Leo begs mercy for offenders and, for all his reserve, does not hesitate to make an emotional appeal: "If anyone is keeping a man prisoner for some offense or other, let him

remember that he is himself a sinner! If he wishes to receive forgiveness for himself, let him rejoice that he has
someone whom he himself may forgive." [17] "What a person
decides with regard to his neighbor, he also decides, by
that very fact, for himself." [18]

Such forgiveness of our fellow-men is in no sense de-
meaning. On the contrary, it is an action by which we share
in the exercise of a divine power. "Forgiveness of one's
fellow-men is a perfectly just and good action whereby a
human being shares in God's own power, so as to determine by his own free act the sentence God will pass on him
and to bind the Lord to the same judgment that he passes
on his fellow servant." [19]

St. Augustine turns to similar themes in his seventh sermon on Lent, which is wholly devoted to the subject of
brotherly love and the forgiveness of offenses. The sermon
begins with a vigorous assertion of the fact that the soul's
salvation, as it struggles against the many temptations be-
setting it, depends on forgiving the offenses done to it by
others:

> These holy days which we spend in the observance of
> Lent make it our duty to speak to you of the harmony
> that must reign among brothers. Anyone who has any
> quarrel with another must put an end to it lest an end
> be put to him. . . . We have made an agreement with
> God and have submitted to a condition that must be
> fulfilled if our debt to him is to be written off.[20]

The forgiveness of offenses, according to Augustine, is
necessary if we are to attain illumination and freedom of
spirit. Appealing to 1 John 3:15, "Anyone who hates his
brother is a murderer," the Saint tells his hearers: "He who
hates his brother walks, goes out and in, and travels where
he wishes; he seems burdened by no chains, locked in no
prison, but he is nonetheless enchained by his crime. Do
not believe that he is not in prison; his prison is his own
heart!" [21]

Almsgiving

One of the most concrete forms of brotherly love is almsgiving, a practice inseparable from authentic fasting. But almsgiving is by no means limited to the material action whereby one gives away one's money. St. Augustine warns against such a narrow interpretation: "It is your duty to intensify your almsgiving during these days. . . . There is a further work of mercy in which one takes nothing from one's store or purse, but expels from the heart that which it is more harmful to keep than to give away. I am referring to the anger one stores up in one's heart against one's brother." [22]

Almsgiving, joined to fasting, also makes possible our union with God in prayer. Commenting on what Isaiah says of fasting (58:3), the Saint concludes: "These are the two wings on which prayer mounts up to God: forgiveness of offenses and alms to the needy." [23]

When St. Augustine speaks of almsgiving, he makes it a condition for union with God in prayer. St. Leo the Great looks upon it rather as a work of mercy that wins us God's forgiveness. "Let us not pass the poor man by, deaf to his groans, but with ready good will show mercy to the needy so that we ourselves may find mercy at the Judgment." [24]

The duty of almsgiving is not limited to helping those who share our faith: "Though the poverty of the faithful should be alleviated first, yet those who have not yet accepted the gospel are to be pitied in their distress, for we must love the one nature that all men share." [25]

To give alms is to participate in the generosity of God himself: "Nothing is worthier of man than to imitate his Creator and to be, as far as he can, the agent of the divine work." [26]

The tenth and eleventh sermons on Lent both end with an exhortation to almsgiving. When man acts mercifully, Pope St. Leo tells us, God sees his own image realized in him. "No zeal on the part of the faithful gives greater joy to God than that which is devoted to his poor. Where he finds a concern for mercy, he sees his own love imaged forth in man."[27]

In a paradoxical turn of phrase, the Saint makes it clear that in his eyes fasting involves far more than mere abstinence from food: "Let fasting Christians grow fat through the distribution of alms and the care of the poor. Let a man give to the weak and the poor what he refuses to spend on his own pleasures."[28]

St. Leo's exhortations during Lent are all marked by his major concerns: brotherly love, forgiveness, and almsgiving. He evidently thinks that his Christians may easily slip into misunderstandings. Perhaps there was danger that a formalistic practice of exterior fasting would become an excuse for a tepid spiritual life. St. Leo does not want this to happen, and he points out the danger in straightforward fashion: "Let us engage in this solemn fast with alert faith and celebrate it, not as a sterile abstinence from food (as bodily weakness or the disease of avarice may suggest), but as a form of great-hearted generosity."[29]

The Saint never tires of emphasizing the real nature and purpose of fasting: "Our fasting does not consist merely in abstinence from food; in fact, there is no profit in depriving the body of nourishment unless the spirit turns from injustice and the tongue abstains from quarreling."[30] To fail in this further abstinence would be hypocrisy, and Pope Leo does not hesitate to agree with non-Christians who criticize Christians in this regard: "Unbelievers will rightly criticize us, and the tongues of the wicked will have a weapon against religion if we fast but our manner of life lacks the purity that perfect abstinence requires" (*ibid.*).

In these pages we have been drawing only upon sermons dealing with Lent. There are, of course, many other sources we could cite, but these will be enough to show how realistically two important Latin Fathers deal with fasting and how much at one they are with our contemporaries in their demand for sincerity and the elimination of all formalism. In a moment, as we endeavor to put our finger on the essential point in fasting, we shall see how a John Chrysostom, for example, likewise rejects formalism.

Fasting without fasting?

In a homily preached on Easter, St. John Chrysostom gives us his interpretation of fasting. He uses the language of paradox, but his hearers must certainly have grasped the essential point he is making.

> During the period when you were fasting, I told you it was possible not to fast while fasting; now I tell you it is possible to fast while not fasting! Is this a riddle? Let me put the truth to you more plainly. How is it possible not to fast while fasting? By abstaining from food but not from sin! And how is it possible to fast while not fasting? By enjoying food while having no taste for sin. This is a far better kind of fasting, and easier as well.[31]

We find the same thought and even some of the same language in St. Leo the Great: "During this time a Christian should do with greater care and devotion what he should be doing at all times. Then the forty-day fast which we have from apostolic tradition will be marked not only by abstinence from food but also and especially by abstinence from sin."[32] St. Augustine uses the same language on several occasions: "If we are truly to fast, we must abstain, above all, from every sin."

Care of the soul

Lent is, most basically, a time of care for the soul. Not only the newcomer to the Catholic faith must be concerned with the growth of his own soul; every Catholic, however long baptized, must have the same concern, since no one is assured of indefectibility. Speaking of those who are soon to be baptized and addressing himself to those already baptized, St. Leo points out of the value and necessity for all of such concern for the soul:

> The former [catechumens] need it [the fast] in order to receive what they do not have as yet; the latter [the baptized] need it in order to preserve what they have

received. For the Apostle says: "Let anyone who
thinks that he stands take heed lest he fall." . . . Let
us therefore make good use, beloved, of this most
propitious of seasons to polish the mirror of our hearts
with greater care.[33]

Fasting consists first and foremost in abstaining from sin,
but it is also to be noted that fasting, in turn, "rescues from
sin those who fast and leads them to ineffable pleasures."[34]

In a homily on the first chapter of Genesis, St. John
Chrysostom quotes St. Paul's Second Letter to the Corinthians: "Though our outer nature is wasting away, our inner
nature is being renewed every day" (4:16), and comments:
"Fasting is the food of the soul. As bodily food makes the
body fat, so fasting makes the soul healthier and makes its
wings light so that it may be borne aloft and be capable of
contemplating what is above."[35]

St. Augustine likewise tells us what he thinks the effects
of Lenten abstinence on the soul are:

When the soul is freed from the burden of excessive
food and drink, it comes to know itself better. For, as
a man cannot tell from a dirty mirror what he really
looks like, so when he is dragged down by food and
drink he thinks himself to be other than he really is.
But when the body is brought to a proper state
through fasting, the soul comes to know itself and
realizes how devotedly it should follow the Redeemer.[36]

In the last analysis, the essential purpose of fasting is that
the soul may be more perfectly configured to the crucified
Christ. Here we have the specific meaning of the Lenten
fast. St. Augustine writes: "Let us also fast and humble our
souls as we near the time when the Teacher of humility
humbled himself and became obedient even to the point of
dying on a Cross. Let us imitate him in his crucifixion by
mastering our appetites and fixing them to the Cross with
the nails of abstinence."[37]

St. Leo uses very similar language in expressing his view of the Lenten season: "The holy apostles, under the inspiration of the Holy Spirit, ordained that a greater fast should be observed during these days, in order that by a common sharing of Christ's Cross we may contribute something to what he has done for us, in accordance with the Apostle's words: 'If we have died with him, we shall also live with him.'" [38]

Fasting is thus a sharing in the suffering of Christ. This is why fasting means a relentless struggle of the kind Christ faced until the moment of his victory. For, "the tempter, always on the alert, attacks more intensely those he sees most careful to avoid sin. Who shall be exempt from his onslaughts, when he dared tempt even the Lord of majesty with his clever tricks?" [39]

There is no point in pushing our inquiry any further, since it will constantly lead us back to the same basic points. Fasting, as the Fathers think of it, belongs to every season and to every moment of life. Their main concern is to eliminate from the practice every taint of the fraudulent and the hypocritical. St. Augustine, for example, does not hesitate to assert that some people make Lent the occasion for sensuality and even abstain from wine for sensual motives:

> There are some who observe Lent more out of sensuality than religion, for they seek to cultivate new kinds of pleasure rather than to chastise their old appetites. They provide themselves with all kinds of abundant and costly fruits and delicacies in order to have a variety of tasty dishes. . . . There are some, too, who do not drink wine but replace it with liqueurs from the juice of other fruits. [40]

Fasting with the entire Church

True Lenten observance has nothing to do with such practices as St. Augustine was rejecting. In fact, it is not even a matter of mere observances at all. The essence and purpose of Lent is rather for the Christian to become like the crucified Christ, to overcome the devil, and to re-establish a proper state of soul through union with God in prayer and with one's neighbor by means of a charity that leads to almsgiving and generous forgiveness.

In his pursuit of this Lenten asceticism, the Christian is not cut off from others, nor is the fruit of his efforts to be found only in his own soul. The entire Church is involved in the struggle, with her attention focused on the catechumens who are preparing to renounce Satan and to put on Christ. In the conflict with the devil, the whole Christian army takes up its weapons and comes to grip with the enemy. "You know that this is the time when the devil rages throughout the world and the Christian army must do battle. If laziness has made some listless or worldly concerns have absorbed their attention, now is the time for them to don spiritual armor and be roused by the heavenly trumpet to enter the struggle." [41]

Completing the temple of God

Thus, it is especially during the season of Lent that the hierarchy and each Catholic — in short, the entire Church — is summoned to cooperate in the redemptive work of the Head. We are "the temple of God, a temple whose foundation is the Founder himself." This place where God himself dwells must be built up in an honorable way.

> There is no doubt but that we cannot begin or complete the building unless its Architect helps us. Yet he who builds it has given us the ability to make the building more perfect by our labors. For the material that God uses in constructing this temple is alive and endowed with reason, and the Spirit of grace inspires it to form, voluntarily, a single structure. . . . Since, then, each believer, and all believers together, form one and the same temple of God, the temple must be perfect not only in all together but in each. [42]

Consideration of fasting thus leads us eventually to the vision that should be our constant guide: the bringing of the Church to completion as the temple of God, until "we all attain to the measure of the stature of the fullness of Christ" (Eph. 4:13). This is the essential purpose of all our religious activity, be it ascetical, mystical, or liturgical. The ultimate purpose of fasting, then, is eschatological.

In the last analysis, fasting does its work in view of the last times. It is a remedy, but a remedy affecting eternal life. Jesus Christ, our Lord and our Head, instituted it for the purpose of healing, strengthening, purifying, and enlightening each and all in the unity of the one Church.

The echo of patristic teaching

It is worth our while to inquire how the immediate successors of the Church Fathers understood Christian asceticism. St. Benedict, whose Rule is steeped in patristic teaching and who often quotes the words of the Fathers, is especially interesting in this respect. He is writing for a community of monks. He thinks of them, however, not as "specialists" in asceticism, but simply as men who are to lead as thorough a Christian life as possible and to seek "the beginnings of perfection."

In chapter 49 of his Rule, St. Benedict deals with the observance of Lent. From the very opening words we can recognize not only the thinking but even some of the characteristic expressions of St. Leo the Great; the whole chapter is evidently inspired by his teaching. Those who have never made the acquaintance of the Rule of St. Benedict will profit by reading this beautiful chapter. It is simple and makes no display of theological learning, but it is certainly the fruit of profound experience in the search for God to the exclusion of all else.[43]

> Although the life of a monk ought to have about it at all times the character of a Lenten observance, yet since so few have the virtue for that,[44] we therefore

urge that during the actual days of Lent the brethren keep their lives most pure and at the same time wash away during these holy days all the negligences of other times.[45] And this will be worthily done if we restrain ourselves from all vices and give ourselves up to prayer with tears, to reading, to compunction of heart and to abstinence.

During these days, therefore, let us increase somewhat the usual burden of our service,[46] as by private prayers and by abstinence in food and drink. Thus everyone of his own will may offer God "with joy of the Holy Spirit" [1 Thess. 1:6] something above the measure required of him. From his body, that is, he may withhold some food, drink, sleep, talking and jesting; and with the joy of spiritual desire he may look forward to holy Easter.

Let each one, however, suggest to his Abbot what it is that he wants to offer, and let it be done with his blessing and approval. For anything done without the permission of the spiritual father will be imputed to presumption and vainglory and will merit no reward. Therefore let everything be done with the Abbot's approval.

St. Benedict is envisaging Lent here, not in terms of the entire Church, but in terms only of the part of the Church that he directs and that is committed to living the complete Christian life. He does not touch on the needs of catechumens. One reason for this is that infant baptisms had become far more numerous by his time; but the chief reason is that monastic life, as he envisaged it, was not directly ordered to the apostolate. His emphasis is on asceticism, or more exactly (in the present passage) on a period when an asceticism that was exercised throughout the year was to be intensified. The point of the Lenten observance, therefore, was not to think up new practices, but to do more perfectly and devoutly what was habitually being done at all times.

Even a superficial reading of the chapter will show the

hierarchy of values that characterized religious life as established by St. Benedict, who was heir to the Desert Fathers and to such monastic lawgivers as Cassian, Pachomius, and Basil. In St. Benedict's view, Lent meant first and foremost a renewed dedication to prayer, reading, and compunction of heart — three essential aspects of monastic life that his Rule frequently emphasizes. Only after these three is abstinence mentioned.

St. Benedict also insists that Lent brings nothing new, but only an intensification (in quantity but especially in quality) of what are constant elements of Christian life. As we have already indicated, the Saint, in speaking of this point, repeats almost verbatim various statements of St. Leo the Great's Lenten sermons. In a similar way, St. Ambrose advises virgins simply to intensify their habitual practices. For, in the last analysis, the important thing is not particular practices but the effort to reach God in detachment from self. The necessity of such detachment is what makes St. Benedict insist that nothing must be done without the abbot's approval.

On all these points, however, what St. Benedict says is hardly distinguishable from the commonplaces of spiritual writers generally. The special ethos of the chapter comes rather from the way in which he characterizes Lent as he wants his monks to live it. The point is made without special emphasis, yet it determines the character of the entire Lenten asceticism: "With the joy of spiritual desire he [the monk] may look forward to holy Easter."

For St. Benedict, as for the Fathers generally and the liturgy, the mortification proper to Lent is part of the movement toward the day of the Lord's resurrection. Asceticism can have but one legitimate purpose: a liberation that consists, not in scorning the body, but in achieving a spiritual balance, a liberation for the sake of unconditional participation in the "great liberation" that is the Passover of the Lord. The purpose, then, is to die with Christ in order to arise with him.

As long as we live in this mortal dwelling, we must con-

stantly strive for the needed balance, and that balance cannot be achieved and maintained without some asceticism.
The asceticism must in turn be reinforced from time to time
by making more intense demands on oneself. The only
valid motive, however, for this Christian asceticism is to
prepare oneself for Easter and for its eschatological fulfillment in the return of the Lord. This is why St. Benedict
speaks of looking forward to Easter "with the joy of
spiritual desire." An asceticism centered on the self cannot
claim, without hypocrisy, to be permeated by authentic joy;
the only joy it will experience is the transient, bitter joy that
springs from satisfied pride in self-mastery. Only the expectation of Easter and of the liberation of man and his world
that Easter means can beget genuine joy — that joy in the
Holy Spirit of which St. Benedict speaks — amid the trials
and difficulties of our present life.

In a preface for the Easter season, the Gelasian Sacramentary makes it clear that in the celebration of the paschal feast, what we should in the last analysis desire, prepare for, and await with joy is the final coming of Christ and
our own "passage" to eternal life: "In your mercy grant, we
pray you, that the more the faithful participate in the paschal sacraments and look forward with longing to your coming, the more may they be faithful to the mysteries by
which they have been reborn, and be drawn into the new
life that these mysteries make possible."[47]

3. THE CHURCH, PLACE OF DIVINIZATION

God's creation is something divine, and he has committed himself to restoring the world so that this divine character may once again be manifest in mankind and in the
world itself. At the same time, however, he wills that man
should be constantly living in quest of the divinization of-

fered to him. It was not enough to redeem man; God also had to give him guidance. It was not enough that the Son should come into our world and die for us; he also had to remain in our world in some fashion or other. It was in order to meet both these needs that the Spirit was sent. The Spirit continues, in the Church, the action whereby God creates a divine reality. This means that the Church in turn is responsible for the divinization of man and of his world.

The Church must therefore have a twofold purpose in all she does. On the one hand, her task is to foster a new creation, a renewal in which death becomes simply a passage to a definitive life; this she does by calling men to faith in him who is the Resurrection and the Life. On the other hand, she must constantly endeavor to preserve and advance in the faith those who have already received the gift and have been trying to make it bear fruit in their lives.

Lent has a place in the achievement of both these purposes. It is a time when those who wish to receive baptism are prepared for the sacrament. It is also a time when the Church revitalizes and rejuvenates the faith of those already baptized, and, if need be, restores life to those of the baptized who have been deadened by sin. Consequently, we find three organizational principles at work in the Lenten liturgy: (1) the liturgy is organized in terms of the catechumenate; (2) it is organized as a preparation for the reconciliation of penitents; (3) it is organized with a view to deepening the spiritual life of those faithful who wish to live more fully by faith and to advance in the concrete practice of the Christian life.

Turning to God

The Church's most important mission is to move men to *metanoia*, or conversion — that is, to bring them to travel a different road and to turn to God. Once the Church was not subject to persecution in the fourth century and was free to organize the forty days of Lent in a detailed way, she would engage in a sweeping revision of the catechumenate, traces of which can be seen at Rome in the third century, as reflected in St. Hippolytus' *Apostolic Tradition.*

It is clear that at this early period the entire local community was responsible for, and concerned about, the conversion of those who felt called to the faith. Hippolytus would die a martyr, for the period of persecution was not yet over; but the Church of Rome did not wait for persecution to end before showing her concern for those who were looking for the divinization for which they had been created. An individual catechesis did not seem adequate for this purpose; the whole ecclesial community had to assist in the recovery of the divine life lost by sin.

Nor was a merely intellectual conversion enough. More had to be done than to open the mind to new ideas, since the purpose of conversion was entry into a new people that regarded itself as chosen by God to be kings and priests, a people that proclaimed the advent of the final age of mankind and did not hesitate to think of itself as belonging to the "race" or "family" of God.

The rather detailed organization we see reflected in Hippolytus' writings is itself a development of what we already know from Justin Martyr in his *First Apology,* which dates from about 150 and was addressed to Emperor Antoninus Pius. Chapters 61 and 62 show the kind of preparation required of those who wished to join the Christian community. They had to believe what was taught to them and promise to live according to their new beliefs. They learned to pray and to seek forgiveness of their sins through fasting. Through all this the community was very much concerned with those seeking admission to its ranks, and it prayed and fasted along with them during their time of preparation for baptism.

Meanwhile, there were also heretical sects that caused confusion of mind among those who wanted to cling to the true faith. The number of Christians was on the increase, but persecution inevitably caused defections. Tertullian worried as he saw Christians joining Gnostic sects, then returning to the Church, and finally rejoining the sects. Evidently a solid formation was needed.[48]

Hippolytus later gives us some detailed information on the state of a catechumenate that was already well organized. By his time catechumens were divided into two classes. The first of these classes consisted of catechumens in the proper sense of the term ("hearers" or "those being instructed"). When individuals sought to enter this group, they were questioned about their way of life and about the reasons why they wanted to enter the Church. Certain demands were made of them; for example, certain occupations had to be abandoned if the practitioners wanted to be accepted into this first stage of the catechumenate.

After this initial examination, those accepted were asked to come for instruction and were presented to the bishop by the members of the community who would be responsible for their detailed Christian education. The period of instruction lasted three years. After each lesson the catechumens prayed together; they did not join the faithful in prayer, nor did they give one another the kiss of peace. The instructor, whether a cleric or a layman, prayed over them and placed his hands on them.

At the end of the three-year period, the catechumen was examined once again concerning his way of life and his practice of charity and good works. If his sponsors gave a favorable report about him, he was admitted to a new stage of the catechumenate and to the group known as the *phōtizomenoi* ("those being enlightened"). During this final period he listened to the Gospel and received a daily imposition of hands. As his baptism became imminent, the bishop himself imposed hands on him. It is very likely that this episcopal laying on of hands took place on Holy Saturday morning, while baptism would be administered during the Easter Vigil, amid prayer and the reading of Scripture.[49]

How is all this related to Lent? The answer is that a good deal of the very substance of Lent is constituted by the prayer and fasting of the entire local community in behalf of those who will receive their divinization during the Easter Vigil. In the last analysis, Lent is organized in terms of this liberation and return to God.

At a later period the Gelasian Sacramentary gives a de-

tailed idea of the organization of Lent and provides the
prayers and the "scrutiny" celebrations proper to the season. The "scrutinies" were not inquiries into the intellectual or moral fitness of the candidates for baptism, but exorcisms that gradually prepared them to become the dwelling
place of the Spirit who would make them adoptive children
of God. The celebrations of the scrutinies took place on
Sundays; in these Masses, the prayers, readings, and parts
of the Canon were slanted in favor of the catechumens and
those in charge of them. As we go through the Sundays of
Lent, we will have the opportunity to examine in greater
detail the information contained in the Gelasian Sacramentary. In any case, extensive use has been made of this latter
book in the current rite of adult baptism.

Clearly, then, Lent is, in the Church's view, not a time
solely for personal meditation and asceticism; rather, it is a
season that opens up wide vistas for the community that is
celebrating it. It is a time of choice, when the community is
summoned to return to God and to bring the world back to
its real source. The entire Christian community prays and
fasts for the true conversion of those who have entrusted
themselves to it and are sincerely looking for the Lord. This
is undoubtedly an aspect of Lent that was much neglected
during the past century, with its emphasis on individual asceticism. When seen in its proper light, Lent is for the
Church a period of great optimism, since it is a time when
Christians recall the true meaning of human life, namely,
that man is destined to enter into the realm of God himself
through rebirth from water and the Spirit.

Metanoia, or conversion

The Christian ideal of man's divinization is not an easy
one to live up to. It is common knowledge that during the
first seven centuries of the Church, Christians were so
awed by what man had become in baptism that he was allowed only one opportunity throughout his life to enter
upon a regime of penitence that would reconcile him with

God through the ministry of the Church. Only in the seventh century did Irish monks begin to give private absolution and to repeat it as needed.

We are rather taken aback by the severity of early Christian practice, since we like to emphasize the infinite mercy of God. The early Christians did not forget God's mercy; they were, however, keenly aware of the tremendous grace of divinization given to man in baptism, and found it difficult to see how those who had reached this new life could fall back into sin.

The time for reconciliation was Lent. On Ash Wednesday the penitent entered the "order of penitents." (Later on, since every Christian could rightly regard himself as a "sinner," the imposition of ashes was universalized.) On Holy Thursday morning, after a period of expiation that might have lasted several years, the penitent was solemnly reconciled to the Lord in the Church. Here again the Gelasian Sacramentary has preserved the texts for this Holy Thursday ceremony. The celebration was somewhat amplified in the twelfth century; the texts and rites were still to be found in the liturgical books until the recent liturgical reform, but they had fallen into disuse. Holy Thursday thus marked the end of Lent. It was followed by an intra-paschal fast that lasted from Good Friday to Communion during the Easter Vigil.

We shall have the opportunity later on in this book to present this penitential ritual with its doctrinally rich texts and moving ceremonies. This will provide a new occasion for enlarging our conception of Lent as a period when sinners are reconciled as the ecclesial community fasts and prays for them.

The Church defines Lent in her prayers

Our earlier sampling of the writings of the Fathers has shown us the wider picture of which fasting was only one part. It is equally instructive to examine the texts of the liturgy, especially the prayers and prefaces, for the

Church's concept of fasting. Even if we were to limit ourselves to the current Roman Missal, we would find a richly
detailed teaching; we must, however, go further and find in
the chief sacramentaries how the Church of a given age
viewed fasting.

We must not, of course, expect to find in these various
books a teaching that is organized into a treatise. The
liturgy, after all, is neither a handbook of ascetical theology
nor a code of law. What we find is something quite different. Like the catechumen who moves forward to the light
of Easter, we come into contact with the thinking that is the
basis of the Church's life during the forty days of Lent. The
catechumen does not receive a ready-made concept of fasting but experiences the Church in her "state of fasting."

Anyone who seeks entrance into the community of God's
new people is already aware that he encounters the Lord by
means of and through signs, and that in the process he
comes into an increasingly closer union with the other
members of the Church. Moreover, he has already heard
the Church herself called a "sacrament." The Church is not
only an institution but also a sign. That is to say, she is not
an institution exactly like the other institutions of this
world; she is an institution that serves as a *sacramentum*, or
sacred, effective sign. On the basis of Christ's incarnation,
death, resurrection, and sending of the Spirit, the Church
has been established as a "sign." In her, through her activity as Spouse of Christ and through her very nature, which
is to be "Christ continued," we are efficaciously touched by
the mysteries of Christ, that is, by all his salvific actions.

We have already seen how St. Leo the Great understood
this *sacramentum*, this efficacious sacred sign or "sacrament." In his view, a sacrament is both an efficacious pro-
longation of Christ's salvific actions and, at the same time,
an abiding reminder of his example. "The living faith of the
Christian assembly not only draws upon the wellspring of
all perfection but at the same time discovers him who is the
model of all perfection." [50]

We can readily apply this teaching to Lent and its fast.

These, too, are sacraments and, as such, have an efficacy that derives from the salvific deeds of Christ. But they are also efficacious in that they render present to us the example of the Savior himself. When the Christian engages in the ascetical practice of fasting, it is impossible for him not to think of Christ fasting for forty days in the wilderness, battling with the demon, and emerging victorious. In fact, the account of Christ's fast in the wilderness is read on the first Sunday of Lent, which marks the beginning of the "sacrament of fasting" that will be effective in us both because of its institution by Christ and because of the encouraging example the Lord himself gives us.

We have also seen that Lent, like fasting, cannot be properly understood if the framework adopted is too narrow; it must be seen rather in the comprehensive perspective of the renewal of the world through the paschal mystery. There is, then, strictly speaking, no "sacrament of Lent and fasting" nor even any "sacrament of the resurrection." There is only a *sacramentum paschale*, a "paschal sacrament," that embraces Lent, the Passion, the resurrection, the ascension, and the sending of the Holy Spirit.

These various points, which we have already met in the Fathers and especially in St. Leo, recur in the Church's liturgical compositions. In these, fasting is part of the paschal sacrament. As such, it is a sign of a grace offered, that is, a sign of efficacious divine action; at the same time it is a sign of, and puts us into contact with, the fasting, struggle, and victory of Christ.

The person who lives from day to day in the spirit of the Church and tries, without preconceived notions, to grasp in the liturgy the wealth of the Church's spirituality will conceive of fasting, not as the ascetical activity of an individual, but as a collective practice. The catechumen who has been enrolled for proximate baptism is not confronted with a requirement of individual asceticism and mortification; rather, he becomes part of an activity of the Church as a whole. The expression "collective practice" could indeed give rise to a false impression or lessen the esteem that the

asceticism in question richly deserves. The danger can be
avoided, however, by realizing that "practice" is not used
here in the devotional sense. By "collective practice," as
we have already indicated and as the Church's prayers during Lent show, we mean that fasting is a "sacrament" for
the Church in its entirety and that its efficacy reaches to the
whole people of God.

It is worthwhile to note the various descriptions given of
Lent in the officially approved Latin edition of the revised
Roman Missal. In the prayer over the offerings on the first
Sunday, Lent is called an "ancient and revered sacrament"
(*venerabilis sacramenti*), the beginning of which we celebrate on this day (the prayer comes from the Gelasian Sacramentary[51]). On other occasions Lent is called an "exercise." Thus the opening prayer for the first Sunday speaks
of "the exercise of the Lenten sacrament" (*quadragesimalis
exercitia sacramenti*), the phrase and indeed the whole
prayer being taken from the Gelasian Sacramentary.[52] On
Ash Wednesday the blessing of the ashes uses the words
"Lenten exercise" (*quadragesimalis exercitatio*), while the
opening prayer on Tuesday of the fourth week speaks of
"the ancient exercise of holy devotion" (*exercitatio ven-
eranda sanctae devotionis*).[53]

The term "observance" (*observantia*) is also used. "Lenten observance" (*quadragesimalis observantia*) occurs in
the blessing of ashes on Ash Wednesday and again in the
prayer over the gifts on the Friday after Ash Wednesday
and in the opening prayer for Wednesday of the third week.
Elsewhere we find the words: "As we rejoice in the annual
celebration of this observance" (*observationis huius annua
celebritate laetantes*).[54] Again, the Lord is asked to sanctify
"our observance" (*observantiam nostram*).[55] Finally, in a
phrase that reveals the true finality of the season as a whole,
Lent is called "paschal observance" (*observatio pas-
chalis*).[56]

God not only bids us observe a season of fasting; he also
gives us the power to undertake it and to persevere in it:
"Lord, protect us in our struggle against evil. As we begin

the discipline of Lent, make this season holy by our self-denial."[57] It is to the Lord that we look for the ability to commit ourselves fully to the mortification that Lent imposes: "Grant, Lord, that we may observe the prescriptions with utter devotion."[58]

Our fasting is thus truly an action of God in us. It is this action that allows us to speak of Lent as a "sacrament" and also as a "mystery." This last term we find used in some older prayers; for example, "Almighty God, we pray you, be present in this holy mystery of fasting."[59] Without the presence of the Lord, the solemn ecclesial act of fasting would have no power to sanctify but would simply be an outward performance.

It is easy to understand that because of this special presence of the Lord in his Church during Lent, the latter should be called "sacrament," "mystery," "solemnity," "feast." The Verona Sacramentary uses the same language in proclaiming the September fast: "Beloved, we are about to celebrate the annual feast of fasting. . . ."[60]

Festive fasting

The name "feast" may well surprise us, since it is at least paradoxical to speak of a fast as a feast. Yet that is precisely how the fast has been seen, especially during the Easter Vigil.

We must bear in mind that the vigil is thought of as a period of waiting for the return of Christ; it is the time when the praying Church awaits the return of her Spouse. In the early Christian centuries the faithful thought that this return would take place during the night between Holy Saturday and Easter Sunday, since that night was the center of Christian life, being the anniversary of Christ's victory and the moment when that victory became present anew. The fast that marked the Vigil, and indeed the whole Lenten fast, is festive because it is leading up to the victory and return of the Spouse.

When Jesus was asked: "Why do we [the disciples of

John the Baptist] and the Pharisees fast, but your disciples
do not fast?" his reply was: "Can the wedding guests
mourn as long as the bridegroom is with them? The day
will come, when the bridegroom is taken away from them,
and then they will fast" (Matthew 9:14-15; cf. Mark 2:19-20;
Luke 5:34-35). We fast because the Spouse is absent. But he
is coming back to us, since he has inaugurated the messianic age and will come again to assert his victory. The
Church, therefore, can fast, yet also celebrate in a festive
way his imminent return. An old preface for the summer or
post-Pentecostal Ember Days recalls the above passage
from the Gospel: ". . . almighty, everlasting God, who . . .
told the children of the Spouse that they were not to fast
before his departure. . . ."[61]

The Christians of the first centuries thus took the passage
as a prophetic instruction that would be valid for the whole
time of the Church. The early Christians found it natural to
be awaiting at every moment the return of Christ.

Fasting from sin

The term "sacrament" is meaningfully applied to fasting
only if the fasting sanctifies. The prayers of the liturgy show
us the negative and positive aspects of this sanctification,
the two often being presented as forming a single whole.

The extensive attention paid to the aspect of struggle and
liberation should not surprise us. After all, Lent begins with
the Gospel account of Christ's struggle with Satan in the
desert, thus putting the whole season under this sign.[62]
Characteristic, too, is the opening prayer for Ash Wednesday: "Lord, protect us in our struggle against evil. As we
begin the discipline of Lent, make this season holy by our
self-denial."[63]

The aspect of struggle, which thus comes to the fore at
the very beginning of Lent, will be an underlying theme
throughout the season. Fasting is intended to strengthen us
against the enemy and is the source of new energy: "Grant,
Lord, that our fasting may fill us with strength, and our abstinence make us invincible to all our enemies."[64]

Fasting is a powerful weapon in this struggle to the death against our foes. With its help and the help of our good deeds, we can win through to victory: "Grant, Lord, that by fasts and good works pleasing to you we may win your help and be able to overcome our enemies."[65]

Liberation from the "enemy" means liberation from sin. The movement here is, as it were, a circular one: our fasting would be illusory if it did not consist above all in avoiding sin, but, on the other hand, fasting is also a powerful help in de-energizing our evil inclinations.

The Book of Isaiah, chapter 58 — a postexilic document — presents an interiorized conception of religious practices. But at an earlier time Amos had already voiced the Lord's disgust with festivals and solemnities in which no interior attitude corresponded to the outward observances (Amos 5:21). The Church, too, is careful to keep reminding the faithful of what an authentic asceticism requires. A preface for the September Ember Days in the Verona Sacramentary reads as follows:

> . . . but if amid our observances we do not abstain from what is harmful and forbidden, you assure us through the prophet that such fasting is not acceptable to you. For not only can bodily mortification not be profitable if the mind is enmeshed in evil thoughts; we are even worse off if the soul does not abstain from sin when its earthly condition has been rendered less burdensome.[66]

The Church is constantly on the alert lest the faithful delude themselves by practicing mortification without a corresponding complete detachment from sin. Such self-deception would be deadly for the Church as well as for the individual. We must be careful, of course, about calling the Church "sinful," but on the other hand we must certainly reckon with sin in the Church. Some twenty years ago this point was well expressed in this way:

> Sin does not arise from the nature of the Church but breaks into her from outside, through the power of the

Evil One at work in men. Sin does not belong to the nature of the Church but must be reckoned as part of the unnatural condition in which she is during her earthly pilgrimage. To put it in the way in which it is usually put: Sin in the Church is that failure in holiness caused by the power of the Evil Spirit through men as members of the Church. Sin in the Church, as part of the Church (as indeed elsewhere), can only be seen as a dark, incomprehensible, ultimately meaningless paradox. But as such it must be taken seriously.[67]

Knowing the mysteries of Christ

Purification, however, is not the ultimate purpose of the Church in its seasons of fasting; it is not an end in itself. To turn away from sin and to believe in, or be faithful to, the gospel (as the new formula for the imposition of ashes bids us do) means to make the effort required in order to know the mysteries of Christ. The opening prayer for the first Sunday of Lent expresses the deeper meaning these forty days should have for the catechumen, for the penitent, and indeed for every Christian: "Father, though our observance of Lent, help us to understand the meaning of your Son's death and resurrection, and teach us to reflect it in our lives."[68]

"Knowing," for the Christian as for biblical man, is first of all a matter of contemplating the God who is Love, thanking him for the wonderful things he has done, and developing a capacity for admiration of his masterpieces in the world and in man's heart, and especially of his extraordinary action in saving mankind. "Knowing" also means entering into close communion with the mysteries of Christ that the Christian experiences through the sacraments. By thus gaining an experiential knowledge of Christ's mysteries — a knowledge fostered by fasting — we actively contemplate and become aware of the benefits we have already received from God and can appreciate their true value. At the same time, we come to realize our own need, and our devotion is deepened as we comprehend the benefits still in store for us. "For when we offer the homage of a suitable observance [i.e., fasting], we become grateful for the gifts we have received and still more grateful for gifts yet to come."[69]

Fasting thus proves enlightening to the spirit. We understand the secrets of the mystery of salvation. We become capable of appreciating the marvelous manifestation of good that the work of mankind's redemption represents. We acquire a clarity of spiritual vision, so that even amid our enthusiasm for the wealth bestowed on us, we do not lose sight of what we must still do to be perfect.

Yet, when confronted with such an outpouring of divine generosity, we feel a certain uneasiness. We are, after all, incapable of implementing by our own efforts such a vision of God, the world, and ourselves, and of progressively making real in our lives the ideal we glimpse. How, then, are we to preserve intact what has been given to us? Indeed, the Church asks herself the same question, for she is well aware of how cowardly and weak the men are who make up her members, and she too feels a certain fear of the responsibility placed upon her to preserve what she has received.

It is precisely the asceticism involved in fasting that will help her guard the treasure bestowed on her. The Verona Sacramentary has a preface for the post-Pentecostal days of fast that reads as follows: "After the joyous days we spent honoring the Lord's resurrection from the dead and ascension into heaven, and after receiving the gift of the Holy Spirit, we are provided with this holy and necessary fast so that our purity of life may assure the permanence of God's gifts to his Church."[70]

During Lent the Lord gradually "fills our minds with . . . wisdom."[71] He "enlightens [us] with the Christian faith."[72]

We can glimpse in such prayers a reflection of the concern for catechumens that presided over the organization of Lent. The scrutinies celebrated for the catechumens have as their purpose a gradual assimilation to the faith, thus creating a pure dwelling in which the Spirit can enlighten those who seek the Lord.

Made like to Christ

There is little reason to fear that the catechumen or the baptized Catholic will become proud on account of the divine life that fills him and the perfection such a life entails. For we know how asceticism will deepen his keen awareness of his own defects, which continue to be many.

But asceticism does more than this. Fasting also helps the catechumen and the Christian to form their souls after the model of Christ himself.

Humility and submission to the Father's will, for example, are two traits to be found in the person who accepts the ascetical life of the Church. The individual does not practice such asceticism in isolation or in whatever way he chooses, for he has before him a model that the liturgy presents to the assembly of the faithful from the first Sunday of Lent on. In their practice of fasting, the catechumen and the baptized believer are inspired by example; they become imitators of Christ. They develop this likeness first and foremost through a humility whose meaning is made clear to them in the asceticism of the Church: "God, you teach us, through fasting and prayer, what is meant by true humility in imitation of your only Son, our Lord." [73]

The same Christ taught an unconditioned submission to his Father's will. By creating in our souls an attitude of detachment, fasting leads us along this path of conformity to the divine will: "Grant, Lord, that through this holy fast we may become completely docile to you." [74]

Change requires a self-conversion

This kind of change does not take place in us without our own cooperation. Unless we ourselves are profoundly committed to the task, God will not divinize us and refashion us in the likeness of his Son, nor will the Holy Spirit enable us to be imitators of Christ. In fact, our conversion is a task that is never finished and done with. That is why the prayer for conversion runs through the Lenten season in the new Roman Missal. Thus, the opening prayer for the third Sunday lists the three activities needed if we are to improve our spiritual condition: "Father, you have taught us to overcome our sins by prayer, fasting and works of mercy." This theme for the season as a whole is set by the liturgy for Ash Wednesday, in which the idea of conversion is central, as is faith, an essential element in conversion. As the new optional formula for the distribution of ashes puts it, echoing the Gospel: "Turn away from sin and be faithful to the gospel" (cf. Mark 1:15). This, of course, cannot be accomplished without a struggle, for we must do battle with all that is evil in us.[75]

It may be that in the past too much stress was placed on corporal penance and fasting. No one would deny that modern life and the demands it makes of us constitute a penance that is often at least as hard as fasting. At the same time, however, we must face up to a permanent fact of our lives, namely, that the soul is so intimately bound up with the body that some training of the body will always be necessary. Doctors and psychologists are becoming more and more aware of this today. Is it not time for Catholics to do the same, with prudence indeed but for specifically gospel motives?

The new Sacramentary, it would seem, has been rather shy when it comes to prayers that speak of chastising the body in order to purify the soul. "God our Father, teach us to find new life through penance."[76] "Lord, as we come with joy to celebrate the mystery of the eucharist, may we offer you hearts purified by bodily penance."[77] The problem, in the last analysis, is an elementary one: to be convinced of our impoverished state and to free ourselves from the bonds of sin.[78] In fact, we should not even dignify with the name "problem" what is often only a simple weakness and a lack of courage in facing up to some proclivity of ours.

On the other hand, we must not stop with such considerations and think of our conversion as a narrowly individual matter. Our conversion is in fact connected with the conversion of the world, and if the celebration of the Eucharist can and does help us in our self-conversion, it is also the source of the world's conversion.[79]

Advancing toward the paschal mystery

The conversion of mankind and of the world in its entirety is possible only through participation in the paschal mystery of death and life. Lent is conceived precisely as a time of progress toward this mystery of liberation and renewal. Its purpose is that we should come with purified souls to the celebration of the paschal mystery.[80] The preface for the first Sunday of Lent turns our attention to Christ and reminds us that "his fast of forty days makes this a holy season of self-denial. By rejecting the devil's temptations he has taught us to rid ourselves of the hidden corruption of evil, and so to share his paschal meal in purity of heart, until we come to its fulfillment in the promised land of heaven."

In the same vein, the prayer over the gifts on the second Sunday asks that through the Eucharistic sacrifice "we may be prepared to celebrate the resurrection." The opening prayer for Thursday of the third week is a petition that we may "be ready to celebrate the great paschal mystery," while the opening prayer for the fourth Sunday urges us to "hasten toward Easter with the eagerness of faith and love."

Put off the old self and put on the new

One of the most humiliating and discouraging things about life is that we tend to become spiritually decrepit, prisoners of habit and of the inclination to follow the path of least resistance. Individuals succumb to this tendency; so do whole groups. Many a community has been enthusiastic in its beginning but quickly yields to routine, which it regards as a simplification of life and sometimes even as a safeguard. Change always involves some risk and is never easy. We are not saying, of course, that we should have contempt for healthy tradition. The latter must not, however, be confused with the pious immobility that only destroys authentic tradition and renders it hateful.

Not only can men become prisoners of habit; they can even return to their sins that sap the soul's strength. We must have the courage to face up to this when it happens and to admit it in ourselves as we do in society at large and in the groups that men form to achieve high purposes.

Lent is a time for cleansing ourselves of any decrepitude and a time of renewal. The postcommunion prayer for Friday of the fourth week puts it thus: "Lord, in this eucharist we pass from death to life. Keep us from our old and sinful ways and help us to continue in the new life." Our whole aim should be "to pass from our old life of sin to the new life of grace" (opening prayer, Monday of fifth week). The Lord must "free us from our sinful ways and bring us new life. May this eucharist lead us to salvation."[81] It is he who must purify us of all that is doomed to destruction and renew his life in us (see the prayer over the gifts, Monday, fourth week).

The real source of renewal is, beyond any doubt, the Lord himself. The Church is very conscious of this fact and asks him to "renew our lives and bring us to salvation" (prayer over the gifts, Wednesday, fourth week).[82]

The sacraments renew us

It is basically and chiefly through his sacraments that the Lord effects his renewal in us. The preface for the fourth Sunday says: "He came among us as a man, to lead mankind from darkness into the light of faith. Through Adam's fall we were born as slaves of sin, but now through baptism in Christ we are reborn as your adopted children." The prayer over the gifts for Saturday of the fifth week makes the same point: "In baptism, the sacrament of our faith, you restore us to life," while the preface for the fifth Sunday speaks in more general terms: "Christ gives us the sacraments to lift us up to everlasting life."

During this season the Lord communicates his strength both to those already baptized and to those who will soon be baptized during the Easter Vigil (see the opening prayer, Saturday, fifth week).[83]

Renewal of body and soul

We would be mistaken to regard all that has been said as the expression of a spiritual vision that concerns only the soul. Let us not fall into that error! The liturgy, like the Bible before it, does not split man into two parts but thinks of renewal as affecting his whole person. The opening prayer for Wednesday of the first week makes this quite clear and in the process gives a very apt expression of the body-soul interaction: "By the good works you inspire, help us to discipline our bodies and to be renewed in spirit."

The Eucharist purifies and renews us in soul, but it also gives strength to the body now and for eternity.[84] In the prayer over the gifts for the second Sunday, we pray that the Eucharist may sanctify us in body and soul and thus prepare us to celebrate the paschal mystery.[85] The post-communion prayer for Monday of the first week emphasizes the truth that one and the same salvation embraces body as well as soul: "Lord, through this sacrament may we rejoice in your healing power and experience your saving love in mind and body."[86]

Renewal for eternal life

The renewal we seek and ask of the Lord, while ourselves working to attain it, is for the sake of life in the world to come. Texts that express this point are numerous; we shall choose only a few of the more eloquent.

The prayer over the offerings on Tuesday of the fourth

week is concise but clear: "Lord, may your gifts of bread and wine which nourish us here on earth become the food of our eternal life."[87] The opening prayer for Monday of the fifth week spells out the requirements for such an entry into eternal life: "Father of love, source of all blessings, help us to pass from our old life of sin to the new life of grace. Prepare us for the glory of your kingdom." The postcommunion for the same day envisages us following Christ more faithfully and thus entering into the joy of the Lord's kingdom.

The Lord gives us pledges of this future life: "Lord our God, may the eucharist you give us as a pledge of unending life help us to salvation" (postcommunion, Wednesday of second week). At the same time, however, even on earth we already possess, in a certain fashion, the blessings heaven has in store for us: "God our Father, by your gifts to us on earth we already share in your life" (opening prayer, Saturday of second week).[88]

4. LENT AND THE MODERN CHRISTIAN

Disordered man

The reader may have had the courage to read the preceding chapters with an unprejudiced mind and may have made the effort to understand them in the light of faith. But is he convinced now that the teaching expounded in these chapters can win a hearing from the men of our day and, specifically, from contemporary Christians? In other words, is it worth our while to try to enter more deeply into the biblico-liturgical theology of Lent, or must we rather regard it as unsuitable and therefore put an end to our study here and now?

Experience and the existential analyses it suggests do not make us especially optimistic about man and his possibilities. Man seems to be a radically disordered being. In fact, that is exactly how St. Paul viewed man when he set down in his Letter to the Romans a number of brutally precise statements based on his experience of himself. He was humble enough to pass on to his readers this existential analysis — and how contemporary it sounds!

> We know that the law is spiritual; but I am carnal, sold under sin. I do not understand my own actions. For I do not do what I want, but I do the very thing I hate. . . . So I find it to be a law that when I want to do right, evil lies close at hand. For I delight in the law of God, in my inmost self, but I see in my members another law at war with the law of my mind and making me captive to the law of sin which dwells in my members (Rom. 7:14-15, 21-23).

The Genesis story that is read at the beginning of Lent does not hide our real condition, and we have tried to assess that condition as objectively as possible. Thus far we have the impression that what Lent teaches is true to what we experience. To this extent, then, we may regard Lent as adapted to contemporary man.

Man renewed

Lent, in brief, shows itself wholly bent on helping man escape from his disordered state and regain union with God. But perhaps the means proposed to us seem inadequate? Perhaps the Church's demands seem too abstract, too unconnected with our real world?

As a matter of fact, given our situation, we may indeed be somewhat put off by the simplicity of the means offered us during Lent. We would prefer methods a bit more striking. We resemble to some extent Naaman the Syrian, who was angry to find that the only cure prescribed for his leprosy was a bath in the Jordan! We must be renewed and attain union with God once again. Fine! The Church, speaking in Christ's name, offers the catechumens a new life. Fine! But the means the Church proposes seem so modest; even the sacramental signs seem out of all proportion to what they are intended to produce.

More specifically, the activities of Lent seem too limited: prayer, almsgiving, mortification. Are these really calculated to suit the condition of modern man? No one doubts that men must change and be converted. But can the practices urged for Lent change the life of a drug addict? Can they calm lust and restore authentic love? Can they change hatred into brotherly harmony? Can they quench the fire of envy? Can they turn fidelity into heroism? No! All in all, experience seems indeed to have demonstrated that the means urged on us by the Church are ineffective.

Such is the critique, but it is itself inadequate as a reflection of the real situation. Christians of today are very much concerned to recover for themselves the values of prayer. They will do so without perhaps making any grandiose claims, but they are well aware that they must indeed learn to pray. Contact with the young, from hippies to the members of "catechumenal" groups, brings home to us their great thirst for prayer and the inner peace they look for in it and claim to find in it. Perhaps the young have not yet realized that what they are really pursuing is their own divinization. In any case, the numerous experiments with communal life and the increasing multiplication of houses of prayer show quite clearly that this means proposed by the Church is being accepted, appreciated, and gradually producing results.

Some individuals are doubtless striking out on the wrong paths. Not every quest is marked by the proper balance, and in some instances neo-romanticism or even illuminism is at work. But we must not overlook the good by concentrating on what is less good. The world seems to be praying again, and in so doing it is rediscovering what should be its primal activity; it is also rediscovering the divinization God intends for it. Through prayer it is getting the poison out of its system. It is slowly regaining a proper scale of values and overcoming its own confusion. Ideologies have less of a fascination for it, and it is beginning to realize that it has everything to gain by developing its contact with God and everything to lose by falling back into practical atheism.

Everyone is aware today of the phenomenon of prayer — even those who do not believe in it or who find it incomprehensible. It is a disconcerting phenomenon. Some people are afraid of it, for they see that its adepts are no longer prisoners of our disordered world but are pursuing a union with God that demands a self-stripping for which not everyone has the courage.

Oddly enough, by God's grace the rediscovery of prayer has not caused its practitioners to turn in on themselves. On the contrary, through their prayer these people have regained the spirit of brotherhood. They have regained it through sharing with others, in the unity formed by the members of the Church as they follow the inspiration of the Spirit. Even more importantly, they pray together; they do not feel distracted by their neighbor but even require their "neighbor" as a visible embodiment and sign of the people that has been gathered again by the breath of the Spirit.

What I have been saying here is not wishful thinking. Everyone who is in contact with the youth of the Church or, more generally, with those who seek, will bear witness to the same phenomenon.

Those who have rediscovered prayer or are in the process of doing so are well aware that they cannot devote themselves to prayer to the exclusion of concern for others and without having developed a profound accord with them. We cannot evade or neglect the needs of our neighbor if we hope to enter into union with the Lord and to taste the fruits of prayer. St. Paul warned the Corinthians that they would not be able to recognize the Eucharistic Body of Christ unless they were also intent on recognizing the Body of Christ which is the Church, and this in the person of their neighbor (1 Cor. 11).

Have people likewise rediscovered the need of mortification? Doctors have always taught us that the body must be mastered. Do Christians really believe this? It would be unjust, of course, to assert that they do not. Mortification has, to be sure, taken different forms than it had in other periods of history; people are less concerned with establishing records than with attaining the right measure. Asceticism is seen as a calculated discipline rather than as a total abstention in one or all areas of life. We can glimpse the ideal being pursued: to have and use what one has, but not to lose one's balance when one does not have it. Doesn't that represent an authentic conversion?

You may object that all this is rather idyllic and represents at best the outlook of a rather small elite. Well, the masses of people doubtless do not look at things in the way described. But then, can a more than superficial Christianity ever become the Christianity of the masses? I am not saying that Christ did not die for all men. I am saying only that in some men and women the Spirit awakens the need for a deeper kind of Christian life. In this regard, our age has made its own a statement emphasized at the Second Vatican Council: that holiness is not linked exclusively to religious life but is an essential goal of the Church in its entirety. We are living today in a Church where many of the laity are seeking holiness and are rediscovering, even amid their human weakness, what it means to be divinized. Thus, there is evidently no basis for thinking or saying that the Church of today does not measure up to the Church of former times.

Whatever the state of the contemporary Church, there will always be room to enter more deeply into the meaning of the Lenten "sacrament" and to follow in faith the path the Church points out to us as leading to our ultimate renewal. It is not primarily with the help of medicine or psychoanalysis or other human arts and sciences that we will achieve this renewal. These things are important enough in themselves, but they are not, like Lent, a "sacrament" that produces divine effects in those who trustingly receive it. We must therefore cease to think of Lent first and foremost in terms of "practices"; we must experience it rather as a time in which we open ourselves to the divine life that God seeks to restore to us. If we do so, and if we bear in mind the various aspects of Lent — for example, the forgiveness of sins and the entry of the catechumens into the faith and the Church — Lent can indeed help us slake our thirst for transcendence.

STRUCTURE AND THEMES OF THE LENTEN LITURGY

5. LENT THEN AND NOW

Lent, a time for self-enlightenment

The themes of the Lenten liturgy soon confront the Christian with a basic question, for they force the Church in its entirety to examine its conscience and rediscover what it truly is. Here is the Christian, a part of the new and ever-growing kingdom of God, but he has come to take for granted the sacred world in which he lives; he moves at ease in it. Now he must ask himself: By what right have secondary things become so important to me?

He must once again look closely at this world and its realities, and realize anew that they have authentic meaning only because they have been inserted into a definitive, lasting, new world. He must also go back over the divine aids and instrumentalities he has received at the successive great moments of Christian life and must examine his conscience on the use he has made of them in the past and the use he is to make of them in the future. Such is the fundamental activity of the Christian in his "state of Lenten asceticism." This activity concerns his relation to God, to others, and to himself.

He soon discovers that he cannot simply "live *his own* Lent" but must live it along with the rest of the Church so that the sinners who have destroyed themselves because they followed an illusory light but found only darkness may regain their place in the Church. He lives Lent along with the Church in its entirety so that she may once again become truly one, shed all formalism, and regain the authentic life in Christ; so that she may grow and prove a welcoming mother to all who are looking for the true path. When the Christian acquires this new perspective, this sense of community, he will discover a new side of Lent that he perhaps never suspected, for he will find himself taking part in the Christian initiation of those who are preparing to put on the light of Christ and work for the building up of the Lord's Church.

If, however, we are to enter fully into the Church's liturgical life, then, not surprisingly, we are forced to acquire a better knowledge of how that life works and how it has evolved. We may at times regret the fact that the Church seems to carry with her so many vestigial organs. This does not justify us in failing to see that a great body like the Church has a history and that the framework of her institutions cannot change as quickly as the moods of our contemporaries. It can only enrich us to know how the Church's inner life has developed in the past. If, then, we are to enter fully into the spirituality of Lent, we must get a clear view of some indispensable points of reference in the complicated development of the Lenten season.

A single celebration

There is in fact but one theme that runs through Scripture, the liturgy, and the Church's life, and that theme is the death and resurrection of Christ in triumph over sin, Satan and eternal damnation. Easter is the high point, the center of convergence, and the outcome or resolution that alone can provide man's history with meaning. The Christians of the first centuries were fascinated by this indubitably real death and resurrection of the God who had come to restore everything in man and the universe. Consequently, they did not see the need for a special celebration of Christ's passover — his death and resurrection — since the rite of the Last Supper, renewed each Sunday by the Savior's command, made that mystery of death and resurrection an ever-present reality.

Yet, men have a hankering for the unusual; repetition

without inner renewal blunts their attention. Even the religious alertness of the soul is not exempt from the slackening that routine causes. Starting in the second century, therefore, the Christian people, for whom Easter was the central, towering event, began to celebrate an anniversary of the Passion and resurrection of Christ with fasting and prayer. Now the year would have a center, and each Sunday, like a stream flowing from an inexhaustible fountain, would remind them of the Great Feast.

The morrow of the feast

We do not like to douse the lights, as it were, after a brilliant festival and return immediately to everyday life. Easter is a moment of such power, its spiritual resonances are so strong and its celebration so much a source of light, that we cannot fail to hear it echoing in our hearts and to see the sparks from its fire. As early as the third century, therefore, the celebration of Easter was prolonged for fifty days, with a final upsurge on the fiftieth day. Beginning in the fourth century, a new feast — Pentecost — focused attention on this final upsurge of the Easter spirit.

Going up for the feast

The paschal festivities require preparation. The soul's joy becomes intense, after all, only when desire has been stimulated and an expectation created. From the very beginning there was a fast (with a paradoxically festive quality to it) in preparation for the annual observance. Soon this fast became longer and longer, and acquired a great importance. Meanwhile, in keeping with an intuition that was the fruit of the Spirit's working, baptism was increasingly reserved for the night of Easter (Easter Vigil).

According to St. Paul, baptism means being conformed to Christ in his death and resurrection. It is because baptism makes real this mystery in each candidate that it incorporates him into the Church, the great, ever-growing Body of

Christ. This doctrine (Rom. 6) quite naturally suggested that baptism should be administered amid the solemnity of the Paschal Vigil. The time which all Christians were to spend in preparation for the celebration of the paschal mystery also became the time of intensive preparation for the catechumens. The preparation for the baptism soon to be received was to be intellectual, moral, and, above all, spiritual.

Initial organization

In the beginning, Christians celebrated a paschal triduum that extended from Good Friday (the death of Christ), through Saturday (Christ in the tomb), to the Sunday of the resurrection. Soon the triduum came to include Thursday (commemoration of the Last Supper), Friday, and Saturday (including the night before Sunday). The Saturday night celebration belongs both to the time when we celebrate the death of Christ and to the beginning of Sunday, when the Lord rises in glory. St. Augustine, for example, understood the liturgy of the Easter Vigil as a kind of hinge connecting the celebration of Christ's death and the celebration of his resurrection.

In the first stage, then, the preparation for the paschal festivities ended on Wednesday of Holy Week. However, it seems (though we cannot prove it) that very soon the whole week came to be directed toward the Paschal Vigil and Resurrection Sunday. The week in its entirety was taken up with the Passion of the Lord.

First extensions

A week seemed quite inadequate as preparation for a solemnity that would last for fifty days. The first addition by way of preparation was three weeks of fasting. The liturgy of this new period was marked by a series of readings from the Gospel of St. John; traces of this are still to be seen.

Christians continued, however, to feel that there was still

an imbalance between the time given over to the celebration of the paschal event and the time allowed to preparation for it. Consequently, from the end of the fourth century on, forty days were set aside for fasting; their beginning was marked by a Sunday whose very title bespeaks the length of the preparation for Easter: the first Sunday of the "quadragesimal" (forty-day) fast.

On Holy Thursday there was now not only the commemoration of the Last Supper but also the reconciliation of public penitents; the first Sunday of Lent became the day on which these individuals were enrolled for their time of penance. Later on, in order that there might be a full forty days of fasting, the Lenten season began on the Wednesday before the first Sunday, or Ash Wednesday (when sinners beginning their public penance had ashes placed on their heads). When the practice of public penance disappeared, all Christians began to receive the ashes on that day; at the end of the eleventh century, Pope Urban II extended this practice to the whole of Christendom.

During the forty days the catechumens underwent a final, detailed, carefully organized preparation. In earlier times there had first been a remote preparation that lasted at least three years; this was the general catechumenate. This was succeeded by a period of proximate preparation for those catechumens who were "chosen" and enrolled for baptism during the Paschal Vigil. At the beginning of the sixth century, the period of remote preparation was dropped. Adult baptisms were becoming infrequent, and the children presented for baptism were born into Christian families. As a result, the whole organization of the catechumenate changed.

Originally there were three "scrutinies." These consisted of exorcisms and instructions. Later on, in the second half of the sixth century, there would be seven of these scrutinies. The scrutinial ceremonies were connected with the first part of the Mass, and, in the time of the three scrutinies, were celebrated on the third, fourth, and fifth Sundays of Lent. At the later period the scrutinies were first shifted to weekdays and finally separated entirely from the Lenten Masses.

This intense preparation of the catechumens and the organization of Lent for the purpose evidently shaped not only the Lenten liturgy but the Lenten spirit as well. The whole community fasted in union with both the public penitents and the catechumens soon to be baptized.

New developments

At the beginning of the sixth century, the fast was extended to seven weeks and Quinquagesima Sunday made its appearance. Counting back from Easter day itself, Quinquagesima is the fiftieth day. The time after Easter and the time before Easter were now in perfect balance.

Things did not stop there. By the end of the sixth century, Sexagesima was being celebrated and, at the beginning of the seventh century, Septuagesima.

Enrichment within the framework

Initially there were celebrations only on Sundays, Wednesdays, and Fridays; on the latter two days, however, this was simply a celebration of the word, without an accompanying Eucharist. Gradually, beginning in the fifth century, celebrations were established for Mondays, Tuesdays, and Saturdays, and from the sixth century on, all these celebrations included the liturgy of the Eucharist as well as the liturgy of the word. Finally, formularies for the Thursdays of Lent were provided in the eighth century.

The liturgy of Lent was thus increasingly enriched. At Rome, with the Pope presiding over congregations of clergy and faithful in the various basilicas of the city, the celebrations were called "stations." In the second century this word meant the fast on Wednesdays and Fridays. It soon came to signify the gatherings for common prayer. Each Lenten celebration took on its own well-defined character, since the formularies and readings were usually inspired

The Lenten Liturgy

both by peculiarities of the place chosen for the station and by the preparation of the catechumens or their sponsors.

Reorganizations and profound changes

As preparation for baptism gradually became less important and was separated from the Lenten liturgy, this liturgy inevitably took on a different character. The original choice of readings and chants had now become less suitable, since the preoccupation with baptism, which had dictated the choice, had faded. Meanwhile, there had already been a number of changes made — for example, in the liturgy of the third, fourth, and fifth Sundays as early as the beginning of the sixth century.

In any event, Lent became first and foremost a period in which Christians already baptized examined themselves in terms of their participation in the life of the Church. The thought of penitence and the catechumenate faded, and Lent took on a quite different character. The gradual suppression of the catechumenal rites meant that the season lost its orientation toward baptism; the theology of baptism no longer played a leading role.

The recent changes initiated by Vatican Council II

Vatican Council II has restored to Lent the dimensions it originally had. It has not revived the reconciliation of penitents on Holy Thursday, but it has restored, at least in Cycle A, the readings and prayers for the five Sundays of Lent as celebrated in antiquity; the preparation of the catechumens has likewise been linked with these Sundays as in the past.

The Church has never thought that her catechumens required a merely intellectual and religious or doctrinal preparation. The efforts of these individuals to absorb the teaching given them and to observe the moral law could be but an imperfect preparation. God himself had to prepare the candidates in a progressive way by causing his grace to

permeate their souls. That is precisely the significance of
the exorcisms that the candidates underwent.

Undoubtedly the exorcisms concentrate, at times in a
rather dramatic way, on the expulsion of the devil; but it
would be a mistake to consider this expulsion as their sole
focus. The expelling of the demon is only the negative side
of the rite and is a way of preparing the soul so that the
light of faith may enter in. These exorcism rites were called
"scrutinies," but "scrutiny" in this instance does not mean
an inquiry into the doctrinal or moral fitness of the candidate. The ritual of the prebaptismal scrutinies is the vehicle
for an important theology that has in large measure been
revived in the new rite for adult baptism.

Until the beginning of the sixth century, three scrutinies
were celebrated, on the third, fourth, and fifth Sundays of
Lent. In fact, the first five Sundays were all organized in
terms of the catechumenate and, inseparably, in terms of a
conversion of life for all Christians. The first Sunday, for
which the Gospel was that of Christ's temptation, was the
Sunday for enrollment in the catechumenate. The enrollment was followed by three years of catechumenal preparation; the immediate preparation took the form of the three
Sunday scrutinies. Once the candidate became associated
with a Christian family, and especially if the candidate
were a child, the enrollment on the first Sunday of Lent
became enrollment for baptism during the coming Paschal
Vigil, that is, after the three Sunday scrutinies and a final
scrutiny on Holy Saturday morning.

Why did the scrutinies not begin immediately, that is, on
the second Sunday of Lent? The answer is simple: The
celebration of the Ember Days was introduced into the first
week of Lent. Now the Ember Saturday, with its six
prophecies and its readings from the Epistles and the Gospel, was celebrated during the night between Saturday and
Sunday, and this meant the suppression of the Sunday
celebration, a fact indicated in the old sacramentaries by
the notation *Dominica vacat* ("the Sunday is empty or

free," i.e., of a liturgical celebration). So the first scrutiny could not take place until the third Sunday.

The exorcisms were connected with the liturgy of the word, and the readings and prayers were chosen with a view to the catechumens. In addition, the catechumens were recommended to the Lord during the Eucharistic Prayer, in the formula that begins *Hanc igitur oblationem* ("Father, accept this offering"), while their sponsors were remembered in the *Memento* of the living.

From the fifth century on, there was also a ceremonial "handing over" (*traditio*) of the Creed. Each article was explained, and the catechumen was obliged to "hand it back" (*reddere, redditio*) at a later point; that is, he had to memorize and recite it. Subsequently there were two further *traditiones*: of the Our Father (likewise explained, petition by petition) and, at the end of the sixth century, of the Gospels; in the latter, a deacon read the beginning of each Gospel and gave a brief commentary.

The formulas for the scrutinial celebrations in the Gelasian Sacramentary show that in most cases the Church was already dealing with infant baptisms. Once this situation became the rule, the three scrutinies, together with their readings and prayers, were transferred from Sundays to weekdays. The Sundays thus deprived took their Gospel pericopes from the weekdays now occupied by the former Sunday scrutinies. Epistles were chosen that would be suitable to the now transformed third, fourth, and fifth Sundays.

It is evident that the features of Lent had now been radically altered; this became Lent as we knew it until the reform initiated by Vatican Council II. Since the children could not personally and actively answer to what was being done over them in the scrutinial ceremonies, the scrutinies were multiplied in a kind of compensatory spirit. The number was doubled to six; the final scrutiny on Holy Saturday morning made seven in all. Gradually the scrutinies became autonomous in relation to the Lenten

Masses. *Ordo Romanus XI* already shows that the close links between the scrutinies and the Mass formularies had been abandoned.[89]

A word needs to be said on the role of St. John's Gospel during Lent. Quite a few exegetes believe that the Gospel was written for use as a baptismal catechesis. In any event, it was certainly used extensively during Lent, especially beginning with the third Sunday. The Roman liturgy has never lost sight of this tradition, and the recent reform has been careful to preserve it.

Since the liturgy of the Sunday scrutinies was to be restored (with adult catechumens in mind), and since the series of readings provided for the scrutinies constitutes a fine catechesis on the paschal mystery, it was decided to form Cycle A out of the readings formerly used on the scrutinial Sundays of Lent. This cycle may be used every year in churches where there are catechumens, but it may also be used every year in other churches. When catechumens are present, the prayers written with them and their sponsors in mind should be used.

It was also decided, however, to provide Lent with two other cycles, B and C. These are less pastoral and in general less satisfactory. Furthermore, in order to form these cycles, texts have been chosen that might usefully have been included in the weekday readings; at times the texts are not entirely suitable, simply because adequate material was lacking.

Given the special character of each cycle, especially Cycle A, we shall study each separately, referring the reader back to the commentary on Cycle A whenever the texts are similar. In order not to interrupt the succession of doctrinal themes proper to the Sundays, we shall study the weekdays, with their single cycle of readings, in a separate section. Similarly, we shall study Palm Sunday and the four following days as a separate unit (Lent ends on the morning of Holy Thursday).

Lent used to begin on the first Sunday. Only later was the beginning set on Ash Wednesday, a day originally geared to the public penitents who were to be reconciled on Holy Thursday morning. In order to give a more unified vision of Lent, we shall begin our discussion of it with the first Sunday. Ash Wednesday will be studied along with the weekdays of the season. It will provide an opportunity for a summing up of the mentality with which the Church wishes us to approach Lent.

TABLE OF READINGS IN THE LITURGY
OF THE HOURS (A Single Cycle)

First Sunday	Exod. 5:1–6:1	The oppression of God's people
Second Sunday	Exod. 13:17–14:9	The journey to the Red Sea
Third Sunday	Exod. 22:20–23:9	The Covenant Code: The law concerning the orphan and the poor
Fourth Sunday	Lev. 8:1-17; 9:22-24	The ordination of the priests
Fifth Sunday	Heb. 1:1–2:4	The Son, heir of all things and exalted above the angels

STRUCTURE OF CYCLE A FOR THE FIRST FIVE SUNDAYS

TABLE OF READINGS IN THE EUCHARISTIC LITURGY

	Old Testament	Apostle	Gospel
First Sunday	Gen. 2:7-9; 3:1-7 Creation and Fall	Rom. 5:12-19 Sin and redemptive grace	Matthew 4:1-11 Temptation of Christ
Second Sunday	Gen. 12:1-4a Call of Abraham	2 Tim. 1:8b-10 Our call to holiness	Matthew 17:1-9 Transfiguration
Third Sunday	Exod. 17:3-7 The thirst of Israel and the waters of despair	Rom. 5:1-2, 5-8 God's love poured into our hearts	John 4:5-42 The Samaritan woman
Fourth Sunday	1 Sam. 16:1b, 6-7, 10-13a The anointing of the king	Eph. 5:8-14 Risen from the dead and enlightened	John 9:1-41 The man born blind
Fifth Sunday	Ezek. 37:12-14 I will put my Spirit within you, and you shall live	Rom. 8:8-11 The Spirit of him who raised Jesus dwells in you	John 11:1-45 Raising of Lazarus

First and Second Sundays of Lent, Cycle A

for years 1978, 1981, 1984, 1987, 1990

6. OUR VICTORY AND TRANSFORMATION IN CHRIST

Temptation of Christ, temptation of mankind

If we are to properly understand the liturgy of the first Sunday, we must go back in spirit to the period when the Christian community closed ranks around the catechumens and when each Christian could remember his own personal history of salvation. That situation is not, of course, to be found only in the distant past; Christian communities in many places can recognize in it their own concrete situation today. In any case, every Christian community must recover something of the same perspective and be united in it with all the other communities.

This opening day of the great catechesis shows the Church preoccupied with two main concerns. She has in mind the essential attitude that must be impressed on the souls of the catechumens; she also is attentive to the basic reactions that must be awakened in the souls of the faithful.

Earlier in this book we discussed the interpretation of the Book of Genesis as read at the beginning of Lent. We return to those reflections now but shall be adding some new considerations.

The mission of Jesus began with a victorious struggle. It took place in the desert during his forty-day fast. The "forty days" evidently had something to do with the traditional choice of this reading to mark the opening of Lent, but Christ's victory over temptation also certainly played a part in the choice.

After his baptism in the Jordan and his official investiture as Messiah by the Holy Spirit, Christ was led into the desert by the same Spirit so that he might be tempted by the devil (Matthew 3:13–4:11). Right from the beginning, then, the Spirit has a very specific activity. Just as he presided over the creation of the world, so he gives rise to the new creation and leads Christ into the desert in order to subject him to a conflict which, unlike that of Adam, will end in victory and be the prelude to the reconstruction and reunification of the world.

In St. Luke's Gospel the succession of pericopes leads to a suggestive juxtaposition. In the latter part of chapter 3, the genealogy of Jesus traces his descent back to "the son of Adam, the son of God." (Luke 3:23-38). Immediately after this comes the account of how Jesus, "the son of Adam," confronts the devil. Ever since the confrontation in paradise, with all its implications for mankind, there had never been another decisive encounter between man and Satan. Now, however, Jesus, "the son of Adam," takes his father's place and, in the name of mankind, confronts the devil once again. This time the conflict ends in a brilliant reversal of the original defeat.

Once this total victory has been achieved, Christ will henceforth be in constant open opposition to Satan. The many cures reported by the evangelists, as well as the expulsions of demons, point to the conflict in which Christ is engaged and are anticipations of his ultimate victory. He must also struggle against all whom the devil dominates. By expelling demons and curing all kinds of illness, Jesus intends to tell us that the reign of Satan is finished[90] and "the kingdom of God has come upon you" (Matthew 12:28); but he tells us the same thing by his opposition to the "brood of vipers" (Matthew 3:7) and to the real "children of Satan,"[91] namely, his proud and unbelieving hearers.

As we know, the Gospel of St. John develops two parallel themes: Jesus progressively reveals himself as Son of God and offers in proof signs that are more and more startling and unmistakable; at the same time, the refusal of the Jews to believe becomes daily more determined. The life of Jesus increasingly becomes a sign to be opposed, and the opposition will reach its climax in his crucifixion.

St. Luke, for his part, is fully aware of how the temptation in the wilderness is linked to the Passion of Christ. At the end of his account of the temptation, he writes: "When the devil had ended every temptation, he departed from him *until an opportune time*" (4:13). Later on, at the Supper, St. John emphasizes the fact that Satan is now entering the lists again: "The devil had already put it into the heart of Judas Iscariot, Simon's son, to betray him" (13:2). Satan now "enters" the soul of Judas, as St. John points out (13:27). For St. Luke, the devil's possession of Judas (22:3) was the opportunity for which Satan had long been waiting. Jesus himself will several times speak of the devil as his Passion draws near: "Now shall the ruler of this world be cast out" (John 12:31); "the ruler of this world is coming. He has no power over me" (John 14:30).

The activity of the "powers of evil" is constantly going on; but the victory of Christ is likewise ever present. His victory becomes ours in our baptism, which is our victory over death.

Victory of Christ, victory of mankind

The Fall in Genesis has its counterpart in the victory of Christ and in our victory as well. In the second reading for the first Sunday of Lent (Rom. 5:12-19), that is the point St. Paul is making when he says that just as all became sinners because one man disobeyed, so all will become just, because one man obeyed. The parallel between the first Adam, natural father of the race, and Christ, Head of redeemed mankind, is dear to St. Paul and to the Fathers.

In the Office of Readings, St. Augustine comments on Psalm 60(61):2-3 and emphasizes the point that we who are tempted in Christ also conquer in Christ:

Christ transformed us in himself when he allowed himself to be tempted by Satan. Just now in the Gos-

pel we heard that the Lord Jesus Christ was tempted
in the wilderness by the devil. Christ, then, was certainly tempted by the devil. Why was he tempted?
Because in him *you* were being tempted. Christ took
his flesh from you and in return gave you the salvation
that resides in him; he took your death for himself and
gave you his life; he took the shame you deserved and
gave you the honor that was his. Consequently, he
took your temptation and gave you his victory. If we
are tempted in him, we also overcome the devil in
him.[92]

In the invitatory, or opening rite of each day's Office, we
sing on this first Sunday of Lent: "Come, let us worship
Christ the Lord, who for our sake endured temptation and
suffering."

Where sin abounded, grace abounded still more — that is
the optimistic vision St. Paul gives us in this reading from
Romans. Our optimism is thus based on Christ's victory,
which has become ours. It is not enough that the victory of
Christ be real; it must also really become our own victory.
What the victory means, as we enter upon the Christian life,
is that we are unconditionally able, by the grace of God
given to us, to regain the balance God intended for us. Victory does not mean that our life on earth will not be a life of
conflict.

Saved in hope

The person who receives baptism is rescued from the
reign of darkness, this "present evil age" (Gal. 1:4) that is
ruled by Satan, "the god of this world [who] has blinded
the minds of the unbelievers, to keep them from seeing the
light of the gospel of the glory of Christ, who is the likeness
of God" (2 Cor. 4:4).

Christ frees the individual who through baptism is conformed to him in his death and resurrection. Before the Last
Supper, Jesus spoke of the coming glorification that his

death would bring: "Now is the judgment of this world, now shall the ruler of this world be cast out; and I, when I am lifted up from the earth, will draw all men to myself." (John 12:31-32). In his First Letter, St. John writes: "We know that . . . the whole world is in the power of the evil one" (1 John 5:19). Christ's resurrection, however, means that the baptized share in his victory: ". . . the ruler of this world is judged (John 16:11); "The reason the Son of God appeared was to destroy the works of the devil" (1 John 3:8).

It is possible for us, however, to lose sight of our real situation as St. Paul describes it: ". . . we ourselves, who have the first fruits of the Spirit, groan inwardly as we wait for adoption as sons, the redemption of our bodies" (Rom. 8:23). We have not regained the power to prevent the body from being autonomous and to subject it to the spirit. That is the hard fact behind the great human drama St. Paul describes when he speaks of the conflict he experiences within himself (Rom. 7:14-25).

We are also forced to admit that even our spirit is not sufficiently subject to God's rule. "The spirit is not sufficiently penetrated by Christ, not united to Christ to the whole extent of its capacity, not yet entirely saturated by grace; and that is why, even after its effective redemption and prior to all personal sin, it still harbours virulent seeds of conflict." [93]

The Christian is now a "child of light" (cf. Eph. 5:8). He lives in the time of grace that precedes Christ's return. "You know what hour it is, how it is full time now for you to wake from sleep. For salvation is nearer to us now than when we first believed; the night is far gone, the day is at hand" (Rom. 13:11-12).

We are already citizens of heaven, and from heaven we eagerly await the coming of the Lord Jesus Christ as our Savior (Phil. 3:20). But that time of waiting is also a time of trial and temptation. Jesus in the wilderness shows us how we should conduct ourselves in the struggle.

We are a little "remnant," historical descendants of the

little "remnant" that came back from captivity in the Old
Testament. Like our Old Testament forebears, we are a remnant chosen by God in his gracious mercy. "But what is
God's reply to him [Elias]? 'I have kept for myself seven
thousand men who have not bowed the knee to Baal.' So
too at the present time there is a remnant chosen by grace"
(Rom. 11:4-5).

Like its Head, this little band must face temptation and
trial. The Church was born from the Savior's side amid trial
and suffering. The Christian's baptism, therefore, is not a
promise of a placid life but a promise of the salvation that
comes through toil and conflict. When James and John
come to Jesus and ask that they might sit at his side in
glory, he answers:

> "You do not know what you are asking. Are you able
> to drink the cup that I drink, or to be baptized with
> the baptism with which I am baptized?" And they
> said to him, "We are able." And Jesus said to them,
> "The cup that I drink you will drink; and with the
> baptism with which I am baptized, you will be bap-
> tized; but to sit at my right hand or at my left is not
> mine to grant, but it is for those for whom it has been
> prepared" (Mark 10:38-40).

Trials and testing, then, describe the condition of the
Church as well as the condition of the baptized individual.
The state of both, even on earth, is heavenly in principle, but
both have many obstacles still to overcome. The Church is
already saved and yet must face persecution and temptation:
"I am coming soon; hold fast what you have, so that no one
may seize your crown" (Apoc. 3:11).

Far from being surprised at trials, the Christian who lives
in Christ should regard them as a sign that he indeed belongs to Christ: "Indeed all who desire to live a godly life in
Christ Jesus will be persecuted" (2 Tim. 3:12). In fact, they
are even more than a sign of belonging; they are necessary
for the development of the Christian, since he gains from
them a new purity and solidity, like gold that is tried in the

fire: "In this you rejoice, though now for a little while you may have to suffer various trials, so that the genuineness of your faith, more precious than gold which though perishable is tested by fire, may redound to praise and glory and honor at the revelation of Jesus Christ" (1 Peter 1:6-7). In short, the Christian must expect to face trouble and suffering, but these are a path to the glory that lies ahead.

Like Christ, the Christian will meet opposition from the world, but he looks for the return of the Lord, and this vision determines his whole moral attitude. In Second Corinthians, St. Paul lists some principles for our guidance: show yourselves servants of God and scandalize no one; be courageous in facing privations and difficulties, hunger and thirst; live a pure life that is guided by an enlightened faith; be patient, kind, and loving (6:1-10, the passage that used to be read on the first Sunday of Lent). "The day is at hand. Let us then cast off the works of darkness and put on the armor of light; let us conduct ourselves becomingly as in the day" (Rom. 13:12-13).

"The young lion and the serpent you will trample under foot"

The warnings given to those who wish to become Christians and the stern reminder addressed to the faithful about the inevitable struggle with Satan may seem extremely harsh. The victory Christ has already won is indeed the basis for a Christian optimism, and every baptized person is aware that he already shares in that victory. Yet his situation in this world may seem somber enough.

Neither catechumen nor baptized Christian should be afraid. The entrance antiphon for the first Sunday of Lent is from Psalm 91 (a psalm also cited in today's Gospel), which is a psalm expressing trust in the divine protection.

As the liturgy of the word gets under way, the Church wants to create an atmosphere of trust, for as the Christian takes his place in the army of Christ and faces the struggle, his heart should be filled with confidence in the divine protection. "When he calls to me, I will answer him; I will be with him in trouble; I will rescue him and honor him. . . . He who dwells in the shelter of the Most High, who abides in the shadow of the Almighty . . ." (Ps. 9:15, 1).

He who engages in the struggle and perseveres in it until the return of Christ is rescued from the fowler's snare and finds a refuge under the Lord's wings. He need fear no arrow, for the Lord's fidelity is a buckler and a shield. The angels will watch over him and protect him from viper and lion and dragon. The psalm ends with a prophecy of paschal victory: "Because he cleaves to me in love, I will deliver him; I will protect him, because he knows my name. . . . I will rescue him and honor him. With long life I will satisfy him, and show him my salvation" (vv. 14-16).

Thus the outcome of the struggle, from the midst of which the Christian cries out to the Lord, is not in doubt; its fruits are glorification and salvation. Commenting on Psalm 90(91), St. Jerome writes: "'He will cover you with his pinions.' He will be raised on the Cross, will extend his hands, and protect us. 'And under his wings you will find refuge,' that is, as you look upon his crucified hands, you will be healed should the serpent bite you." [94]

"Restore to me the joy of thy salvation"

Psalm 51, "Have mercy on me, O God, according to thy steadfast love," has been chosen as the responsorial psalm after the first reading (Genesis). Its central theme is the sin that separates us from God in our earthly lives. The second reading, from Paul's Letter to the Romans, will show how Christ has rescued us from our sinful state.

The entire psalm takes the form of a confession that is both individual and communal. By the time the psalm was composed, Israel had developed to the point where each Israelite could recite it in private prayer as well as with the community in the liturgical celebration. The sin of which the psalm speaks consists in opposition to God: "Against

thee, thee only, have I sinned, and done that which is evil
in thy sight." The point of this verse is that the sinner sees
his sin to be his own and acknowledges that he is responsible for it. He asks to be purified of it, knowing that the Lord
alone can accomplish this.

We find in this psalm the vocabulary for any penitential
liturgy; read the psalm through and this will become clear.
The verses chosen for the first Sunday of Lent emphasize
the aspect of purification: "Create in me a clean heart, O
God." They also ask for wisdom and strength: "Put a new
and right spirit within me. Cast me not away from thy presence, and take not thy holy Spirit from me."

Such a purification will restore to man the special joy
proper to being saved: "Restore to me the joy of thy salvation." When the return to the Lord is effected, a man cannot
but break out into thanksgiving: "O Lord, open thou my
lips, and my mouth shall show forth thy praise."

Psalm 51 proves extraordinarily powerful and stirs profound spiritual emotion not only when sung by the Church,
with Christ, to the Father, but when addressed directly to
Christ himself. If we use the psalm in this second manner,
we immediately recapture a dimension of sin of which the
New Testament was aware: sin is sin against Christ.

Transfiguration (Gospel, second Sunday)

He who makes his decision and accepts conflict is also
destined to be transformed into the likeness of Christ.

Moses fasted for forty days, and later Elijah did the same;
both ascended the holy mountain. In the Mass of the second Sunday they appear to the apostles in the company of
the transfigured Christ: "He was transfigured before them,
and his face shone like the sun, and his garments became
white as light. And behold, there appeared to them Moses
and Elijah, talking with him" (Matthew 17:2-3).

How significant that Moses and Elijah should be found in
intimate conversation with Christ! During their life on

earth they had already been invited to this intimacy with the Lord, and it was a fast of forty days that prepared each of them for their meeting with God.

After only a few days of Lent, catechumens and baptized alike have had the opportunity to see more deeply into the reality of Christian existence. On the first Sunday we have been present at the tempting of the Lord. Then the Church has shown us not only the attentive care of the Lord for his people but also the struggles, trials, and austerities they must embrace if they are to walk with him. Now we move on to the transfiguration, where we find Moses and Elijah with Christ.

The choice of this particular pericope is important, and we must dwell on it for a moment. Here the Church has her catechumens gathered before her. She has already introduced them to an austere life like that of Moses and Elijah. Now she takes them, along with the apostles, to the transfiguration. Christ will indeed be glorified, but he will reach that state by passing through suffering and death. The Church thus presents a program embracing the whole life of anyone who wants to enter the baptismal font and model his life upon that of Christ.

Evidently, on the very first Sunday of Lent we find ourselves already at the heart of the paschal mystery, for this mystery can be summed up by saying that through his Cross Christ entered into his glory. Observe that Peter, James, and John, who witness the transfiguration, will also see Christ in his agony. A further point to be noted is that this episode follows upon Peter's faith-inspired answer at Caesarea to Christ's question: "Who do men say that the Son of man is? . . . But who do you say that I am?" (Matthew 16:13, 15). At the transfiguration, Peter finds his profession of faith in Christ confirmed by the Father's words: "This is my beloved Son, with whom I am well pleased; listen to him" (Matthew 17:5).

St. Luke's account of the transfiguration tells us what Christ was speaking of with Moses and Elijah: "[They] spoke of his departure, which he was to accomplish at

Jerusalem" (Luke 9:31). More simply, they spoke of his
exodus, his passover. This is all the more striking in that the
whole account of the transfiguration begins with the words
"After six days" (Matthew 17:1) or "Now about eight days
after these sayings" (Luke 9:28), that is, about six or eight
days after Jesus had foretold his coming Passion.

Once again, then, the transfiguration of the Lord focuses
our attention wholly on the paschal mystery. But we are to
attend to it in a more than narrowly contemplative manner,
as if we were simply watching Jesus dying and rising and
thus accomplishing "his" passover or passage. No, we are
meant to approach it in an active way, as a mystery that
involves us, a mystery that we are to accomplish with Christ.
The Christian and the catechumen are to spend the
forty days with Moses and Elijah in order to ascend the
mountain with them. We must enter upon our own exodus,
not simply contemplating the transfigured Christ, as the
disciples did, but being transfigured with him.

St. Ambrose, commenting on the postbaptismal rite in
which the newly baptized receive their white robe, writes:
"He who is baptized is purified according to the law and
according to the Gospel. . . . According to the Gospel, because the garments of Christ were white as snow when he
showed himself, in the Gospel, in the glory proper to his
resurrection. He, therefore, whose sins are forgiven becomes whiter than snow." [95]

In the first volume of this series, when reflecting on
Christ's baptism in the Jordan, we already discussed certain
aspects of the transfiguration and especially the Father's
words; we refer the reader to that discussion. Here we need
only note that the transfiguration is connected with the ac-
complishment of the Father's will. In a sermon that is read
in the Office of Readings for the second Sunday of Lent, St.
Leo the Great gives a fine commentary on the transfiguration and the profound significance it has for us:

> [The Lord] gave solid grounds for the Church's hope
> so that the whole Body of Christ might understand the
> transfiguration bestowed upon it and that the mem-

bers might be assured of sharing in the honor which shone out in their Head. With regard to this sharing, the Lord himself had said, when speaking of his coming in majesty: "Then the righteous will shine like the sun in the kingdom of their Father." St. Paul asserts the same when he says: "I consider that the sufferings of this present time are not worth comparing with the glory that is to be revealed to us." And again: "You have died, and your life is hid with Christ in God. When Christ who is our life appears, then you also will appear with him in glory."[96]

Obey the call

God's call of Abraham and his choice of Abraham's posterity (first reading, second Sunday of Lent) has always had a profound significance for Christians, who see in it a prefigurement of their own call and the choice of the Church.

In this passage as in many others, the text of Genesis shows the influence of three traditions concerning the event. The account nonetheless emerges as a unity, while the absence of anecdotal detail allows the figure of Abraham to stand out in all its religious splendor. He will forever be the man whom a loving God chose in order to bless him and entrust the divine promises to him. That is the way the Yahwist source wishes us to see him.

God's act of friendship, however, implies demands to be made on Abraham; the friendship must be returned. And the patriarch, amid the many trials and difficulties of his long life, does manifest a faith that men will always regard as an unparalleled model for their own faith. It is this moral stature of Abraham that the Elohist source wishes to bring home to us.

God's covenant with Abraham and his descendants must have its outward sign. The Priestly tradition, which is the third source for the narratives concerning Abraham, will emphasize the fact that God changes this man's name from Abram to Abraham, meaning "father of multitudes." He is chosen in order that he might be a "father." The sign of the covenant for his posterity will be their circumcision (Gen. 17:4-14).

God chooses. It is impossible to read this account and not apply it to ourselves by asking whether God's choice extends to our own time and embraces anyone who seeks the truth. Do I see myself in this Abraham, who is the figure or model not only of Jesus Christ but of every person whom God calls? The whole history of salvation thus involves choice and call. We know the outcome of that history, and to us Abraham appears as the starting point of a divine action whose full extent we shall understand only at the end of time.

Suddenly God takes the initiative and speaks to Abraham. Abraham is now a man called, and immediately his life is changed. This man, a descendant of Shem, finds that he now belongs to God and must abandon his native land; he must depart from Ur. For God is a jealous God and sets apart anyone whom he chooses: "Go from your country and your kindred and your father's house to the land that I will show you. And I will make of you a great nation" (Gen. 12:1-2).

If we ask why it should be Abraham to whom these words were addressed, we will receive no answer. He is chosen from among many others, but not for any exceptional qualities we can discern in him. There is only one possible answer to our question: God chooses because he loves.

Abraham "went," for his going is the condition for receiving the fullness of God's gifts and becoming father of a posterity that will end in the new people of God of which the First Letter of Peter speaks (2:9). The road Abraham is to travel is unknown to him; he is in God's hands. The Letter to the Hebrews emphasizes this point: "He went out, not knowing where he was to go" (11:8).

Believe in love

"He went out, not knowing where he was to go." Reliance on God presupposes faith in him and his love, and it implies a return of love. The person who is called accomplishes nothing great unless God helps him to accomplish it. His own contribution is simply to grow in love. If he does, all else necessary will come from the God who anticipates us in our every action. The readings of the Lenten season will cast an indispensable light on the faith of Abraham and on the Christian imitation of that faith in daily life; this enlightenment will enable the Christian to avoid possible deviations.

Such deviations certainly can occur. The mere fact of being a descendant of Abraham gives one no guarantee that deviations will surely be avoided. No, the simple belonging must turn into a genuine giving of self to God. Jesus makes this point in an almost brutal way when speaking to the Jews: "I know that you are descendants of Abraham; yet you seek to kill me. . . . You are of your father the devil, and your will is to do your father's desires" (John 8:37, 44).

Those seeking the Catholic Church and those who belong to it both need to be reminded that juridical membership is not enough. We must not only belong to the stock of Abraham; we must be children of Abraham as well and do the works of the Father.

Even here, however, we can fall into a snare. To do the works of the Father in a formalistic way guarantees nothing, as Jesus points out on many occasions. In Christian life it is God who gives us the power to act, and to act out of love for him; the first and fundamental "observance" consists in charity. That is the point St. Paul is making in 1 Corinthians 13:1-13 (which used to be read on Quinquagesima Sunday).

The unconditional faith of Abraham is one of the best known themes of the Old Testament and one of the most important for every one of us. The trials Abraham had to undergo show how God was taking the initiative in the work of salvation. Indeed, Abraham himself was fully aware that he had not been called because of any special merits or qualities of his own. The birth of Isaac brought home to him how God had a special destiny in mind for his posterity. Isaac was the fruit of an impossible conception, and

Abraham saw in his birth a sign that God would indeed fulfill his promises (Gen. 21:1-8).

According to a number of scholars, the account of the sacrifice of Isaac (Gen. 22) was revised to some extent at a later time. In it we read that God ordered Abraham to offer up his own son in sacrifice. As a matter of fact, we know that the Canaanites did at times sacrifice children as part of their cult. In any case, the emphasis in the Genesis account is on two points. The first is that Abraham submits to God in faith and is ready to sacrifice his son: "Now I know that you fear God, seeing you have not withheld your son, your only son, from me" (Gen. 22:12). Christian tradition will see in the sacrifice of Isaac a prefiguration of the sacrifice of God's only Son. The Church here is once again advising those who wish to become her members that their faith will have to be unconditional.

The second point stressed in the account (a point of less importance here) is that God intervenes to put an end to the practice of sacrificing children. The re-editing of the account highlights this condemnation, one the prophets had often proclaimed. But this didactic aspect of the account in no way detracts from the faith of Abraham.

Under the covenant, God has the initiative to such an extent that even when it comes to offering him a sacrifice, he is the one who "will provide himself the lamb for a burnt offering" (Gen. 22:8). Abraham himself makes this point, for after he has offered in Isaac's place a ram that had been trapped in a nearby thicket, the account tells us: "Abraham called the name of that place The Lord will provide; as it is said to this day, 'On the mount of the Lord it shall be provided'" (Gen. 22:14).

The same principle applies to the sacrifice of Christ and his Church. God always provides the Victim, thus keeping the initiative in the work of salvation and making the liturgy his own. It is always the only Son that is offered, and it is always God that provides the Victim and hands him over for the salvation of the world.

God's oath

There is an air of joy about Genesis when it tells us that "the Lord had blessed Abraham in all things" (Gen. 24:1). Chapter 22 tells us of the oath God swore after he had intervened to save Isaac:

> By myself I have sworn, says the Lord, because you have done this, and have not withheld your son, your only son, I will indeed bless you, and I will multiply your descendants as the stars of heaven and as the sand which is on the seashore. And your descendants shall possess the gate of their enemies, and by your descendants shall all the nations of the earth bless themselves, because you have obeyed my voice (Gen. 22:16-18).

As we know, a single individual was to fulfill the promise and be *the* descendant of Abraham. The stock of Abraham proved unfaithful, and the history of the Old Testament is the history of its infidelities and of God's repeated efforts to bring it back to faith, love, and fidelity. His repeated efforts were failures. Thus, at first sight, God's blessing on Abraham seemed a failure. Its success becomes clear only when we move on to "the time of fulfillment."

The Church frequently speaks to us of "Abraham's bosom." The phrase comes from St. Luke's parable of Dives and Lazarus; the latter "was carried by the angels to Abraham's bosom" (Luke 16:22). The Church wishes her children to end in the same way; our present liturgy for the dead prays that the soul of the deceased may be led "to Abraham's side."

The Christian of today is heir to the promise given to Abraham, but he is an heir through, and because of, Christ. In Christ alone was the promise completely fulfilled; he alone became the heir of the promise.

St. Paul speaks of these fundamental ideas in chapter 3 of his Letter to the Galatians. His line of thought is quite clear. Abraham "believed God, and it was reckoned to him as righteousness" (3:6). In Abraham all nations were to be blessed, but only those that have faith would effectively be blessed along with Abraham, the man of faith (3:8-9). Observance of the law avails nothing, for "it is evident that no man is justified before God by the law; for 'He who through faith is righteous shall live'" (3:11). Christ "redeemed us from the curse of the law, having become a curse for us . . . that in Christ Jesus the blessing of Abraham might come upon the Gentiles, that we might receive the promise of the Spirit through faith" (3:12-14).

Clearly, then, the promise was fulfilled in a single man. And yet God could rightly speak of a multitude of descendants because through Jesus Christ the many also become heirs of the promise. Christ adds that Abraham himself had a consoling vision of the complete fulfillment of the divine promise: "Your father Abraham rejoiced that he was to see my day; he saw it and was glad" (John 8:56).

All who are united to, and identified with, Christ are heirs to the promise with him: "For as many of you as were baptized into Christ have put on Christ. There is neither Jew nor Greek, there is neither slave nor free, there is neither male nor female; for you are all one in Christ Jesus. And if you are Christ's, then you are Abraham's offspring, heirs according to promise" (Gal. 3:27-29).

Family of Abraham, family of Christ

A suitable catechesis must bring home these points to those who seek to draw near to Christ and the Church. The baptism they wish to receive is the sacrament of faith. Once they have put on Christ, they will become children of the promise. Each of them will be "no longer a slave but a son, and if a son then an heir" (Gal. 4:7).

Here, once again, the liturgy offers the world a broad synthetic vision of the problem of salvation and the possibilities for its solution. The direction of the solution is clear and can be summed up in a phrase: the Lord's love for men. God loves, chooses, and calls. The appropriate re-

sponse is unconditional faith, and the reward for such faith
is that man in Christ becomes an heir to the promise. God's
love, which created mankind, still seeks to gather men into
his kingdom, the kingdom that the heirs to the promise in
Christ will possess.

Two loves

The Christian is the constant object of this divine love
that makes him an heir to the promises and a child of the
kingdom. But being a child and an heir presupposes, on his
part, an unremitting effort to respond to the love that God
pours out on him. Love alone gives meaning to the history of
salvation, and love alone gives meaning and coherence to a
Christian's life. First Corinthians, chapter 13, to which we
alluded earlier, says this in an uncompromising way:

> If I speak in the tongues of men and of angels, but
> have not love, I am a noisy gong or a clanging cymbal.
> And if I have prophetic powers, and understand all
> mysteries and all knowledge, and if I have all faith, so
> as to remove mountains, but have not love, I am noth-
> ing. If I give away all I have, and if I deliver my body
> to be burned, but have not love, I gain nothing (1 Cor.
> 13:1-3).

There can be no room for illusion here. Love is essential;
nothing can avail without it, not even a faith powerful
enough to move mountains. Love, or charity, then, is a
comprehensive program for Christian life. It is, moreover,
man's answer to God's love that has been revealed in so
many divine initiatives in the Old and New Testaments.
God has always loved us first; he is the fountainhead of
love. St. John explains this by telling us in the fourth chapter of his First Letter just what love is: "In this the love of
God was made manifest among us, that God sent his only
Son into the world, so that we might live through him. In
this is love, not that we loved God but that he loved us and
sent his Son to be the expiation for our sins" (1 John 4:9-
10).

Love has been fully revealed to us in the person of Jesus and has reached its climactic expression in his death on the Cross. But Christ did not simply reveal to us the Father's love for us; he also showed us how we are to love the Father and one another.

In 1 Corinthians 13, St. Paul goes on to describe the specific qualities of love. He tells us that love for God is signified and expressed in love for our brothers and sisters:

> Love is patient and kind; love is not jealous or boast-ful; it is not arrogant or rude. Love does not insist on its own way; it is not irritable or resentful; it does not rejoice at wrong, but rejoices in the right. Love bears all things, believes all things, hopes all things, en-dures all things (1 Cor. 13:4-7).

Since we all belong to the one family of Abraham and have all put on Christ, this kind of fraternal love is indeed a touchstone, as St. John insists: "Beloved, if God so loved us, we also ought to love one another" (1 John 4:11); "If any one says, 'I love God,' and hates his brother, he is a liar; for he who does not love his brother whom he has seen, cannot love God whom he has not seen. And this commandment we have from him, that he who loves God should love his brother also" (1 John 4:20-21).

This basic law of Christianity allows no loopholes: we must love God and our neighbor. "By this all men will know that you are my disciples, if you have love for one another" (John 13:35).

The story of Abraham, which stands in such sharp con-trast to the story of Adam, who is the very image of dis-obedience, points out the road the believer must travel: the road of faith, hope, and obedient love. Not only is there a contrast between Adam and Abraham; there is also a paral-lel between Abraham and Christ. The New Testament looks upon Christ as the fulfillment of the promise. Peter, in one of his sermons, tells his hearers that Christ belongs to Abraham's posterity: "You are the sons of the prophets and of the covenant which God gave to your fathers, saying to

Abraham, 'And in your posterity shall all the families of the earth be blessed.' God, having raised up his servant, sent him to you first, to bless you in turning every one of you from your wickedness" (Acts 3:25-26).

Our holy calling

"Our Savior Christ Jesus . . . abolished death and brought life and immortality to light through the gospel" (2 Tim. 1:10). Thus does St. Paul speak to us in the second reading for the second Sunday. In Christ, "God saved us and called us with a holy calling" (2 Tim. 1:9). This is important both for those preparing for baptism and for all the rest of us.

The first point about this calling that needs to be emphasized is that it is entirely free on God's part. If God has saved us and given us a call to holiness, it is not because of any merits of ours, says the Apostle. The idea of God's freely given call is a favorite of St. Paul; he speaks of us as being called to holiness (Rom. 1:7; 1 Cor. 1:2) and to charity (Gal. 5:13). In all this, however, God has a plan that he is bent on carrying out, a plan that he reveals to us in his Son Jesus. In this context St. Paul speaks of "the mystery," meaning the divine plan that was hidden through the ages but has now been made known to all in Christ. And what is that plan? It is a plan to give mankind the victory over death and the gift of life and immortality — in short, the paschal victory.

We are called, then, to holiness, and if we respond to the call as Abraham and Jesus did, we shall eventually reach our triumphal transfiguration.

Such, then, is the global vision of the history of salvation as presented in the readings for the first two Sundays of Lent. We were created that we might be holy and glorify the Father; we fell in Adam and we succumbed to personal temptation. Now we are filled with the grace of Christ and called anew to holiness and to a glory that will be a sharing in the transfiguration of Christ himself. Baptism has given us the *rudimenta gloriae*, "the elements of our own future glorification," to use an expression from the Gelasian Sacramentary.[97]

The entry into the catechumenate

After a certain amount of pre-evangelization and a careful study of each adult who wishes to enter the Church, the local church celebrates in ritual the entry of the candidate into the catechumenate. The community that accepts responsibility for him is present, especially those individuals whose task it will be to guide and help him. The rite is connected with a liturgy of the word and may be followed by the Eucharist or held separately.[98]

The candidate is asked what he seeks from the Church and then is given a brief exhortation in which he is told that the way of the gospel is now opening before him, the way of faith that will lead him to love and eternal life. He is now asked whether he is ready to enter upon this way. Thereupon, the sponsors and the whole assembly are asked whether they are willing to help the catechumen. The celebrant offers a short prayer of thanksgiving, to which all respond with the words "We praise and bless you, Lord!"[99]

The signing of the catechumen's forehead with the cross belongs to the oldest part of the catechumenate ritual. The priest and the sponsors trace the sign, and the celebrant says: "N., receive the cross on your forehead: by this sign of his love (or: of his triumph) Christ will be your strength. Learn now to know and follow him."[100] This is followed by the (optional) signing of the catechumen's various senses: ears, eyes, lips, breast, and shoulders. This part of the ritual is then concluded by one or other of two prayers. The first is from the Gelasian Sacramentary: "Let us pray. Father, we pray for these catechumens N. and N. who have been signed with the cross of our Lord Jesus Christ; by its power, keep them safe. May they be faithful to your initial teachings and, by keeping your commandments, come to be reborn in glory."[101]

The alternate prayer is of recent composition: "Almighty

God, you have given life to your people by the death and resurrection of your Son. May these catechumens take up their cross, live always by its saving power and reveal it in their lives."[102]

If it be appropriate to do so, a new name is given to the catechumen. Then he is conducted into the church, where a liturgy of the word is celebrated. After the homily (an innovation in relation to the tradition, which postpones the homily to a later point), the candidate is given the book of the Gospels, and the congregation offers a litanic prayer for him. The celebrant then concludes the whole rite with a prayer. Two options are given. The first prayer suggested is again from the Gelasian Sacramentary, though it has been slightly revised: "(God of our fathers and) God of all creation, keep your servants N. and N. joyful in hope and faithful in your service. Lead them, Lord, to the waters of baptism that give new life. May the eternal joy you promise be the reward of all who spend their lives in good works."[103]

The alternate prayer is one of recent composition: "God and Father of all creation, since you created man in your own likeness, receive with love these men (and women) who come to you today. May they who have listened to the word in this community be renewed by its power and come to reflect the image of Christ."[104]

When the catechumens have been dismissed, the Eucharist may be celebrated.

During the catechumenate and their period of instruction, the catechumens take part in further liturgies of the word that are celebrated specifically for them.

The priest, the deacon, and even the catechist may impose hands on the catechumens and pronounce "minor exorcisms" over them. The ritual provides a number of such prayers of exorcism, as well as formulas for blessing the catechumens.

The "handing over" or "presentation" (*traditio*) of the Creed, etc., may be anticipated. We shall speak of it, however, at the point where it should ordinarily be celebrated in accordance with the ancient tradition. It is also permissible to anoint the catechumens with blessed oil on the breast, on the hands, and even on other parts of the body if desirable.

After the period of the simple catechumenate comes the enrollment of the catechumens for their final preparation; this enrollment takes place at the beginning of the Lent immediately preceding their baptism. At this point the catechumenate in the strict sense is at an end, since the candidates cease to be simply "catechumens" (i.e., "hearers") and become "elect" (i.e., chosen for proximate baptism). (Thus the ancient tradition; we shall continue to use here the general term "catechumen.")

The priest or other person responsible for the initiation of the catechumens presents them to the community. The sponsors are then questioned about the fitness of the candidates, and the catechumens are asked whether they indeed wish to be baptized at the next Easter Vigil. The community then offers a litanic prayer for them, and the celebrant ends the ceremony with a prayer.

Two concluding prayers are provided, and again the first is from the Gelasian Sacramentary, while the alternate is of recent composition. "God our Father, you created the human race that you might also be the One who makes it ever new. Count these adopted children as sons (and daughters) reborn to your new covenant. Make them children of the promise. Although they cannot reach eternal life by their own nature, may they come to share it by the power of your love."[105] "All-powerful Father, God of love, you wish to make all things new in Christ and to draw all men to him. Guide and govern these men (and women), chosen through the ministry of your Church. Keep them faithful to their calling, help them to be built into the Kingdom of your Son, and prepare them to be sealed with the promised Gift of the Holy Spirit."[106]

The "elect" are then dismissed and the Eucharist is celebrated.

The enrollment for baptism was regarded in the past as highly important. The Book of Exodus had spoken of heavenly tablets on which the names of God's elect were written (Exod. 32:32-33). St. Gregory of Nyssa alludes to this when speaking of the catechumens enrolling for baptism: "Give me your names so that I may write them down in ink. But the Lord Himself will engrave them on incorruptible tablets, writing them with His own finger, as He once wrote the Law of the Hebrews." [107]

We will note that the catechumens and the elect are dismissed before the Eucharistic liturgy begins. The point of the dismissal is not to keep the Eucharistic celebration secret nor simply to restore an ancient practice for its own sake. The intention is rather to emphasize the fact that normally one may not be present at the celebration of the Eucharistic banquet unless one is worthy to eat of it. For this, one must be a baptized Catholic, and more.

Once enrolled, the catechumens begin a kind of retreat in preparation for baptism. In her *Diary of a Pilgrimage*, Egeria writes: "It is the custom here, throughout the forty days on which there is fasting, for those who are preparing for baptism to be exorcized by the clergy." [108] (Egeria was writing at the end of the fourth century and describing the liturgy at Jerusalem insofar as she could observe it.)

Third Sunday of Lent, Cycle A

for years 1978, 1981, 1984, 1987, 1990

7. THE THIRST FOR THE WATER OF LIFE

Living water

No better Scripture texts could have been chosen than those of this third Sunday for telling the catechumens how

their thirst will be quenched. In these passages they meet
the Lord as the Rock from which water flows forth in the
desert (Exod. 17:3-7), and they draw near to Christ, who is
living Water for those who believe in him (John 4:5-42).

The bitter water at Marah had earlier stirred the anger of
God's people on their journey away from Egypt. On that
occasion, a piece of wood thrown into the water had
rendered it sweet (Exod. 15:22-26). Now, a little while later, the lack of water is again being felt. The place is Mas-
sah and Meribah, two names given to Rephidim to mark it
as the place where the people were tested and where they
quarreled with Moses and their God.

The reading brings that tragic story home to the imagina-
tion and heart of the catechumens. The people of God are
weary; they have been on the march for a long time, they
are fatigued and have nothing, they have no sense of unity,
no efficient organization. It is quite understandable then,
humanly speaking, that they should rebel. What is less understandable is that they should rebel against the God who
has already done so much for them. They forget the past
and the Lord's constant care for them, and, with mindless
violence, begin to complain and grow angry: "Give us
water to drink" (Exod. 17:2). Their cry, addressed to Moses
and through him to God, might have been a confident appeal in time of trial, a request inspired by optimism and
sure of a saving answer. In fact, it was a kind of curse uttered in despair.

Thus the people of Israel were turning away from their
God. Here was a crucial moment in their journey, and a sin
of despair that would forever leave its mark on them. The
psalms will remind Israel later on of this moment of infidelity: "Yet they sinned still more against him, rebelling
against the Most High in the desert. They tested God in
their heart by demanding the food they craved. They spoke
against God, saying, 'Can God spread a table in the wilderness?'" (Ps. 78:17-19).

The rock stands before the people, solid and inexorable.
Apparently there is no human solution. Even Moses him-

self does not seem too sure of the Lord's omnipotence, and Aaron shares his uneasiness. And for this both will be punished, as the parallel account in the Book of Numbers tells us: "Because you did not believe in me, to sanctify me in the eyes of the people of Israel, therefore you shall not bring this assembly into the land which I have given them" (20:12).

The power of the Lord does manifest itself, despite the weakness of Moses' faith: "Pass on before the people, taking with you some of the elders of Israel; and take in your hand the rod with which you struck the Nile, and go. Behold, I will stand before you there on the rock, and water shall come out of it, that the people may drink" (Exod. 17:5-6). All trust must be in the Lord, but the trust is justified: "Water came forth abundantly" (Num. 20:11).

The religious wonder roused by this event would last through the centuries: "He cleft rocks in the wilderness, and gave them drink abundantly as from the deep. He made streams come out of the rock, and caused waters to flow down like rivers" (Ps. 78:15-16). Isaiah speaks in the same tones: "They thirsted not when he led them through the deserts; he made water flow for them from the rock; he cleft the rock and the water gushed out" (Is. 48:21).

The water gushing from the rock was to play a key role in the life of Israel, for it was a sign of how much they were loved by that Lord who would henceforth be called the "Rock of salvation": "O come, let us sing to the Lord; let us make a joyful noise to the Rock of our salvation!" (Ps. 95:1).

The Fathers offer two different interpretations of this extremely important episode. Some see the water, taken in conjunction with the manna, as a prefiguration of the Eucharistic wine. St. John Chrysostom interprets it this way when commenting on 1 Corinthians 10:4 and on the connection between the crossing of the Red Sea and baptism:

> After speaking of the sea, the cloud, and Moses, Paul adds: "And all ate the same supernatural food." He means: Just as you came up from the pool and ran to

the table, so they came out of the sea and approached a new and miraculous table (I am referring to the manna). And just as you have a marvelous drink, the Savior's Blood, so they had a miraculous drink. They found no springs or rivers, but they did receive abundant water from the hard, dry rock.[109]

St. Ambrose follows the same line of thought in his two catechetical works, *De sacramentis* and *De mysteriis*; for him, too, the water of Horeb prefigures the Eucharistic wine. He expresses his thought quite clearly in the *De sacramentis*:

> "They drank from the supernatural Rock which followed them, and the Rock was Christ." Drink, you too, that Christ may follow along with you. See the mystery! Moses is the prophet; his staff is God's word. The priest [Moses] touches the rock with the word of God and water flows, and the people drink. So, too, the priest [in the Eucharist] touches the chalice and water flows in the chalice and leaps up for eternal life.[110]

St. Augustine accepts the same parallelism.[111]

There is, however, another patristic interpretation that sees baptism prefigured in the water flowing from the rock at Horeb. While the first interpretation was based on St. Paul (1 Cor. 10:4), this one appeals to St. John. St. Cyprian is one of the most important proponents of this interpretation:

> Every time that water alone is mentioned in the Holy Scripture, it refers to Baptism. God foretold through the Prophet [Isaiah] that while they were among pagan peoples and in dry places water would gush forth and fill the chosen people of God, that is, those who had been made his children by Baptism. The Prophet says: "They thirsted not in the desert when he led them out: he brought forth water out of the rock for them, and he clove the rock, and the waters

gushed out" (Is. 48:21). This was fulfilled in the Gospel
when the side of the Lord, who is the Rock, was
pierced by a lance during his Passion. He recalls what
had been said of him by the Prophet when he
exclaims: "If anyone thirst let him come to me and
drink. He who believes in me, from his belly shall
flow living waters." To emphasize that the Lord is
speaking not of the chalice but of Baptism, Scripture
adds: "This he said of the Spirit, which they were to
receive who believed in him" (John 7:37-39). And we
receive the Spirit in Baptism.[112]

"If you knew the gift of God"

It is an easy step from the account of the miraculous
water in the Book of Exodus to Jesus' words on the true
"living water" in John's Gospel (4:5-42). The meeting of
Jesus and the Samaritan woman is fascinating indeed. Back
in the Book of Exodus we saw the Israelites full of com-
plaints and standing before the Rock that would save them;
we might, as we read, think ourselves transported to the
dawn of creation, when God first encountered his fallen
creatures. Here, in the Gospel of St. John, Christ meets one
of his sinful creatures and, in her person, encounters mankind, which he intends to create anew.

St. Augustine has a fine commentary on the episode, as
he describes the wearied Creator confronting the creature
whom he is bent upon creating anew through his weariness
and suffering:

> It was for you that Jesus was wearied from the jour-
> ney. We find Jesus strong but also weak: a strong
> Jesus and a weak Jesus. Strong, because "in the be-
> ginning was the Word, and the Word was with God,
> and the Word was God. He was in the beginning with
> God." Would you know how strong this Son of God
> is? "All things were made through him, and without
> him was not anything made that was made," and all

these things were made without effort. What can be stronger than him who made all things effortlessly?

Do you want to see him weak? "The Word became flesh and dwelt among us." The strength of Christ created you, the weakness of Christ created you anew. The strength of Christ brought into existence what was not; the weakness of Christ prevented what was from perishing. He created us in his strength; he searched us out in his weakness.[113]

The baptismal typology in the story of the Samaritan woman is clear at several points. Thus: "Whoever drinks of the water that I shall give him will never thirst; the water that I shall give him will become in him a spring of water welling up to eternal life" (John 4:14). In other words, water by itself does not give life, but only water that has been transformed by Christ. The real "water from the well" is Christ.

We should bear in mind here one of the interpretations the Fathers gave to the rock at Horeb. They saw in it the side of Christ that was opened to let water flow out (see the passage above from St. Ambrose).

St. Augustine, for his part, writes: "The rock is a pre-figurement of Christ. . . . Moses struck the rock twice with his staff, and the two blows signify the two arms of the cross."[114] His interpretation looks to both baptism and the Eucharist, and enables us to better understand why John 4:14 should be chosen as a Communion antiphon for the Mass of the third Sunday: "Whoever drinks the water that I shall give him, says the Lord, will have a spring inside him, welling up for eternal life."

As even unbelievers can see when they meet Christians fervent in their faith, the latter do not hesitate, in whatever circumstances, to ask the Lord for "a sign of thy favor, that those who hate me may see and be put to shame because thou, Lord, hast helped me and comforted me" (Ps. 86:17). When these Christians find themselves in the arid wastes, they feel no need to complain, as the Israelites did, but say simply: "Lord, give us water." And when they receive the Eucharist, they hear Christ say to them: "Whoever drinks of the water that I shall give him will never thirst."

The Christian is thus led to interpret the gift of water to the Samaritan woman in the same way as the gift of water to the Israelities at Horeb: It is a source of nourishment and strength. As the catechumens hear the Gospel, it is as though they heard St. John himself telling them that the water the Lord gives is the water of rebirth.

The Mass for this third Sunday evidently has the catechumens very much in mind. If we but think of these readings and chants in the context of the scrutiny, with its special prayers for the Mass, we will have no difficulty in discerning the spirit in which the Mass formulary for the third Sunday was compiled. The catechumen, like the baptized Christian, is a human being who thirsts for God, a human being on a journey.

The prophet Isaiah links the episode of the rock at Horeb with the new exodus. The water that flowed from the rock becomes, in his eyes, a symbol of the salvation that God will give in the messianic age (see Is. 35:6; 41:18; 43:20; 48:21). At the well of Jacob, Jesus tells the Samaritan woman that the messianic age has come and that "I who speak to you am he [the Messiah]" (John 4:26).

The promises are now fulfilled. The Israelites had asked for water, and the Lord now gives it anew, but it is a mightier water than before. Now water will be the instrument of salvation, the source of life, a well out of which man is reborn as one emerging with Christ from the tomb and entering upon a new life that is itself the pledge of eternal life. For baptism is not an end but a beginning, a rebirth leading to a struggle that will last until Christ returns. Water becomes a spiritual drink and is transformed into the blood of Christ that was poured out to ransom the multitude. Baptism and Eucharist together constitute a complete initiation into the life of God.

The major themes of the conversation with the Samaritan woman

It will be worth our while to review briefly the major themes of this Gospel passage, which is certainly one of the most beautiful in the Fourth Gospel. This will also provide an opportunity to observe once again how the liturgy makes use of Scripture. If one were to approach the text purely as an exegete, it would be difficult to see in it any reference to the sacraments. And yet the Church, following the Fathers, reads the text precisely in this way when she uses it on the third Sunday of Lent, the day of the first scrutiny for those to be baptized. In such a reading, two sections are of special interest: the dialogue with the Samaritan woman (4:7-26) and the dialogue with the disciples (4:31-38).

In the first dialogue we find a favorite method of St. John at work: the conversation takes place on two levels, as it were, allowing two ways of understanding what is said. The Samaritan woman interprets the water and what is said of it as applying to man's natural thirst, whereas Jesus sees in the water a sign. He promises a "living" water (vv. 7-15) that is God's gift. But the gift of living water is connected with the knowledge of Jesus, who, at a later point in this dialogue, will reveal himself to be the Messiah (v. 26, "I who speak to you am he").

Water is an important theme throughout the Scriptures. In the prophetic books it is a symbol of the blessings the Messiah will bring (Zech. 14:8; Joel 4:18). In the sapiential books water is equated with wisdom (Prov. 13:14; etc.), or else it symbolizes the fruit derived from the study of the law (Sir. 24:22-31), that is, wisdom from on high. In the New Testament, similarly, living water symbolizes the teaching of Christ.[115] In the dialogue with the Samaritan woman, then, when Jesus speaks of water, he is continuing the Jewish symbolism according to which water stands for wisdom. The wisdom now, however, is the wisdom of Christ.

At this point we pass to a new level. The water is the

revelation that Jesus brings and is not given solely to the Samaritan woman. Rather, says Jesus, "whoever drinks of the water that I shall give him will never thirst" (John 4:14). The Church, in her liturgy, sees in this water the sacramental water of baptism that associates a believer with the death and resurrection of Christ. In so doing, the Church is not distorting the meaning that the exegete finds in the text but is simply applying it to the life of the believer.

In his first dialogue with the Samaritan woman, Jesus also shows himself to be a prophet (vv. 16-19) and, most importantly, the Messiah (vv. 20-26). It is in this context that a statement is made that is very important both for the Christian's understanding of prayer and liturgical action and for the catechumen's ongoing education. Christ makes reference to a dispute over where men should worship. The Samaritans were convinced that men should worship on Mount Gerizim, where Noah had built an altar after the Deluge and where Abraham, too, had offered sacrifice (Deut. 27:4-8). The temple the Samaritans had built here was a rival of the Temple at Jerusalem. No Israelite could accept that there should be two temples, and therefore the Samaritan woman's question was a relevant one: Where was true worship to be offered?

Jesus' answer is decisive: The time has come when worship will no longer be connected with a temple, since "true worshipers will worship the Father in spirit and truth" (John 4:23). Does this mean that Christ is condemning all rites and all outward signs? Men have so interpreted his words at certain critical moments when an exaggerated ritualism had cast its pall over Christian worship. The Reformers, for example, appealed to this text in order to condemn all external worship.

The key to the proper interpretation of the text is contained in the words "in spirit." If the meaning is that authentic worship is to be purely spiritual, stripped of all material components, then any liturgy is to be condemned. In this reading of the text, Jesus is emphasizing the element of inwardness that all Christian prayer should have. In point of fact, however, when Jesus speaks of worship "in spirit," he means prayer that the Holy Spirit prompts us to offer. He is saying what St. Paul says in his Letter to the Romans when he reminds his readers that the Spirit makes it possible for them to speak to God and call him "Father" (8:26-27).

We may also ask what Jesus means by worship "in truth." Does it mean genuine worship that replaces worship under the Law, worship that was only a prefiguration of the real thing? To reach an answer, we must inquire into what "truth" means in the language of the Fourth Gospel. In this Gospel, "truth" is the message that Jesus came to bring us. In fact, in the last analysis "truth" is Jesus himself, for he declares himself to be both Truth and Life. Authentic worship, then, is worship offered in and with Christ at the prompting of the Holy Spirit, who alone makes it possible.

The second dialogue is that of Jesus with his disciples, who return to the scene after Jesus' conversation with the woman (vv. 31-38). The first dialogue had made it clear what it means to be thirsty and to drink. The second will explain what it means to "eat." There is a food to be eaten of which the disciples are ignorant. In response to the disciples' question, Jesus launches upon a theme that is very prominent in St. John's Gospel: doing the Father's will. "My food is to do the will of him who sent me, and to accomplish his work" (v. 34). When, contrary to prevailing prejudice, he spoke to the Samaritan woman and thus surprised and almost scandalized his own disciples, he was doing the Father's will and engaging in the work of salvation.

Another reason for the choice of this Gospel pericope in today's Mass is the evangelist's summarizing statement: "Many Samaritans from that city believed in him because of the woman's testimony. . . . And many more believed because of his word. They said to the woman, 'It is no longer because of your words that we believe, for we have heard for ourselves, and we know that this is indeed the Savior of the world'" (vv. 39-42). These verses are important because they emphasize the universality of Jesus' work and of the work of the Church, and thus reassure those who are coming to the faith.

God's love poured into our hearts

The second reading in the Mass of the third Sunday brings out the full spiritual meaning of the Gospel pericope. The latter speaks of the water that leaps up to provide eternal life, while the first reading had shown us the thirsty Israelites despairing and rebelling. With St. Paul we are caught up by hope (Rom. 5:1-2, 5-8). "And hope does not disappoint us," he tells us, "because God's love has been poured into our hearts through the Holy Spirit who has been given to us" (v. 5). In other words, we have within us the wellspring from which the life-giving water flows, and it — he! — justifies us through faith. This is, of course, a mystery of love that we really cannot comprehend. Paul underscores the incomprehensibility: "Why, one will hardly die for a righteous man — though perhaps for a good man one will dare even to die. But God shows his love for us in that while we were yet sinners Christ died for us" (vv. 7-8).

This Sunday of the first scrutiny thus focuses on the gift of the love that quenches our thirst. It is indeed a "sacramental Sunday." That is doubtless how the Church thinks of it, without in any way distorting the objective meaning of the texts she has us read. Water is a sign of a gift, and the gift is the love that justifies us through the action of the Spirit. How could the Church fail to link this water with the sacramental water of baptism?

The first scrutiny

As we pointed out earlier, the scrutinies began on the third Sunday of Lent. Scrutiny, let us remember, does not here mean an inquiry; it means an exorcism that prepares the catechumen to receive the Spirit in baptism. The new rite for adult baptism has restored the scrutinies. When catechumens are actually present and a scrutiny is to be held, the opening prayer of the Mass is for the catechumens: "Lord, you call these chosen ones to the glory of a new birth in Christ, the second Adam. Help them to grow in wisdom and love as they prepare to profess their faith in you." [116]

The readings and chants are those of Cycle A. After the homily the catechumens and their sponsors come before the celebrant; he invites the sponsors to pray silently for the catechumens and then asks the catechumens likewise to pray silently; they bow or kneel to show their repentance. This period of silent prayer is followed by prayer for the catechumens in the form of a litany and by the exorcism.

The exorcism has been completely rewritten. The exorcism given in Gelasian Sacramentary and in the baptismal rite for both adults and children down to our own time could hardly have been taken over into a revised rite, given its rather medieval emphasis on the power of the demon. That power is indeed not to be underestimated, but it can be presented in ways that would only antagonize our contemporaries. Let us look first at the old formulas; we will then be in a position to appreciate the adaptation that has been deemed necessary. The older rite contained a prayer followed by an exorcism proper; there were separate prayers for men and women. At the end the priest added a closing prayer.

Prayer over men: "O God of Abraham, God of Isaac, God of Jacob, you appeared on Mount Sinai to your servant, Moses; you led the children of Israel out of Egypt, graciously appointing an angel to guard them day and night. We ask you, Lord, to send your holy angel from heaven to guard in the same way your servants, N. and N., and to lead them to the grace of your baptism. Through Christ our Lord. Amen." [117]

Exorcism of men: "Therefore, accursed devil, acknowledge your condemnation, and pay homage to the living and true God; pay homage to Jesus Christ, his Son, and to the Holy Spirit, and keep far from these servants of God, N. and N., for Jesus Christ, our God and Lord, has called them to his holy grace and to the font of baptism. Accursed devil, never dare to desecrate this sign of the holy cross which we are tracing upon their foreheads. Through the same Jesus Christ our Lord, who is to come to judge the living and the dead and the world by fire. Amen." [118]

Prayer over women: "O God of the heavens and the earth, God of the angels and the archangels, God of the patriarchs and of the prophets, God of the apostles and of the martyrs, God of the confessors and of the virgins, God of all who live holy lives, God to whom every knee bends of those in heaven, on earth, and under the earth: I beg you, Lord, to protect these your servants, N. and N., and to lead them to the grace of your baptism. Through Christ our Lord. Amen." [119]

Exorcism of women: "Therefore, accursed devil . . ." (same as exorcism of men).

Concluding prayer: "Lord, holy Father, almighty and eternal God, source of all light and truth, I humbly beg your never-ending and most holy mercy upon these servants of yours, N. and N. May it please you to grant them the light of your own wisdom. Cleanse them and make them holy. Give them true knowledge, so that they may be made worthy to come to the grace of your baptism. May they maintain firm hope, sound judgment, and a grasp of holy doctrine, so that they may be able to receive your grace. Through Christ our Lord. Amen." [120]

Here now are the formulas in the new rite. It can be said that they are derived from the old prayers, but they have been adapted to a new and different audience of Christians and candidates for baptism. It will be noted, too, that they make explicit reference to the three readings of the Mass.

After the litanic prayer for the catechumens, the celebrant turns to the latter and says:

God our Father, you sent your Son to be our Savior: these men (and women) preparing for baptism thirst for living water as did the Samaritan woman. May the word of the Lord change their lives too, and help them to acknowledge the sins and weaknesses that burden them. Keep them from relying too much on themselves and never let the powers of evil deceive them. Free them from the spirit of falsehood and help them recognize any evil within themselves, that with hearts cleansed from sin they may advance on the way to salvation. We ask this through Christ our Lord. Amen.

He then extends his hands over the candidates and continues:

Lord Jesus, you are the fountain we thirst for; you are the teacher we seek; you alone are the Holy One. These chosen ones open their hearts honestly to confess their failures and be forgiven. In your love, free them from evil, restore their health, satisfy their thirst, and give them peace. By the power of your name, which we call upon in faith, stay with them and save them. Command the spirit of evil to leave them, for you have conquered that spirit by rising to life. Show your chosen people the way of life in the Holy Spirit that they may grow closer to the Father and worship him, for you are Lord for ever and ever. Amen.[121]

After the scrutiny the candidates leave the assembly, and the Eucharistic liturgy begins. But even though the catechumens have left, the community continues to pray for them and their sponsors (godparents). The following are the special prayers for the third Sunday when a scrutiny is celebrated at the Mass.[122]

Prayer over the gifts: "Lord God, give faith and love to your children and lead them safely to the supper you have prepared for them."

During the Eucharistic Prayer, when Eucharistic Prayer

I is used, special forms of the *Memento* of the living and of the *Hanc igitur* are used: "Remember, Lord, these godparents who will present your chosen men and women for baptism. . . . Lord, remember all of us. . . ." "Father, accept this offering from your whole family. We offer it especially for the men and women you call to share your life through the living waters of baptism."

Prayer after Communion: "Lord, be present in our lives with your gifts of salvation. Prepare these men and women for your sacraments and protect them in your love."

The theology of these prayers (which include the opening prayer cited earlier) is simple but substantial. The opening prayer summarizes very briefly the effects of the baptism for which the candidates are preparing: They will be reborn and have restored to them their original dignity (lost by original sin). Such a change is evidently a work possible only to God. When man is born into the world, he is in connivance, as it were, with evil as well as with good. He is incapable, by his own powers, of changing these relationships to the milieu into which he is born; only God can dissolve this solidarity with evil.

In thus changing man, God restores him to his true dignity and bestows true wisdom upon him. "Wisdom" here has nothing to do with the wisdom of the philosophers but is specifically Christian, being identical with the personal experience of God in and through the community. Man's restoration to the state that God originally intended for him has but one ultimate purpose, namely, that man may praise God's glory.

The prayer over the gifts likewise shows God taking the initiative in the transformation that the catechumen will undergo. The catechumen must indeed have faith and love, but it is God who invites him to share in the Eucharist and gives him the sacraments of baptism and confirmation as the way by which he gains full access to the Lord's Supper.

The special prayers in the Canon are indicative of the importance the Church attributes to the work of the godparents. Their names are read out in the *Memento* of the living, since they will not only present the candidates for baptism but will also have a responsibility for them once they are baptized. At the same time, the Church bids the whole community play its part in the great task of giving divine life to others.

It is evident that when the Church administers a sacrament, she does not think of herself as simply entrusted with powers whose use she supervises. She does not think of the sacrament as merely a tool she uses and whose application she regulates, while herself remaining, as it were, completely external to it. For when the Church administers a sacrament, she can only do so as the Body of Christ; this means that her role in the sacrament is literally a vital, i.e., life-giving, role. She is fully aware of this fact, and the way in which she associates the whole community with the baptism shortly to be administered is a stirring proof of it.

The prayer for those to be baptized, in the *Hanc igitur*, supposes that their names, too, have been mentioned. In this prayer the typical biblical word "call" indicates both God's initiative in salvation and the situation of the Christian over against the world. Christians live in the world, but they live there as people set apart because they have been chosen and called.[123]

Fourth Sunday of Lent, Cycle A

for years 1978, 1981, 1984, 1987, 1990

8. THE LIGHT OF TRUTH

Finding the light

The Gospel for the fourth Sunday (John 9:1-41) is a deeply moving one, and its teaching is rich in meaning for each of us.

In general terms, here is what it tells us. All of us have been born blind, and the catechumens, despite their desire to attain to the truth, are still blind. But now the Lord tells them: "As long as I am in the world, I am the light of the world" (John 9:5). Of himself, man can do nothing, for, as Jesus says, "For judgment I came into this world, that those who do not see may see, and that those who see may become blind" (John 9:39). He alone is the Light, and he alone can give light because he alone has been sent by the Father to do so. Is there anything we can do? Yes, "go, wash in the pool of Siloam" (v. 7). Then man's eyes are opened, and he who was born blind can see. This is the Lord's doing.

In his catecheses St. Ambrose gives an enthusiastic comment on this passage from the Fourth Gospel. His words are addressed to Christians recently baptized, but they also show us how the Saint preferred to approach baptism.

> When you had yourself registered, he [Jesus] took some clay and spread it on your eyes. What does that mean? It means that you were forced to acknowledge your sin, examine your conscience, do penance for your faults — in short, you had to admit to the state that the whole human race shares. For although the person approaching baptism makes no confession of sins, he does nonetheless admit his sins by asking for the baptism that justifies and by asking to pass from sin to grace.
>
> Do not think that this act is useless. There are those — I know at least one, who, when we told him: "At your age you have a greater obligation to be baptized," replied: "Why should I be baptized? I have no sins. I have never committed a sin, have I?" Such a man had no clay, because Christ had not spread it on his eyes; which is to say that Christ had not opened his eyes. For, in fact, no man is without sin.
>
> Consequently, anyone who takes refuge in baptism acknowledges that he is but human. Christ, then, put

mud on you, that is, he gave you a reverential fear, prudence, and a consciousness of your own weakness, and he said to you: "Go to Siloam." What is "Siloam"? It means (says the evangelist) "Sent." In other words, then: Go to the fountain where they preach the Cross of Christ the Lord; go to the fountain in which Christ has paid the ransom for the sins of all.

You went, you washed, you came to the altar, you began to see what you had not seen before. In short, your eyes were opened in the fountain of the Lord and by the preaching of the Lord's Passion. You seemed previously to be blind of heart; now you began to see the light.[124]

In his forty-fourth sermon on the Fourth Gospel, St. Augustine offers this commentary:

If, then, we reflect on the meaning of this miracle, we will see that the blind man is the human race. The blindness struck the first man because of sin, and he became for us the source not only of death but of sin as well. . . . The evangelist makes a point of telling us the name of the pool, and the fact that the name means "Sent." You already know, of course, who the "One sent" is. Unless he had been sent, none of us would have been freed of sin. . . .

Ask a man, "Are you a Christian?" If he is a pagan or a Jew, he will answer, "I am not." But if he says, "I am," then ask him, "A catechumen or one of the faithful?" If he says, "A catechumen," then he has been anointed but not washed. But how did he get anointed? Ask him and he will tell you. Ask him in whom he believes, and because he is a catechumen he will say, "In Christ." Now, I am speaking, of course, to both faithful and catechumens. What did I say of the spittle and mud? That the Word became flesh. That is what the catechumens learn. But it is not enough for them to have been anointed; let them hasten on to the font if they seek the Light.[125]

The second reading in the Office of Readings for this day is from this same commentary on St. John. Part of the passage reads as follows:

> We too, brothers, have now been enlightened, for the salve of faith has been rubbed on our eyes. First there was the spittle mixed with earth with which the man born blind was anointed. But we too, as sons of Adam, were born blind and need him to enlighten us. . . . We shall have joy in the Truth when we see him face to face, as we have been promised. . . . You are not told: Strive to find the way so that you may reach the truth and the life. That is not what you are told! Rise up from your laziness! The way itself has come to you and roused you from your sleep . . . rise, therefore, and walk![126]

The man Jesus

How clear and simple is the answer the man born blind gives to the Pharisees when they asked about his cure: "The man called Jesus made clay and anointed my eyes and said to me, 'Go to Siloam and wash'; so I went and washed and received my sight" (John 9:11). But the man himself was not the only one to know what had happened; the crowd saw and was amazed that the man born blind could now see (vv. 8-13). Evidently he who worked this wonder must have been a prophet or even the Messiah (vv. 40-43). The people were disturbed, for they could not come to a clear judgment on just who the man Jesus was.

The authorities of the synagogue refused to see anything at all. Their reaction is entirely juridical in character: We are disciples of Moses; this man Jesus is a sinner, since he has not observed the laws governing the Sabbath, and God does not listen to sinners. In the end they can only assert: "As for this man, we do not know where he comes from" (v. 29). The blind man, on the other hand, is quite logical in his thinking: "If this man were not from God, he could do nothing" (v. 33). As a result, he is expelled from the synagogue as a sinner and a rude mocker.

The Son of Man, Light of the world

By healing the man born blind, Jesus shows himself to be Son of Man and Light of the world. The very purpose of the sign, indeed, is to show others what he really is. He is the Light of the world, the Light that enlightens every man (John 1:9). The works that he does and that prove him to be the Light are nothing but the carrying out of the Father's will. We must even say that they are God's own works rendered visible through signs.

The main point of the whole narrative, then, is to show that Jesus is the Son of the Father and the Light of the world, and that he has been sent to carry out the Father's plan of salvation.

Here, once again, we see the difference between a purely exegetical reading and a liturgical reading. From the purely exegetical viewpoint, the aim of the passage is to show the divinity of Christ through a sign that he has given. The liturgical reading of the passage does not deny this first aspect, but it focuses on something else. The mention of the pool of Siloam and the fact that a man is cured of blindness resulted in the account being used, from a very early period, as a baptismal catechesis. The liturgy thus emphasizes not only the revelation of Jesus' person but also the sign itself, with its relation to baptism, and the effect the sign had, that is, the curing of blindness. Because the sacrament does have this effect, the baptized are described as "the enlightened."

"Christ shall give you light"

The liturgical significance of the Gospel pericope determined the choice of the second reading, the passage from the Letter to the Ephesians in which St. Paul tells the faithful that they were once darkness but are now light in the

Lord, and that consequently they must live as children of the light (Eph. 5:8-14).

The Christian has become light; that is, he has been wakened from the dead and enlightened by Christ. The statement is not vaguely poetic; it is real and a source of joy, but it also brings serious obligations. It is no easy matter to be, with Christ, a light for the world. Yet such is the responsibility of the entire Church and in a special way of all those in the Church who continue the work of the apostles. This second group must not, however, be made to bear the whole burden. Each of us is in his own way a light; that is what our baptism means.

St. Paul contrasts the time of darkness, before baptism, and the time of light that follows upon, and results from, baptism. In this time of light we must bear the "fruit of light," which "is found in all that is good and right and true" (v. 9).

The Lord chooses his Anointed One

The first reading for the fourth Sunday (1 Sam. 16:1b, 6-7, 10-13a) brings out once again the fact that in the Gospel reading the Church has a special interest in the cure of the blind man as a sign of baptism. It is impossible to establish any concrete link between the first reading and the other two, and yet a broadly conceived but coherent connection does exist.

The first reading emphasizes the fact that God chooses those whom he wills to draw to himself and consecrate. There is evidently an allusion here, in the liturgical context, to the gift of faith that God freely gives to the catechumens. His choices are manifested in a very personal way; that is, God has his own way of choosing and judging, and his judgments are not superficial, like those of men, who can only judge by externals. The person chosen for the gift of faith is not chosen because of any merits on his part; in fact, the gift is often a thorough surprise to others looking on and even baffles them completely.

This element of free choice is the point to be emphasized in this reading, as I see it. At the same time, we cannot forget the anointing, which can be related to the anointing of the eyes of the man born blind. Such a parallel may seem forced, however, and we need not insist on it.

The prayer after Communion tells us in a few words what our prayer should be: "Father, you enlighten all who come into the world. Fill our hearts with the light of your gospel, that our thoughts may please you, and our love be sincere."

The second scrutiny

The Gelasian Sacramentary (and the older baptismal liturgy) supplies us with the rite for the second scrutiny, which was celebrated on this fourth Sunday of Lent. Here is the exorcism proper:

> Hear, accursed Satan, I adjure you by the name of the eternal God and of our Savior Jesus Christ, depart with your envy, conquered, trembling, and groaning. May you have no part in these servants of God, N. and N., who already have thoughts of heaven and who are about to renounce you and your world and achieve a blessed immortality. Therefore give honor to the Holy Spirit who, descending from the high throne of heaven, comes to upset your wiles and to make perfect the hearts cleansed at the divine fountain, temples and dwelling places dedicated to God. And thus entirely freed from the harmful effects of past sins, may these servants of God give thanks always to the eternal God, and bless his holy name forever and ever. Amen.[127]

In the Gelasian Sacramentary the exorcism of women was preceded by the following prayer: "God of Abraham, God of Isaac, God of Jacob, God who instructed the tribes of Israel and freed Susanna from a false accusation, I humbly pray you to free these your servants and in your mercy lead them to the grace of your baptism."[128] To be noted here is the reference to Susanna; her story had been read on the preceding day, Saturday of the third week.

In the new rite for adult initiation, the scrutiny is celebrated according to the same pattern as the first (on the third Sunday). The two prayers of exorcism are notable both for clarity and for wealth of teaching. The celebrant turns to the candidates and with hands joined says: "Father of mercy, you helped the man born blind to believe in your Son and through that faith to reach the light of your Kingdom. Free your chosen ones from the falsehoods that surround and blind them. Let truth be the foundation of their lives. May they live in your light forever."

With hands extended over the candidates, he continues: "Lord Jesus, you are the true light that enlightens all men. By the Spirit of truth, free all who struggle under the yoke of the father of lies. Arouse the good will of these men (and women) whom you have chosen for your sacraments. Grant them to enjoy your light like the man whose sight you once restored, and inspire them to become fearless witnesses to the faith, for you are Lord for ever and ever. Amen.[129]

Fifth Sunday of Lent, Cycle A

for years 1978, 1981, 1984, 1987, 1990

9. ARISE AND LIVE

"Your brother will rise again"

Christ is still saying to us: "Your brother will rise again." But he does not now say it to the members of the Church in the same way that he once said it to the sisters of Lazarus. The latter were indeed trustful as they listened to the Lord, but they were also forced to be passive; they could only await what sign the Lord might give. Now, however, Christ speaks his words to the Church, and it is with the entire Church and each of her members that he raises his voice in prayer to the Father. On the day of baptism the Church says to the catechumen, as she does also to the Christian who has fallen into sin: "Lazarus, come out!" Christ and the Church together say: "Unbind him, and let him go," and the bonds of sin fall away at the words of Christ and his Church.

Christ is the Light of the world (John 11:9-10), and now, through the Church, he is also the Resurrection and Life of the world (vv. 25-26). Along with Christ, the Church is "deeply moved in spirit" before the tomb of Lazarus, the sinner, and her prayer unties the fetters of sin and restores Lazarus to life.

When we read that Christ was "deeply moved in spirit and troubled" at Lazarus's tomb, and when we hear it asserted that the Church is troubled along with him, we should not see in the phrase merely the expression of profound human and spiritual love and concern. The deep sorrow of Christ, the God-Man, is a sorrow at what sin has done to man. In Christ, God is recalling the Adam he once made in his own image, a creature radiant with life and beauty of body and spirit. Now Christ finds himself confronted with the failure of that first creation, and the Church must always experience the same disturbance of soul as she sees what that initial disaster has done to mankind. She can see these evil effects at every moment, for she need only look at the pagan world and at her own members, since they too are less than fully alive because of sin.

In his forty-ninth discourse on the Fourth Gospel, St. Augustine comments on the raising of Lazarus. In Lazarus he sees a great sinner and emphasizes the fact that the man has now been buried for four days. Why this emphasis? Because for Augustine the four days represent original sin, sin against the natural law, sin against the law of Moses, and sin against the law set down in the gospel.[130] "This interpretation will leave its mark on numerous texts of the liturgy. For example, the preface for the consecration of cemeteries speaks of 'the fourfold weight of sin.'"[131] An old preface for the fifth Sunday uses similar language: "Being a weak man like us, Jesus wept for Lazarus. Then by the power of his divinity he restored the man to life and raised mankind up when it was buried under the fourfold weight of sin."[132]

In the discourse already mentioned, St. Augustine highlights something that is quite important, namely, the necessity of faith if we are to have and preserve the life that Christ gives. The Gospel about the raising of Lazarus (John 11:1-45), which is read on the fifth Sunday of Lent, develops this point quite forcefully. No life without faith — faith is an indispensable condition, but on the other hand its effect is sure: "Whoever lives and believes in me shall never die" (John 11:26).

St. Augustine asks, and answers, another question:

> Someone may say, "How can Lazarus be a symbol of the sinner and yet be so loved by the Lord?" Let the questioner listen to the Lord: "I came not to call the righteous, but sinners"! If God did not love sinners, he would not have come to earth.
>
> On hearing of Lazarus's illness, Jesus said: "This illness is not unto death; it is for the glory of God, so that the Son of God may be glorified by means of it." Such a glorification of the Son of God did not really increase his glory, but it was useful to us. He says, then, "This illness is not unto death." The reason is that even the death of Lazarus was not unto death but happened for the sake of the miracle, the performance of which would lead men to believe in Christ and so avoid real death. Consider here how the Lord indirectly calls himself God, having in mind those who deny that he is God.[133]

In his commentary St. Augustine stresses the glorification of the Son. Jesus tells Martha: "Did I not tell you that if you would believe you would see the glory of God?" (v. 40). We are reminded here of the familar yet always inspiring words of St. Irenaeus: "Man fully alive is the glory God seeks" (*Gloria Dei, vivens homo*). For when man is fully alive, the covenant and the second creation are a success. It is to that success that the raising of Lazarus points.

Jesus is "deeply moved in spirit and troubled" at the sight of God's first creation fallen into disorder, death, and destruction. His own glory, on the other hand, will shine out most fully in the Passion, when he shows himself Master of death and Master of life, and does so at the time and place he himself has decided on. The miracle of the raising of Lazarus presupposes the whole work, past and yet to come, of Jesus, and is a sign of it. Now the catechumen is urged to see his own glory as implied in the glory of Jesus and of the Church. The glorification of Christ is completed in the glorification of Christians: "I am glorified in them," says Jesus in his priestly prayer (John 17:10). The raising of Lazarus is a sign of the restoration of creation to its original splendor.

When Christians receive the Body of Christ, they sing of their own resurrection, for of that the Eucharist is their pledge. "When Jesus saw her [Mary] weeping, and the Jews who came with her also weeping, he was deeply moved in spirit and troubled. . . . Jesus wept. . . . he cried out with a loud voice, 'Lazarus, come out.' The dead man came out, his hands and feet bound with bandages, and his face wrapped with a cloth" (John 11:33, 35, 43, 44).

"That you may believe"

The choice of this Gospel for the fifth Sunday was motivated by the desire to give prominence to an important form of baptismal typology: the resurrection of Lazarus as a figure and type of the resurrection of Jesus and of our twofold resurrection (our resurrection to divine life in baptism and our later, definitive resurrection at the end). The sign of Lazarus is a good example of how St. John conceives of such signs. The sign is done in response to faith and for the glory of God. With regard to faith, not only is the sign a response but it also moves men to a still deeper faith, as Christ's own words bring out (11:11-26). As a matter of fact, John's entire Gospel is written for the purpose of rousing faith (see 20:31).

Martha's faith is implied in her regretful words, "Lord, if you had been here, my brother would not have died" (v. 21). She believes in the power and presence of Jesus; when he is there, we may hope for anything and everything. In fact, even now her words show that her hope is still alive, for cannot Jesus do anything he wishes? It is at this point that Jesus begins his catechesis; as so often in John, the Lord uses for his point of departure a misunderstanding he himself has deliberately allowed his interlocutor to fall into. He thus leads Martha from belief in the resurrection on the last day (which Jews accepted and to which Jesus himself seemed to be referring) to a belief in himself as the Resurrection and Life of all who believe in him (11:25-26).

The resurrection of Jesus, prefigured in the raising of Lazarus, is a sign of our own resurrection. Martha moves from faith in a Christ who can work miracles to a faith in the word of him whom the Father has sent. This is the act of faith that every person makes at baptism: he believes in the Word, the Christ who died and was raised from the dead. The second reading (Rom. 8:8-11) emphasizes this faith in the power of the Spirit of the risen Christ, the Spirit who dwells in us and will cause us likewise to rise from the dead.

Mary's faith is like that of her sister Martha. When she leaves the house on hearing of Jesus' arrival, she does not go to weep at her brother's tomb, as the Jews believe, but goes to meet Jesus and falls at his feet. Then we hear from her the same profession of implicit faith as her sister had uttered: "Lord, if you had been here my brother would not have died" (v. 32).

It is at this point that the evangelist shows us a Christ who is troubled and deeply moved both by the sorrow of his friends and by their profession of faith.

Jesus and death

It is important to observe how Jesus the man acts in the face of death. We are told that he is moved by deep emotions and that he weeps (vv. 33-35). Despite this, when he raises Lazarus, he does so in order that God may be glorified. If Martha has faith, she will see this glory of God (v. 40). He also raises Lazarus in order to move men to faith and to draw them gradually to a belief in his own resurrection, which is a sign of our final resurrection that will give death a new meaning for the Christian.

The fact, however, that death will have, and indeed already has, a new meaning in no way lessens the human compassion of Jesus in the face of the brutal reality of death. This is not the place for a disquisition on how Jesus viewed death; that is not why this Gospel was chosen. The important thing here is how Jesus relates death to what will follow it, namely, the resurrection that will give glory to God. To the Christian, death is a passage to a new life, a passage from a bodily, material life to a spiritual life, a passage that takes place in Jesus, by the power of his Spirit. This, as we said above, is the point being made in the second reading.

The Spirit and life

The first reading has already focused our attention on God's will to bestow life on men (Ezek. 37:12-14). St. Jerome points out that the prophet's image shows a belief in the future resurrection and that the Church's use of the passage shows her sharing this belief: "The image of the resurrection would never have been used to signify the restoration of the Israelite people unless there was indeed a resurrection and unless men believed that it would come to pass, for no one proves the uncertain by the nonexistent." [134]

The words "I will put my Spirit within you, and you shall live" (Ezek. 37:14) immediately bring to mind the passage

of Romans (8:8-11) that has been selected as the second
reading. Both passages speak of a gift and an activity of the
Spirit who makes alive. We have Christ living in us; consequently, though our bodies are condemned to death because of sin, the Spirit is our true Life, now that we have
been justified and sanctified. He who raised Jesus from the
dead will also restore life to our mortal bodies by the power
of his Spirit who dwells in us.

The passage from Romans provides the clearest and most
complete commentary on the entire liturgy of the fifth Sunday: Once we are baptized, the Spirit of Jesus dwells in us
and we have the pledge of resurrection and life. That says
everything, and if we really want to understand the attitude
of Jesus toward death, we must approach it in the light of
St. Paul's words in Romans 8. The Christian does not look
upon death as other men do; for him, death means the beginning of a new life or, more accurately, the further unfolding of a life that is already his, once he has been justified by baptism and has Christ living in him.

The third scrutiny

On this Sunday the Church continues her proximate
preparation of the catechumen for baptism. The celebration
of this third scrutiny follows the same format as that of the
first two scrutinies on the two preceding Sundays.

After the intercessions for the catechumen, the celebrant
turns to the candidates and prays:

> Father of eternal life, you are a God, not of the dead,
> but of the living: you sent your Son to proclaim the
> good news of life, to rescue men from the kingdom of
> death and to lead them to resurrection. Free these
> chosen people from the power of the evil spirit who
> brings death. May they receive new life from Christ
> and bear witness to his resurrection. We ask this
> through Christ our Lord.

Then, having silently laid hands on each candidate, he
extends his hands over them all and says:

Lord Jesus, you raised Lazarus from death as a sign that you had come to give men life in fullest measure. Rescue from death all who seek life from your sacraments and free them from the spirit of evil. By your Holy Spirit fill them with life; give them faith, hope and love that they may live with you always and come to share the glory of your resurrection, for you are Lord for ever and ever.[135]

The "presentations"

It was in connection with the celebrations on these Sundays and during the weeks of Lent that the Church introduced and gradually organized what were called the "presentations" (*traditiones*): of the Creed, or profession of faith, of the Lord's Prayer, and of the Gospels. These were celebrations in which these texts were read to the catechumens and some commentary on them was given. The new rite of Christian initiation of adults has restored the practice of the presentations, though in a simplified form. We think it worthwhile to provide the reader here with the text of these ceremonies in their ancient form.

Presentation of the Creed

Here begins the presentation of the Creed to the candidates. Before reciting the Creed, address them as follows:

Dear sons and daughters, you are about to receive the sacrament of baptism and to be begotten as new creatures of the Holy Spirit. Welcome wholeheartedly the statement of the faith that will justify you if you truly believe. With your souls now changed by a true conversion, draw near to God who enlightens our minds, and receive the sacrament of the evangelical Creed that the Lord inspired and the apostles established. Its words are few, but it contains great mysteries. For the Holy Spirit, by dictating these truths to the teachers of the Church, created so concise and eloquent a statement of our saving faith that what you are to believe and constantly pay heed to cannot be too much for your understanding or your memory.

Exert yourselves, then, to learn the Creed. What we ourselves have received we hand on to you. Write it down, not on a material substance that can decay, but on the pages of your heart. This, then, is how the confession of the faith you have received begins. . . .[136]

When this has been done [when the acolyte, with his hand on the catechumen's head, has recited the Creed], *the priest continues*:

That is the summary of our faith, dear sons and daughters; those are the words of the Creed that are not the fruit of human wisdom but are true and divinely ordered. No one is incapable of understanding and observing them. According to this Creed, the power of God the Father and the power of God the Son is one and equal. It tells us that the only-begotten Son of God was born, according to the flesh, from the Virgin Mary and the Holy Spirit; that he was crucified and buried and that he rose on the third day; that he ascended into heaven and is seated at the right hand of the Father's majesty, and will come to judge the living and the dead. In this Creed we acknowledge that the Holy Spirit possesses, inseparably, the same divine nature as the Father and the Son. And finally we confess the calling into being of the Church, the forgiveness of sins, and the resurrection of the flesh.

Now, beloved, you are being changed from your old self to a new self; you are beginning to be no longer carnal but spiritual, no longer earthly but heavenly. Believe with constant assurance that the resurrection accomplished in Christ will be accomplished in all of us as well, and that what the Head first experienced, the whole Body will experience later on. The very sacrament of baptism that you are soon to receive gives expression to that hope, for in baptism we celebrate a death and a resurrection, as the old self is laid aside and a new one received. A sinner enters the waters, a man justified comes forth from them. We reject him who brought us to death and accept him who brings us back to life and through whose grace you become sons of God, begotten now not by the desire of the flesh but by the power of the Holy Spirit.

You must adhere with all your heart to this very brief yet very full confession so that you may use it as a safeguard at all times. It is a weapon whose power is always invincible and will help us to be good soldiers of Christ despite any ambush the enemy may lay. Let the devil, who never ceases to tempt man, find you always shielded by this confession of faith. Then you will overcome the enemy you renounce, and, under the protection of him whom you confess, you will preserve the grace of the Lord incorrupt and stainless until the end. Finally, in him from whom you receive the forgiveness of your sins, you will also attain to the glorious resurrection.

Beloved, you now know the Catholic Creed that has been presented to you; go and be obedient to its teaching, without changing a single word of it. For the merciful God is mighty. May he guide you as you advance to the baptismal faith, and may he bring us, who hand the mysteries on to you, to the kingdom of heaven in your company, through the same Jesus Christ, our Lord, who lives and reigns for ever and ever. Amen.[137]

Presentation of the Lord's Prayer

Presentation of the Lord's Prayer. The deacon exhorts the candidates:

In addition to other salutary instructions, our Lord and Savior Jesus Christ gave his disciples a formula of prayer when they asked him how they should pray. The reading we just heard has made you more fully cognizant of this prayer. Listen now, beloved, to how the Lord teaches his disciples to pray to God, the almighty Father: "When you pray, go into your room and shut the door and pray to your Father who is in secret." "Room" does not refer to a hidden part of the house but reminds us that the recesses of our heart are known to God alone. To shut the door in order to worship God means to turn a mystical key and exclude evil thoughts from our minds, and to speak to God with closed mouth and pure heart. Our God listens to our faith, not to our words. We must therefore use the key of faith to close our hearts to the snares of the enemy and open them to God alone, whose temple they are, so that he who dwells in us may be our Advocate as we pray.

Christ, our Lord, who is the Word of God and the Wisdom of God, has taught us this prayer. Here, then, is how we should pray:

Here you are to comment on the Lord's Prayer:

Our Father, who art in heaven. These are the words of a free man, and full of confidence. You are to live in such a way that you may indeed be children of God and brothers and sisters of Christ. For who would be rash enough to address God as his Father while failing to do God's will? Beloved, show yourselves worthy of adoption by God, for it is written: "To all who received him, who believed in his name, he gave power to become children of God."

Hallowed be thy name. The meaning is not that our prayers make God holy, for he is always holy. Rather do we ask that his name be made holy in us so that, after being sanctified in his baptism, we may continue as we have begun.

Thy kingdom come. But when does our God not reign, since his reign is unending? Therefore, when we say "Thy kingdom come," we are asking that our kingdom may come, the kingdom promised us by God and won for us by the blood and suffering of Christ.

Thy will be done on earth as it is in heaven. Thy will be done in the sense that what you will in heaven, we who dwell on earth may accomplish in an irreproachable way.

Give us this day our daily bread. The "bread" here is to be understood as spiritual bread. Our real bread is Christ, who said: "I am the bread which came down from heaven." We speak of it as "daily" because we must always be asking to be preserved from sin so that we may be worthy of heavenly food.

And forgive us our trespasses as we forgive those who trespass against us. The sense of this petition is that we cannot win forgiveness of our sins unless we first forgive those who have offended us. As the Lord says in the Gospel: "If you do not forgive men their trespasses, neither will your Father forgive your trespasses."

And lead us not into temptation. That is, do not let us be led into temptation by the tempter, who is the source of all corruption. For, as the Scriptures tell us, "God . . . tempts no one." The devil is the real tempter. So that we may overcome him, the Lord tells us: "Watch and pray that you may not enter into temptation."

But deliver us from evil. He says this because, as the Apostle remarks, "We do not know how to pray as we ought." We must so pray to the one all-powerful God that in his mercy he would grant us the power to overcome the evil that human weakness is powerless to guard against and avoid. This we ask of Jesus Christ our Lord, who lives and reigns as God in the unity of the Holy Spirit, for ever and ever.

Then the deacon exhorts the catechumens: Remain in order and silence, and listen attentively.

You have heard, beloved, the holy mysteries of the Lord's Prayer. When you depart from here, renew them in your heart so that, as men and women who are perfect in Christ, you may be able to ask and receive the merciful favor of God. For God our Lord has power to lead you, runners toward the faith, to the waters of rebirth, and to bring us, who have handed on to you the mystery of the Catholic faith, into the kingdom of heaven along with you — he who lives and reigns with God the Father in the unity of the Holy Spirit, for ever and ever.[138]

The new rite of Christian initiation suggests readings for each of the two presentations. Each ends with a prayer over the candidates. The prayer at the end of the presentation of the Creed is as follows: "Father, all-powerful and ever-living God, fountain of light and truth, source of eternal love, hear our prayers for N. and N., your servants. Cleanse them of sin, make them holy, give them true knowledge, firm hope and sound teaching, so that they will be prepared for the grace of baptism. We ask this through Christ our Lord."[139]

In that earlier time, the presentation of the Creed took place on Wednesday of the fourth week of Lent. The readings for the Mass during which the presentation was made were Ezekiel 36:23-28, Isaiah 1:16-19, and John 9:1-38. If we bear in mind the theme of the first two readings (the renewal, through baptism, of the person who obeys the Lord's commands) and if we take the trouble at this point to reread the Gospel, especially the end of it, we will be struck by the unity between the Mass proper and the presentation of the Creed. The end of the Gospel is especially appropriate. Jesus hears that the blind man whom he cured has been expelled from the synagogue; he seeks the man out, and the following dialogue takes place: "'Do you believe in the Son of Man?' He answered, 'And who is he, sir, that I may believe in him?' Jesus said to him, 'You have seen him, and it is he who speaks to you.' He said, 'Lord, I believe'" (John 9:35-38).

Note the question Christ asks, and also his statement: "You have seen him." The text is evidently appropriate also in relation to the scrutiny (celebrated at this same Mass), in which the community prayed that the candidates' minds and hearts might be opened to the light of faith. At the beginning of the Gospel, Jesus says: "I am the light of the world" (John 9:5). The catechumens can glimpse the light dawning for them and continue on their way to full enlightenment.[140]

The presentation of the Lord's Prayer seems to have taken place on Saturday of the fourth week of Lent. This conclusion is suggested by the readings once assigned to that day. The new rite of Christian initiation of adults has revived the presentation of the Lord's Prayer, while adapting it to our day. A liturgy of the word precedes the ceremony of the presentation of the Lord's Prayer. The deacon then reads the passage from St. Matthew's Gospel (6:9-13) in which Christ teaches his disciples the Our Father, and the celebrant gives a homily explaining the meaning and importance of the prayer. The ceremony concludes with a prayer: "Almighty and eternal God, you continually bless your Church with new members. Deepen the faith and understanding of these candidates chosen for baptism. Give them a new birth in your living waters and make them members of your family. We ask this through Christ our Lord."[141]

Presentation of the Gospels

This was the last of the presentations to be introduced into the liturgy. Here is how the ceremony was conducted during the period when the Gelasian Sacramentary was in use:

> *Here begins the explanation of the Gospels to the candidates so that their ears may be opened.*
> *First, four deacons emerge from the sacristy, preceded by candle-bearers and censer-bearers and carrying the four Gospels; these they place on the four corners of the altar. Then, before any of the deacons reads, the priest speaks as follows:*
> Dear sons and daughters, we are about to open to you the Gospels, that is, the acts of God. First, how-

ever, we must tell you in an orderly way what a Gospel is, where it comes from, whose words it contains, why four men wrote of these acts, and who the four are whom the Holy Spirit appointed in accordance with prophecy. For if we do not proceed in an orderly fashion, we may leave you confused. You came here that your ears might be opened; we must not begin by blunting your minds.

A Gospel is literally "good news." Specifically, it is the good news of Jesus Christ our Lord. It is called "good news" because it proclaims and manifests the coming in the flesh of him who spoke through the prophets and foretold: "In that day they shall know that is I who speak; here am I." That, briefly, is what a Gospel is. As we explain now who the four were whom the prophet had foretold, we shall link their names to the symbols the prophet used for them. The prophet Ezekiel says: "Each had the face of a man in front; the four had the face of a lion on the right side, the four had the face of an ox on the left side, and the four had the face of an eagle at the back." There can be no doubt that these four figures are the evangelists. The names of those who wrote the Gospels are Matthew, Mark, Luke, and John.

A deacon then proclaims: Remain silent and listen attentively.

He then starts the reading of Matthew and reads from the beginning to the words: "He will save his people from their sins."

After the reading, the priest comments thus: Dear sons and daughters, lest we keep you too long in suspense, we shall explain to you the reason for the symbol assigned to each evangelist, and why Matthew has the face of a man. The reason is that at the beginning of his Gospel he gives the full genealogy of the Savior and tells us of his birth. His Gospel begins with the words: "The book of the genealogy of Jesus Christ, the son of David, the son of Abraham." You see, there is reason for making a man the symbol of Matthew, since he begins with the birth of a man, and for identifying Matthew with the symbol in the prophet.

Another deacon then proclaims, as before: Remain silent and listen attentively.

He then reads the beginning of the Gospel according to Mark, down to the words: "I have baptized you with water; but he will baptize you with the Holy Spirit."

Then the priest continues: Mark the evangelist, who is represented by a lion, begins in the desert, for he says: "The voice of one crying out in the wilderness: Prepare the way of the Lord!" An added reason is that the lion reigns unconquered in the desert. We find many examples of this lion, so that this prophecy, for instance, is not without meaning: "Judah is a lion's whelp; from the prey, my son, you have gone up. He stooped down, he couched as a lion, and as a lioness; who dares rouse him up?"

A third deacon makes the same proclamation as before. Then he reads the beginning of the Gospel according to Luke, down to the words: "To make ready for the Lord a people prepared."

Then the priest continues: Luke the evangelist has the features of the ox, to which our Savior in his sacrifice is to be compared. In reporting the good news of Christ, Luke begins with Zechariah and Elizabeth, the elderly parents of whom John the Baptist was born. Luke is compared to an ox because in him we can see two horns, that is, the two Testaments, and, in a nascent state, young and vigorous, the four hooves which are the four Gospels.

The fourth deacon makes the same proclamation as before. He then reads the beginning of the Gospel according to St. John, down to the words: "Full of grace and truth."

The priest then continues: John is like an eagle because he seeks great heights. Does he not say: "In the beginning was the Word, and the Word was with God, and the Word was God. He was in the beginning with God"? Then, too, David says of Christ: "Your youth is renewed like the eagle's," that is, the youthfulness of Jesus Christ who rose from the dead and ascended into heaven.

Having conceived you, the Church that bears you in her womb rejoices that the celebration of her liturgy is leading to new beginnings for Christianity. As the holy day of Easter approaches, may you be reborn in the bath of baptism, and merit, like all the saints, to receive the incorruptible gift of sonship from Christ our Lord, who lives and reigns for ever and ever.[142]

10. THE DELUGE AND THE COVENANT

Cycle B is not as carefully constructed as Cycle A. On the first two Sundays the classical themes of the temptation and transfiguration of Jesus have been kept, as they have been in Cycle A and will be again in Cycle C. In Cycle B the pertinent passages are from the Gospel of Mark.

The waters of destruction

> The Lord saw that the wickedness of man was great in the earth, and that every imagination of the thoughts of his heart was only evil continually. And the Lord was sorry that he had made man on the earth, and it grieved him to his heart. So the Lord said, "I will blot out man whom I have created from the face of the ground, man and beast and creeping things and birds of the air, for I am sorry that I have made them" (Gen. 6:5-7).

So widespread has corruption become that Yahweh regrets ever having created man and his world! Note how the account sees not only man but subhuman creatures too as a single object of God's intention to destroy. We saw earlier that Adam in paradise was a person with links to the entire cosmos, that he was not created to be an isolated individual but the ancestor of a race and steward in charge of the subhuman world. Sin effects a radical upheaval of the unity proper to creation; consequently, God's intention to destroy his creature embraces not only man himself but all that is connected with him.

STRUCTURE OF CYCLE B FOR THE FIRST FIVE SUNDAYS

TABLE OF READINGS IN THE EUCHARISTIC LITURGY

	Old Testament	Apostle	Gospel
First Sunday	Gen. 9:8-15 Deluge and covenant	1 Peter 3:18-22 Deluge, an image of saving baptism	Mark 1:12-15 Temptation of Jesus
Second Sunday	Gen. 22:1-2, 9, 10-13, 15-18 Sacrifice of Abraham	Rom. 8:31b-34 God gave his Son for our sake	Mark 9:2-10 This is my beloved Son
Third Sunday	Exod. 20:1-17 The law given by Moses	1 Cor. 1:22-25 The crucified Messiah, wisdom, yet a stumbling block	John 2:13-25 Destroy this temple, and in three days I will raise it up
Fourth Sunday	2 Chr. 36:14-16, 19-23 Exile and liberation; God's anger and mercy	Eph. 2:4-10 Dead through sin, raised up by grace	John 3:14-21 The Son sent to save the world
Fifth Sunday	Jer. 31:31-34 The new covenant with forgiveness of past sins	Heb. 5:7-9 Christ's obedience, cause of eternal salvation	John 12:20-33 The grain of wheat that dies bears fruit

The Deluge is in fact the second destructive act, and, like the first, is a response to the disorder in man. The first resulted from Adam's disobedience, the second from the deepening corruption of his posterity.

Although the Lord tells Noah that "never again shall all flesh be cut off by the waters of a flood" (Gen. 9:11), he will continue to use water as a means of punishing men. At the time of the Exodus, for example, water will engulf the soldiers of Pharaoh (Deut. 11:14; Ps. 106:11; Wis. 18:5). Indeed, punishment by water will be the habitual way for God to exercise a just vengeance: "The possessions of his house will be carried away, dragged off in the day of God's wrath" (Job 20:28).

There will, moreover, be another deluge. At least, that is how Isaiah describes the invasion by the Assyrians, who come from the region of the Euphrates and punish Israel for its lack of faith:

> Because this people have refused the waters of Shiloah that flow gently, and melt in fear before Rezin and the son of Remaliah; therefore, behold, the Lord is bringing up against them the waters of the River, mighty and many, the king of Assyria and all his glory; and it will rise over all its channels and go over all its banks; and it will sweep on into Judah, it will overflow and pass on, reaching even to the neck; and its outspread wings will fill the breadth of your land, O Immanuel (Is. 8:6-8).

Water, then, is the instrument God uses when he turns in wrath upon a corrupt world. This does not mean that water does away with the wickedness of men. Wickedness constantly springs up anew; the world's situation can be described in images of the Tower of Babel, the confusion of tongues, and the dispersal of the peoples, for all these are consequences of original sin that destroyed the world's unity and so frustrated God's plan.

The waters of salvation

We noted earlier that the liturgy never bids the faithful meditate on sin without reminding them that sin is also the starting point of redemption. The attitude of the Church in her liturgy is always that expressed in the *felix culpa* of the Easter Proclamation. This does not mean that corruption is ever glossed over. Anyone who wishes to draw near to God and to achieve the conversion that will turn him to the Lord must be aware of the world's, and his own, corruption. When candidates prepare to enter upon the intensive forty-day catechumenate of Lent, the Church does her duty and forces them to face the reality of the world's sinfulness. At the same time, however, she always emphasizes what the Lord has done and is still doing in order to eliminate evil.

The Church takes the same view of the Deluge. Just as sin is always seen in the perspective of healing, so punishment is always seen as part of the process of rebuilding.

Throughout Lent, and especially during the Easter Vigil, the liturgy gives prominence to the theme of the "waters that save." From the beginning of this season, the Church offers a synthetic view of the history of salvation both to those who are preparing for baptism and to the rest of us who have already received the sacrament.

Water can destroy, but life always emerges from the punishments that God inflicts. Only men experience the sad necessity of inflicting a punishment that leads only to death. That is not God's way. Water can indeed destroy, for like every other creature it is entirely at God's service: "If he withholds the waters, they dry up; if he sends them out, they overwhelm the land" (Job 12:15); "He rebukes the sea and makes it dry, he dries up all the rivers" (Nahum 1:4). But water can also save, and the Deluge, as it turns out, sets a pattern that recurs throughout the history of salvation: Men sin; God punishes and destroys the world, but he also leaves a "little remnant" that will be the nucleus of a new people. In saying that the Deluge sets a pattern, we are not denying, of course, that the account in Genesis underwent revisions that were intended precisely to bring out the pattern that would recur later on.

In Sirach, Noah is quite clearly presented as a "remnant": "Noah was found perfect and righteous; in the time of wrath he was taken in exchange; therefore a remnant was left to the earth when the flood came. Everlasting covenants were made with him that all flesh should not be blotted out by a flood" (Sir. 44:17-18).[143]

The New Testament and the Fathers' commentaries on it see the Deluge as prefiguring baptism and salvation. The account of the Deluge, which presents in an exemplary form the divine ways of bringing man to salvation, is a special favorite of the Fathers because it serves the catechumens both as a doctrinal summary and as an image of Lent itself. For, like Lent, the purifying Deluge lasted forty days: "And rain fell upon the earth forty days and forty nights" (Gen. 7:12); "The flood continued forty days upon the earth" (Gen. 7:17); "At the end of forty days Noah opened the window of the ark which he had made" (Gen. 8:6).

Once again, then, Scripture itself tells us how we are to understand Scripture.

Deluge and baptism

As the reader may be aware, many exegetes regard the First Letter of Peter as a baptismal catechesis. In chapter 3 we find a reference to the close connection between the Deluge and baptism. After recalling the ark in which "a few, that is, eight persons, were saved through water" (v. 20), the writer goes on to say: "Baptism, which corresponds to this, now saves you" (v. 21). We must not overlook the phrase "saved through water": the same water that destroys sinners is a source of salvation for the little remnant.

The Letter stresses the correspondence between the Deluge and baptism. In this correspondence, the Deluge is the "type." We must, however, be on guard against a simplistic view of types, as though they were mere examples or illustrations. A type, for the Bible, is the beginning of a historical process, of a saving action that is still going on. The connection between the Deluge and baptism is more than that between an image in the past and something we see now occurring. Baptism is in close continuity with the Deluge; the former is truly and effectively what the latter was. In fact, baptism is the full realization of all that the Deluge was, so that now baptism is the true Deluge. If, then, there is evidently a distinction and a contrast between type and reality, we must nonetheless see in the type more than a mere image, for the type contains the seed of a reality that will some day achieve its full stature.

It is easy enough to see the correspondences between the Deluge and baptism. At the same time, however, we should not press details of the relation between type and reality. It should be enough, from the standpoint of a spirituality of baptism, to see how anticipations of baptism existed millennia ago. If we push the correspondences too far, we may end up with unreliable and factitious conclusions. The Fathers did not always avoid moving in this direction. St. Justin, for example, sees in the explicit mention of eight people being saved a symbol of the ogdoad or eighth day, the day of the resurrection. The person who descends into death with Christ in baptism also rises with Christ. "St. Justin gave this symbolism definitive form. Noah with his wife, his three sons and the wives of his sons form the number eight and provide the symbol of the eighth day, the day of the manifestation of the resurrection."[144]

We must not, however, be too hard on St. Justin. This same passage from his writings provides a very interesting commentary: "In the Deluge the mystery of mankind which was to be saved was present." Evidently Justin understands the true status of a biblical type. "Christ, as the First-born of every creature, became the Head of a new race to which he gave birth through water, faith, and the wood that contains the mystery of the Cross, just as Noah was saved by wood and carried on the waters with his family."[145]

The Deluge as type of baptism, the ark as type of the

Church, the dove as symbolizing the Holy Spirit — these are constant themes in the Fathers. Here we need cite only two classic texts. The first is from Tertullian's treatise on baptism:

> After the waters of the Deluge had cleansed away the ancient iniquity and thus baptized the world, as it were, a dove was sent from the ark and returned with an olive branch. Even the pagans regard this as a symbol of peace. Thus it heralded the appeasement of heaven's wrath. By a similar ordinance aiming at a wholly spiritual effect, the Dove that is the Holy Spirit is sent from heaven, where the Church (prefigured by the ark) dwells, and flies down to bring God's peace to earth, that is, to our fleshly nature as we emerge from the bath after being cleansed from our old sins.[146]

We should note Tertullian's emphasis on the dove as a symbol of the Spirit and on the ark as a figure of the Church. Scripture itself, of course, offers us no commentary on either the dove or the ark. Yet patristic tradition is of one mind in developing this typology, especially as it concerns the ark, and the liturgy took it over at an early date.[147] The typology is evidently an attractive one and expresses something that remains true for us today.

The second classic commentary is from the pen of St. Ambrose. This Father wrote a treatise on Noah and the ark,[148] a passage of which was read at Matins in the monastic breviary on what used to be Sexagesima Sunday. But it is in the two little works *De sacramentis* and *De mysteriis* that we find the most interesting and best known passages.[149]

In *De sacramentis* we read:

> In the Deluge, too, there was already a prefiguration of baptism. We were just beginning to explain this yesterday.[150] What is the Deluge, after all, but a means of preserving the just man so that he might propagate justice, and of destroying sin? That is why

> the Lord, seeing the sins of men being multiplied,
> spared but a single just man, along with his children,
> and commanded the waters to rise over the moun-
> tains. In the Deluge, then, all fleshly corruption
> perished, and only the race and example of the just
> man survived. Does the Deluge, then, not resemble
> that other deluge which is baptism, in which all sins
> are wiped away, while only the soul and grace of the
> just man are raised to life?[151]

Ambrose is evidently adopting the basic theology of the
First Letter of Peter, without reading into it anything more
than it says. In both the Deluge and baptism he sees water
at work destroying corruption and at the same time preserv-
ing "the race and example of the just man."

In *De mysteriis*, Ambrose repeats some of Tertullian's
favorite themes:

> Here is another testimony. All flesh had become cor-
> rupt because of its sin, and so the Lord said: "My
> spirit shall not abide in man for ever, for he is flesh."
> He thus shows that fleshly uncleanness and the stain
> of more serious sins are a bar to spiritual grace. Wish-
> ing to restore what he had originally given, God
> therefore caused a Deluge and bade Noah, a just man,
> to enter the ark. When the Deluge has ceased, Noah
> released a crow, which did not return; then he re-
> leased a dove, which did return, carrying, we are told,
> an olive branch. You see the water, the wood, and the
> dove. Can you have any doubt of the mystery they
> contain?
>
> The water is that in which the flesh is immersed so
> that all fleshly sin may be washed away; in the water
> all sin is buried. The wood is that to which the Lord
> Jesus was nailed when he suffered for us. The dove is
> the one in whose likeness the Holy Spirit descended
> (as you learn from the New Testament) in order to in-
> still in you peace of soul and tranquillity of heart. The
> crow is a figure of sin, which departs and does not

return, provided you imitate the observance and example of the just man.[152]

Water and the end of time

There is another point in the Genesis story that the First Letter of Peter especially emphasizes: the divine patience that made God wait before imposing sentence. "God's patience waited in the days of Noah during the building of the ark" (1 Peter 3:20). The Second Letter of Peter makes the same point:

> First of all you must understand this, that scoffers will come in the last days with scoffing, following their own passions and saying, "Where is the promise of his coming? For ever since the fathers fell asleep, all things have continued as they were from the beginning of creation." They deliberately ignore this fact, that by the word of God heavens existed long ago, and an earth formed out of water and by means of water, through which the world that then existed was deluged with water and perished. But by the same word the heavens and earth that now exist have been stored up for fire, being kept until the day of judgment and destruction of ungodly men.
>
> But do not ignore this one fact, beloved, that with the Lord one day is as a thousand years, and a thousand years as one day (2 Peter 3:3-8).

This passage is in fact repeating Jesus' own commentary on the "patience of God": "For as in those days before the flood they were eating and drinking, marrying and giving in marriage, until the day when Noah entered the ark, and they did not know until the flood came and swept them all away, so will be the coming of the Son of man" (Matthew 24:38-39).

The Deluge, then, in both the New Testament and the Fathers, has an eschatological dimension. The Second Letter of Peter indicates a parallel between the time before the

Deluge and the time still separating us from the final judgment. The delay that God in his patience provides, has for
its purpose to bring men to repentance: "The Lord is . . .
forbearing toward you, not wishing that any should perish,
but that all should reach repentance" (2 Peter 3:9).

We must observe, however, that if in the eyes of the
Fathers the Deluge has an eschatological meaning and is a
preparation for the coming judgment, baptism has the same
significance. It too prepares for and prefigures the judgment
at the end of time. Origen writes: "In rebirth through the
bath of water we were buried with Christ. . . . Through the
regeneration effected by that bath, in which fire and Spirit
are at work, we become like the glorious Christ as he sits
upon his throne of glory, and we too sit upon twelve
thrones with him." [153]

The obstacles to salvation

Evidently the plan of salvation meets with difficulties;
there are obstacles to the fulfillment of the purposes God
has in his work. The evil powers and the spirit of the world
combine to try to frustrate him.

The catechumen who is seeking to reach the Light has
been presented in the liturgy with a synthesis of the mystery and history of salvation. The need, for the catechumen
and for every Christian, is to enter into, and become part of,
the mystery that concerns him so intimately. For only the
just man will be saved, that is, the man found worthy to
enter the ark; all others will be destroyed. In principle, of
course, the baptized person has entered the ark, which is
the Church; he continues, however, to be a man and subject
to the human condition. St. Augustine brings out the tragic
character of man's paradoxical condition:

> Now we begin already to be *like to God*, since we
> have the first-fruits of the Spirit; and yet we are *still
> unlike* because the old Adam is still with us. . . . Now
> we have the first-fruits of the Spirit, and so have al-
> ready really become the sons of God. For the rest, it is

in hope that we are saved, and renewed, and, in the same way, become sons of God: because we are not yet saved in all reality, we are not yet fully renewed, not yet even sons of God, but sons of this world. . . . Let all that then be consumed that keeps us still sons of the flesh and of the world, and let all that be perfected that makes us sons of God and renewed in the Spirit.[154]

On this first Sunday of Lent, both the seeker of light and the baptized are confronted once again with the mystery of salvation. This salvation is a gift of rebirth, but its completion comes after a long process of maturation during which God patiently waits for us to manifest our active good will. Gregory of Nyssa points out: "Each human being is born by his own choice. Thus we are to some extent our own fathers, because we freely beget ourselves as we wish to be."[155]

Covenant and sacrifice

The global vision of the mystery of salvation offered us would have a serious lacuna if nothing were said of covenant and sacrifice. After all, the reason why God exercises patience is that he may eventually be reunited to men and bring them into a covenant whose sign is sacrifice. On this point, once again, the account in Genesis has been re-edited, and the covenant that is really to begin in its full form with Abraham has been projected back and connected with the salvation offered to Noah and his posterity.

The account of the Flood in Genesis shows us a Noah who, after the forty days, is a new man; he is the father of a new race, and thus he is a new Adam and a figure of Christ. The Church delights in showing to her faithful and to all who seek the light this figure of man renewed. At the same time, she emphasizes the fact that the covenant is sealed by a sacrifice: "Then Noah built an altar to the Lord, and took of every clean animal and of every clean bird, and offered burnt offerings on the altar. And when the Lord smelled the pleasing odor, the Lord said in his heart, 'I will never again curse the ground because of man'" (Gen. 8:20-21).

The sacrifice brings the covenant into existence, for by sacrifice creation pays homage to the God who takes the initiative. God accepts the sacrifice, and the covenant is concluded:

> Then God said to Noah and to his sons with him, "Behold, I establish my covenant with you and your descendants after you, and with every living creature that is with you, the birds, the cattle, and every beast of the earth with you, as many as came out of the ark. I establish my covenant with you, that never again shall all flesh be cut off by the waters of a flood, and never again shall there be a flood to destroy the earth." And God said, "This is the sign of the covenant which I make between me and you and every living creature that is with you, for all future generations: I set my bow in the cloud, and it shall be a sign of the covenant between me and the earth" (Gen. 9:8-13).

Second and Third Sundays of Lent, Cycle B

for years 1979, 1982, 1985, 1988, 1991

11. GOD HAS HANDED OVER HIS SON FOR US

"This is my beloved Son"

These words of the Father in the story of the transfiguration are full of meaning for us. The same words were spoken at the Epiphany, and our study of the Epiphany liturgy has already given us the opportunity to discuss certain aspects of them.

We can hear in the words an echo of Abraham's words as he offers the Father his only son. In the case of Christ, the Son has come and offered himself, but he has done so out of obedience and the desire to do the Father's will, thus counteracting the disobedience of Adam. For his obedience Christ is rewarded with the transfiguration; the latter becomes then the sign of the transfiguration every man will experience who chooses to walk the paths of God and do the Father's will.

The account of the transfiguration raises a number of problems, but these are not our concern here, since we intend to be faithful to our purpose, which is the liturgical reading of the Scriptures. In Cycle A the transfiguration was seen as resulting from the response to a call. On this second Sunday of Cycle B, the theme is somewhat different: now the transfiguration crowns the response to a call, but a response that includes the offering of sacrifice. This is the theme of the first reading, on the sacrifice of Abraham. It is also the theme of the second reading, in which St. Paul reminds us that God has handed over his own Son for our salvation. It is Christ's willingness to sacrifice himself that gives full meaning to the words, "This is my beloved Son."

There is a point I would like to raise here concerning the Gospel pericope, although it is not a point that determined the choice of the Gospel for the second Sunday of Lent. I am referring to the secrecy that Christ imposed on his disciples after the transfiguration (Mark 9:9-10). This is not the only occasion, of course, on which Christ imposes secrecy on the witnesses of his miracles, his exorcisms, and even his parables. St. Mark has his special way of dealing with this whole matter. He emphasizes the secrecy, and notes, on this particular occasion, that the witnesses do observe the secrecy, though they do not understand "what the rising from the dead meant" (v. 10).

Perhaps Christ's intention in ordering secrecy is to make a slow initiation possible. His action would then be part of

a catechetical and pastoral method. The truth is admittedly
one, but there are degrees of fullness in presenting it. We
see Jesus acting and speaking in one way with a small
group of disciples, in another with a larger group of followers, and in still another with the crowd. He chooses to reveal his messiahship in varying degrees.

By emphasizing this aspect of Jesus' method, St. Mark
and the early Church reply to the accusation that Jesus
manifested nothing of the glory and splendor that should
surround the coming and work of the Messiah. Their answer is that Jesus did indeed manifest his glory, and in several degrees, but that he also did not want all to know of
this glory.

The Gospel itself can be read with varying degrees of
comprehension. Christ, then, provides us with the example
of a prudent catechesis that respects the pace each hearer
keeps in attaining full understanding of Christian teaching
or of the inspired word of God.

The sacrifice of Abraham

In the story of Abraham preparing to sacrifice his son,
there is a striking sentence that prepares us for the second
reading, in which we will hear of the Son sent to save us:
"God will provide himself the lamb for a burnt offering"
(Gen. 22:8). Abraham went ahead with the preparation that
would lead to the sacrifice of his son because he believed
in God's promise, even though everything seemed to be
preventing its fulfillment.

The sacrifice of Abraham became a theme in the
Eucharistic liturgy; the Eucharistic Prayers, especially the
Roman Canon (the first of our present four Eucharistic
Prayers), often mention it. The *De sacramentis* of St. Am-
brose contains the nucleus of the Roman Canon, and there
we already find reference to Abraham and his sacrifice:

> And the priest says: "Mindful, therefore, of his most
> glorious Passion and his resurrection from the dead
> and his ascension into heaven, we offer you this spot-

less Victim, this spiritual Victim, this unbloody Victim, this holy bread and chalice of eternal life, and we ask and pray that you would accept this offering on your altar on high, through the hands of your angels, as you deigned to accept the gifts of your just servant Abel, the sacrifice of our father Abraham, and the offering your high priest Melchisedech made to you." [156]

This prayer is evidently very close to the passage that follows immediately upon the consecration in the Roman Canon. The only real difference is that the reference to the angels and the altar on high now comes after the mention of Abel, Abraham, and Melchisedech.

The Son handed over for us

St. Paul in this passage (Rom. 8:31-34) simply mentions the gift of the Son to us without discussing it. He sees it as part of God's saving plan and a sign of the Father's love for us. God sacrifices his own Son as part of his plan for the reconstruction and reunification of the world (see Rom. 16:25-26). From our creaturely point of view, the Father's gift of his Son to us is a revelation of the "mystery," that is, the secret plan of salvation that has been hidden in God from eternity.

The purpose God has in giving us his Son is to make us likewise his children after the image of the only-begotten Son. That is why the Word takes to himself a human nature like ours (see Rom. 8:3). God handed his Son over to death for the sake of us all. Consequently, there can be no further accusation against us: "If God is for us, who is against us? . . . Who shall bring any charge against God's elect? . . . Who is to condemn?" (Rom. 8:31-34). Jesus, after all, has died for us; more than that, he rose to life for us and is now seated at God's right hand. Here we are prepared for the Gospel of Jesus' transfiguration and prediction of his resurrection.

Psalm 116, the responsorial psalm for the second Sunday, expresses very well the sentiments of Abraham and Christ, and our own sentiments too: "O Lord, I am thy servant; I am thy servant, the son of thy handmaid. Thou hast loosed my bonds. I will offer to thee the sacrifice of thanksgiving and call on the name of the Lord" (vv. 16-17).

It is not easy to discern the unity of the three readings for the third Sunday in Cycle B, and we must not try to force them into a pattern.

Jesus crucified, a stumbling block for the world

The second reading (1 Cor. 1:22-25) brings out the power inherent in Christian witness, but it also emphasizes the great obstacle: Christ is seen by many as foolishness and a stumbling block. The Apostle is not saying that the Christian should love what makes no sense; we cannot imagine God requiring his followers to be stupid. The thing that eludes human comprehension is that God should love us to the point of sending his Son to save us.

St. Paul confronts us with a fact: "Jews demand signs and Greeks seek wisdom, but we preach Christ crucified" (vv. 22-23). The Church's message is that Christ was crucified for our salvation, and she will keep on preaching that message to the end of time as her dearest possession, even though it is a message that wins her no sympathy from unregenerate man. On the other hand, "to those who are called, both Jews and Greeks, Christ [is] the power of God and the wisdom of God. For the foolishness of God is wiser than men, and the weakness of God is stronger than men" (vv. 24-25).

The language of this last sentence is strong and will not let us slip by unattentively. The message and the reality to which it points condition our lives; we cannot ignore them. This, after all, is the only message we really have for men, and what a demanding message it is! All who believe in Christ must also walk in his steps, but this means that they will be in conflict and that a radical detachment will be required of them. The foolishness of God must become our foolishness. It is evidently impossible to maintain such an attitude unless we believe unconditionally in the resurrection of Christ. Consequently, when St. Paul writes in his Letter to the Romans: "If you confess with your lips . . . that Jesus is Lord and believe in your heart that God raised him from the dead, you will be saved" (Rom. 10:9), he is but repeating an ancient confessional formula and expressing the basic belief without which Christianity would simply not exist.

Belief in, and knowledge of, the risen Christ are the reason why the Gospels can present the life, work, suffering, and death of Jesus as still real and operative. The crucifixion has always been a stumbling block; today the resurrection is, too. This is not the place to raise problems proper to Easter day, but we must at least ask ourselves how real the resurrection is and whether it makes any difference in our lives. Only on condition that the resurrection is real in every possible sense of the word can we proclaim Christ crucified and sacrificed, in accordance with the Father's will, for the sake of our salvation.

The sign of the temple

It is because of the key importance of the resurrection that the liturgy proposes to us as a Gospel reading for the third Sunday a passage in which Christ foretells his own resurrection (John 2:13-25). In dealing with this passage, we must, once again, not get overly involved in details of historical exegesis. The point is not that these details are negligible but that our purpose is rather to discern the point of view the liturgy takes in proposing this reading for the third Sunday of Lent.

The main reason why the reading has been chosen is Jesus' prophecy of his resurrection: "Destroy this temple, and in three days I will raise it up" (v. 19). Later on, Jesus would be accused of wanting to tear down the Temple in Jerusalem (Matthew 25:61; Mark 14:58). To make clear what Jesus really meant, St. Mark expands Jesus' words:

"We heard him say, 'I will destroy this temple that is made with hands, and in three days I will build another, not made with hands'" (Mark 14:58). Jesus is evidently referring to the building of a new eschatological temple.

St. John, who always chooses words that are more exact and richer in meaning, uses here, not the Greek word *oikodomân*, "to build" (as in Mark), but the verb *egeirein*, "to awaken, to raise up," which can refer both to the material reconstruction of the temple building and to the raising of his own body from death. Christ's hearers do not understand and begin to mock him: "It has taken forty-six years to build this temple, and will you raise it up in three days?" (v. 20).

St. John himself explains what Jesus meant: "But he spoke of the temple of his body" (v. 21). This does not mean that the apostles immediately understood at the time the meaning of Jesus' words. We have every reason for thinking that they understood only after Jesus had risen from the dead and they themselves had been enlightened by the Holy Spirit.

The body of the risen Jesus will be the new temple, the spiritual temple in which men will worship in Spirit and truth (John 4:21). St. John was the first to understand that the new temple was the risen body of Jesus, but the entire New Testament uses the symbol of the temple, especially St. Paul when speaking of the Church (Eph. 2:19-21; etc.)

St. John emphasizes the faith of those who see the signs Jesus gives. As everyone is aware, in his writings generally and especially in his Gospel, St. John develops a theology of the place of such signs in Christian life. The sign is given either in response to faith or in order to rouse faith. The faith thus roused may be full and perfect, or it may be still unsure. It is to a still imperfect faith that John is referring when he says: "Many believed in his name when they saw the signs which he did; but Jesus did not trust himself to them, because he knew all men" (John 2:23-24). We must speak, then, of a faith that is roused by the word and a faith that is roused by signs.

The law that frees

St. Paul speaks of the law as a yoke: "We were confined under the law, kept under restraint until faith should be revealed" (Gal. 3:23). The law, however (that is, the law proper to the old covenant), "has but a shadow of the good things to come" (Heb. 10:1). We know how Paul likes to contrast the law and faith: We are no longer under the law (Rom. 6:14) but are dead to the law (Rom. 7:4) so that we may live for God (Gal. 2:19); Christ has redeemed us from the curse of the law (Gal. 3:13), having in his own flesh, abolished the law (Eph. 2:15). Paul writes of the Christian in confrontation with the law (Rom. 7) and of our salvation as coming through faith, not through the law (Gal. 3). For his part, St. John tells us that the law came through Moses, but grace through Jesus Christ (John 1:16-17).

In contrast to these various New Testament approaches, the passage read from Exodus on this third Sunday speaks of the law as something that liberates, as a road leading God's people to freedom. The Old Testament contains several codes of law, but the one in Exodus 20 is the most important. We will recall that Jesus himself quotes passages from it to the rich young man who asks him what must be done to attain eternal life (Mark 10:17-25).[157]

The Ten Commandments are in fact signs of God's love and a means of liberation. Psalm 81 recalls the Decalogue in the context of Israel's birth into freedom (Ps. 81:7). In a similar way, today's reading from Exodus begins by reminding us: "I am the Lord your God, who brought you out of the land of Egypt" (v. 2). The law that the Lord promulgates gives life and brings the people of God into existence.

In the light of the last statement, we can grasp the connection between this reading and the other readings for this Sunday, although we shall not be emphasizing the connection. The law is an intermediate, transitional stage; it cannot give life or the justice that is God's gift (Gal. 3:21). It was given, therefore, to call attention to sin and to prevent it. Being concerned only with transgressions, the law is imperfect. On the other hand, Christ came to fulfill the law by making its purpose possible, viz., radical intimacy with God; we must therefore acknowledge that the law led to Christ. The goal of the law is Christ, through whom comes the justice (forgiveness of sins, holiness) that is promised to everyone who believes (Rom. 10:4). But Christ also puts an end to the law by fulfilling all its precepts in his great act of obedience (Gal. 3:13). Christ became a man among the Jews so that he might submit to their law and thereby ransom them from their slavery (Gal. 4:4-5).

The responsorial psalm that follows this first reading glorifies the law as perfect, trustworthy, and a source of wisdom for the simple (Ps. 19:8). A passage from Origen shows us that if we are to have a true knowledge of the Decalogue, we must already have reached a certain level of holiness:

> Of every one who has learned to scorn the present world ("Egypt" in figurative language) and has been carried up (to use the scriptural term) by the word of God so that he is no longer to be found here because he is hastening toward the world to come — of every such soul the Lord says: "I am the Lord your God, who brought you out of the land of Egypt, out of the house of bondage." These words, therefore, are not directed solely to those who once came out of Egypt. Much more does the Lord say to you who hear them now, provided you have indeed left Egypt and no longer serve the Egyptians: "I am the Lord your God, who brought you out of the land of Egypt, out of the house of bondage." Consider: Are not worldly affairs and fleshly deeds a house of bondage? On the other hand, are not the abandonment of worldly concerns and a life according to God a house of freedom? The Lord tells us so in the Gospel: "If you continue in my word, you are truly my disciples, and you will know the truth, and the truth will make you free." [158]

Fourth and Fifth Sundays of Lent, Cycle B

for years 1979, 1982, 1985, 1988, 1991

12. THE SALVATION OF THE WORLD

The Son sent to save the world

This theme, which is elaborated in the Gospel for the fourth Sunday (John 3:14-21), was already broached and developed in the readings for the second Sunday, especially the first (Gen. 22:1-2, 9, 10-13, 15-18) and second (Rom. 8:31b-34). Today's Gospel reading has its problems, but these are of only remote concern to its use in the liturgy.

For example, when we read chapter 3 of the Fourth Gospel, we easily see a notable difference of style between verses 1-12 and verses 13-21. In this second section, which we read today, there is still question of man achieving rebirth through the death and resurrection of Jesus. But the style is different. The speaker is now "we" rather than "I": "You do not receive our testimony" (v. 11). From verse 13 on, Jesus no longer converses about Nicodemus, but is spoken of in the third person. Moreover, there is an emphasis on the exaltation of the Son of Man that has only a vague connection with the first part of the chapter.

The passage suggests, then, that these verses are a catechesis of John himself and that he has composed them. This is a position taken in German exegesis and represented by a number of authors whom we need not cite here. It does seem that John has at least rewritten the passage, although we cannot hope to determine just which words were spoken by Jesus and what John himself added — all under the inspiration of the Holy Spirit. This is a problem that runs throughout the Fourth Gospel. I do not mean that John introduces his personal fantasies (the contrary has

often been shown) but that, under the guidance of the
Spirit, he goes back over the words and deeds of Jesus in
order to shape them into a catechesis that will stimulate
faith. That is what has happened in the passage with which
we are dealing now.

The basic theme of today's liturgy is the rebirth of man, a
rebirth that depends on the sending and coming of the Son
and on his exaltation, that is, his crucifixion and triumphant
resurrection. Such is God's love-inspired plan for mankind.
The love that God has for us is the starting point of the
entire work of salvation. Yet the salvation must also be accepted — and when the light came, men preferred the
darkness! This response, elicited by Christ's coming, turns
into a condemnation of the world. Men condemn themselves because, in their desire to continue in their evil
ways, they refuse the light.

Rebirth, therefore, requires certain attitudes in man; the
renewal offered us does not take place mechanically. Christ
came to give life, but the gift must be accepted or it will
turn into a condemnation. We must act according to the
truth if we want to reach the light. But what does it mean to
"act according to the truth"? "Truth" is a favorite word of
St. John. But how are we to interpret it, since in the Greek
text *alētheia*, "truth" in the intellectual sense, was used to
translate the Hebrew '*emet*, which means "truth" in a moral
sense. Which of the two does St. John have in mind?

Take verse 21: "He who does what is true comes to the
light." We might rephrase this and say: "He who acts well
(*or*: uprightly) comes into the light." Then we are choosing
the Hebrew meaning of '*emet*, "fidelity," of which the Old
Testament provides so many examples (see Gen. 32:10;
47:29; etc.), and we are restricting "truth" to its moral
meaning. Does such a limitation fit in with the mentality St.
John shows throughout his Gospel? When he writes:
"When the Spirit of truth comes, he will guide you into all
the truth" (John 16:13), John means precisely truth, not
fidelity; that is, he means knowledge of the reality Jesus has
made accessible to us, the eternal reality he has revealed to

men. In fact, Christ does not simply reveal this reality to us; he himself *is* this reality in its definitive form (see John 14:10).

The Son has thus brought the truth to man's world, and this action produces light (a light which, again, he himself is in its definitive form: the "true" light). We must live and act in accordance with this truth if we are to reach the light and be reborn. We can see how important such a text is with regard to the sacraments: A sacramental sign is not a magical gesture but always supposes the recipient's faith and acceptance of truth in the light.

"God so loved the world"

In this same passage from the Fourth Gospel there is a short sentence that leaps out from the page when the people of our day read it: "God so loved the world." No one has ever denied what the sentence says, but there has always been, and still is, a spirituality that puts more emphasis on the fact that we must love God than on the fact that we are loved by him. Yet John frequently stresses God's love for us, as revealed in the salvific activity of his Son. He writes, for example: "In this the love of God was made manifest among us, that God sent his only Son into the world, so that we might live through him. In this is love, not that we loved God but that he loved us and sent his Son to be the expiation for our sins" (1 John 4:9-10).

The priority of God's love for us is one of the most deeply moving truths Christianity preaches, for it presupposes that God is full of mercy toward weak and sinful man. John does not tire of preaching this love: "By this we know love, that he laid down his life for us" (1 John 3:16). Recognition of God's freely given love becomes characteristic of the believing Christian: "So we know and believe the love God has for us" (1 John 4:16). This awareness on the part of the Christian is not a fleeting thing but a necessary and constant part of his make-up: "God is love, and he who abides in love abides in God, and God abides in him" (*ibid.*).

He, on the other hand, who does not believe is already condemned, because he has not accepted the Son (John 3:18). The reason for the condemnation is clear: the Light came into the world, but men loved the darkness more (John 3:19).

The struggle between light and darkness, a favorite theme of the Fourth Gospel, reveals the drama in every Christian's life. The Christian is faced with a choice he cannot evade.

The wrath and mercy of God

The account read in the first reading for this fourth Sunday shows us the unfaithfulness of Israel: "All the leading priests and the people likewise were exceedingly unfaithful" (2 Chr. 36:14). The passage also tells us that all scorned the messengers that God sent, and mocked the prophets. The passage thus illustrates what the Gospel will say: Men refused the light because they loved the darkness. God's wrath at Israel's infidelity will lead to the destruction of the Temple and the deportation to Babylon of those who had escaped the slaughter.

But the Lord is also a God of love, and the passage from Chronicles alludes to the way in which his love would later gain the upper hand over his wrath (vv. 22-23). Seventy years later, Cyrus, king of Persia, would rebuild the Temple and permit the people of God to return to Jerusalem.

The responsory psalm for this reading gives admirable expression to the sentiments of the Israelites in exile; it can be the expression of our own sentiments as well: "How shall we sing the Lord's song in a foreign land? If I forget you, O Jerusalem, let my right hand wither!" (Ps. 137:4-5).

Awareness of not having acted toward God as truth requires, along with suffering and expiation — these make it possible to return to the good graces so characteristic of the God of the Old Testament and the New, for he is a God who pardons and raises up. This is the point emphasized in the second reading (Eph. 2:4-10) for this fourth Sunday.

Dead through sin, raised up by grace

In his Letter to the Ephesians, St. Paul uses strong language: "God, who is rich in mercy, out of the great love with which he loved us, even when we were dead through our trespasses, made us alive together with Christ (by grace you have been saved), and raised us up with him, and made us sit with him in the heavenly places" (2:4-6).

Here is the full reality and effectiveness of that divine love the Gospel speaks of. As the Letter to the Romans puts it: "God shows his love for us in that while we were yet sinners Christ died for us" (Rom. 5:8). We know what Paul's own experience had been, and we can glimpse something of his profound feeling when he writes, in the verses immediately preceding the verse just quoted: "While we were yet helpless, at the right time, Christ died for the ungodly. Why, one will hardly die for a righteous man — though perhaps for a good man one will dare even to die" (Rom. 5:6-7).

We are now alive, and alive with Christ: "God . . . even when we were dead through our trespasses, made us alive together with Christ" (Eph. 2:5). Elsewhere Paul expands that statement: "And you were buried with him [Christ] in baptism, in which you were also raised with him through faith in the working of God, who raised him from the dead" (Col. 2:12).

Not only are we risen with Christ but we also experience our ascension with him: "[He] raised us up with him, and made us sit with him in the heavenly places" (Eph. 2:6). For St. Paul, the ascension is the sign of Christ's glorious state after the act of obedience that brought him to death (Phil. 2:9). But Christ's ascension is also ours, not only as an encouraging promise that will be fulfilled at the end of our life but as a reality that has already begun. Baptism is the beginning of our ascension, because in baptism we rise with Christ.

On this fourth Sunday, then, we contemplate the superabundant grace the Father has bestowed on us. We are saved by grace; this grace is inexhaustibly rich and makes our actions good in God's sight.

Such is the wealth of teaching given on this fourth Sunday of Lent. As we contemplate it, we must grasp the marvelous coherence of God's plan of salvation; but, more than that, we must ask ourselves how we are to live out the mystery in our everyday lives.

The seed that dies when its "hour" comes

The fifth Sunday continues to spell out the work of salvation in which we are participating. The grain dies and bears fruit, and the fruit, cultivated by obedience, is eternal salvation, a new covenant based on God's forgetfulness of our past sins. In this or a similar way we can sum up the message of the fifth Sunday.

The theme of the seed that is buried in the ground and then bears fruit is found in the Synoptics as well as in John. But John here gives the parable a special twist: the seed is Jesus himself, who by dying will give life to mankind. We would therefore lessen or even destroy the meaning John gives the image if we were to draw from it only a moral lesson, seeing in it simply a call to humble and mortify ourselves so that we may bear fruits of holiness. That would indeed be a profound misinterpretation, for what the image conveys in John is a Christology.

The Synoptics have parables dealing with seed and use them chiefly because of the development a seed undergoes; see, for example, the parable of the mustard seed, in Mark 4:30-32 (see other parables in Mark 4:1-9 and 26-29, with the parallels in the other Synoptics). John, however, emphasizes chiefly the death and burial of the seed, that is, of Christ, and the fruit that springs from this self-giving of the Lord. Here the seed is a Person.

We would even be mistaken if we gave a merely moralistic interpretation to such words as these: "If any one serves me, he must follow me; and where I am, there shall my servant be also; if any one serves me, the Father will honor him" (John 12:26). The real point in this whole section of the Gospel is the journey taken not only by Christ but by the Christian after him. The catechumen's baptism imprints on him the image of Jesus in the Spirit, so that it is now natural and inevitable for him, too, to pass through death in order to reach resurrection.

We should note, at the beginning of the passage, the desire of the Greeks "to see Jesus." They mean simply that they want to see a man who draws crowds and enjoys a certain success. Jesus' answer, however, clearly summons the Greeks to advance to a new level, for he tells them that he is one who dies, rises, and is glorified, and that to follow him means traveling the same road.

The petition of the Greeks draws from Jesus the mention of another favorite theme of St. John: the "hour" that is coming and is already at hand. The presence of this theme gives the parable of the dying seed a special tonality.[159]

The "hour" is here linked with the "glorification," a term that, as John uses it, includes the Passion, death, resurrection, and ascension of Jesus. Verse 23 of the passage brings the two terms together: "The hour has come for the Son of man to be glorified."

John's Gospel traces the stages within this "hour." At the marriage feast of Cana, Jesus says that his "hour" has not yet come (2:4). Chapter 7 contains three mentions of this hour that has not yet come (vv. 6, 8, 30). Chapter 8 repeats the theme: "But no one arrested him, because his hour had not yet come" (v. 20). Now, at last, the hour has come, and it is the hour of Jesus' glorification, this last term having the various complementary meanings John assigns to it. Christ has come to this hour so that now the Father may glorify his own name through him.

It is important to emphasize the connection between the "hour" and the glorification. Several passages of John bring the two terms together: "The hour has come for the Son of man to be glorified" (12:23); "When he [Judas] had gone out, Jesus said, 'Now is the Son of man glorified, and in him God is glorified'" (13:31); "Father, the hour has come;

glorify thy Son that the Son may glorify thee" (17:1). In these passages the hour and the glorification are connected, and the glorification refers to the mystery of the Christ's death and resurrection.

The voice of the Father that is heard in the pericope we are discussing foretells the glorious Passion of the Son. Immediately after the Father's words Jesus proclaims judgment upon the world — judgment through the Cross, which will be victorious over evil. When Jesus is "lifted up" (and John is careful to explain what being "lifted up" means: it refers to the manner of his death), he will draw all men to himself.

What more explicit statement than this could we want to prove that God indeed wills to save all men? The seed, then, that dies when its hour comes, saves the world and all mankind.

Christ saves mankind by his obedience

This universal salvation was made possible, however, only because the Son obeyed to the point of dying. This theme has been the subject of so much commentary that there seems to be no point in dwelling on it here, and yet it is a theme that situates us at the very center of the history of salvation. The Fathers saw in Christ's obedience the counterweight to Adam's disobedience. We have already discussed the parallel and contrast that St. Paul emphasizes so heavily: by one man sin entered the world, and by one man grace renewed the world.

The Letter to the Hebrews may surprise us with the statements it makes in the passage read on the fifth Sunday. We read, for example: "Although he was a Son, he learned obedience through what he suffered; and being made perfect he became the source of eternal salvation to all who obey him" (5:8-9). The author of the Letter sees further perfection possible for Christ in the line of obedience. The Christ shown us here is the Christ who, though Son, shared our human nature in all things except sin; consequently, he was called to the experience of suffering and obedience. This is not an abstract Jesus. At the same time, however, the author is careful to stress the harmony that existed between the attitudes of the transcendent Christ and those of the Christ visible to us in the Gospel. The author can therefore assert that all who obey the Christ visible among us will have eternal salvation through the Christ who was obedient unto death.

"I will remember their sin no more"

Infidelity, divine wrath, establishment (or renewal) of a covenant — here is a pattern that runs through the entire Old Testament. Now, in the New Testament, there is question again of a covenant, but now it is a "new" covenant.

The new covenant is described for us by Jeremias in the first reading for the fifth Sunday: "I will be their God, and they shall be my people" (31:33). The theme is one that would be taken up by later prophets (Ezek. 11:20; 14:11; 36:28; 37:23-27; Zech. 8:8), and it occurs a number of times in Jeremias himself (24:7; 30:22; 31:1; 32:28). Here the relations between the Lord and Israel are clearly defined. We have already seen how the prophet Osee expresses the relations between the Lord and his people through the image of betrothal and marriage or the image of a father's dealings with his son (Osee 2:2; 3:1; 3:4; 11:1-4). In Jeremias the covenant is also connected with knowledge of the Lord: "They shall all know me, from the least of them to the greatest" (v. 34).

But what is "new" about this covenant? It is new because the covenant will be written in men's hearts, and this makes it notably different from the old covenant. In the latter, God's will was expressed from outside, as it were; here each person will carry the Lord's law in his heart. In consequence, knowledge of, and union with, the Lord will no longer be reserved to an elite, especially the prophets, but will be accessible to all. "They shall all know me, from the least of them to the greatest"; recall here what the Gospel says about Jesus drawing all men to himself. The new covenant will also bring the forgiveness of sins: "I will remember their sin no more" (v. 34).

To this last-quoted text Psalm 51 responds with a prayer: "Wash me thoroughly from my iniquity, and cleanse me from my sin! . . . Create in me a clean heart, O God. . . . Restore to me the joy of thy salvation" (vv. 2, 10, 12).

The grain of wheat is buried in the ground when its hour comes, and it then bears its fruit. So the obedience of Christ gives his followers access to eternal life, and in his new covenant God remembers past sins no more.

First and Second Sundays of Lent, Cycle C

for years 1980, 1983, 1986, 1989, 1992

13. THE FAITH THAT TRANSFORMS

Tempted but victorious through faith

As in the other two cycles, we read the account of the temptation of the Lord on the first Sunday of Lent in Cycle C. Here the temptation acquires a special meaning, inasmuch as the trial that Christ undergoes ends in a victory, a victory of confidence in the Father and of the will to do what the Father has determined. Man does not live on material bread alone; in fact, the important bread, which he absolutely must eat, is the Father's will as made known through his living word (Is. 55:1). For Jesus, the word of God is a bread we must eat daily (Matthew 4:4); to that word we must commit ourselves in faith (John 6:35-47), for we must worship the one God by doing his will, without asking him to explain himself to us.

This kind of faith in God turned Israel into a great nation. Even when the nation had been reduced to slavery, Israel's God listened to his people, rescued them, and led them into a land flowing with milk and honey. The first reading for today tells us of Israel's faith and how the nation was saved through tribulation (Deut. 26:4-10). Psalm 91 serves as a response to this reading, and in it we hear the triumphant cry of a nation that has been tried and led into slavery: "Say to the Lord, 'My refuge and my fortress; in God, in whom I trust'" (Ps. 91:2). The psalm also gives us God's response in turn: "Because he cleaves to me in love, I will deliver him; I will protect him, because he knows my name. When he calls to me, I will answer him; I will be with him in trouble, I will rescue him and honor him. With long life I will satisfy him, and show him my salvation" (vv. 14-16).

STRUCTURE OF CYCLE C FOR THE FIRST FIVE SUNDAYS OF LENT

TABLE OF READINGS IN THE EUCHARISTIC LITURGY

	Old Testament	Apostle	Gospel
First Sunday	Deut. 26:4-10 Faith of the people of Israel	Rom. 10:8-13 Faith in Christ	Luke 4:1-13 Temptation of Christ
Second Sunday	Gen. 15:5-12, 17-18 Abraham's faith and the covenant	Phil. 3:17–4:1 Our transfigured bodies	Luke 9:28-36 Transfiguration of Christ
Third Sunday	Exod. 3:1-8a, 13-15 The Lord rescues his people	1 Cor. 10:1-6, 10-12 The desert journey, an example for us	Luke 13:1-9 Be converted or perish
Fourth Sunday	Josh. 5:9a, 10-12 The Passover celebrated in the promised land	2 Cor. 5:17-21 Reconciled to God in Christ	Luke 15:1-3, 11-32 The prodigal son
Fifth Sunday	Is. 43:16-21 Dream not of the past; a new world is here	Phil. 3:8-14 Rising with Christ	John 8:1-11 The woman taken in adultery

Those who believe in Christ should be animated by a similar confidence. In the second reading St. Paul encourages us against times of trial and suffering: "'The word is near you, on your lips and in your heart'" (Rom. 10:8; cf. Deut. 30:14). The entire passage, in fact, is a cry of trust and of certainty that deliverance will come: "If you confess with your lips that Jesus is Lord and believe in your heart that God raised him from the dead, you will be saved. For man believes with his heart and so is justified, and he confesses with his lips and so is saved" (Rom. 10:9-10).

Paul's words of encouragement touch us in the details of our everyday life. There is no single moment at which we cannot be sure of our salvation, provided that we believe and call upon the name of the Lord, who is generous to all who invoke him.

The central thought of this first Sunday is "salvation" through faith; faith and salvation are the two dominant themes. We must be careful, however, to note that the message is addressed to all mankind: "There is no distinction between Jew and Greek; the same Lord is Lord of all and bestows his riches upon all who call upon him. For, 'every one who calls upon the name of the Lord will be saved'" (Rom. 10:12-13, citing Joel 3:5). Salvation is not reserved to a single people or to a single race; it is not reserved even to the people of the promise. Christ shows us a far vaster and deeper conception of the economy of salvation than the one with which Abraham, Moses, and Israel were familiar.

In verses 5 and 6 of chapter 10, which are not included in today's reading, St. Paul contrasts the justice that comes from the law with the justice that comes from faith. The law proved incapable of really saving those who tried to achieve salvation through their own works (Rom. 10:3; see also Rom. 9:32). In faith, on the other hand, the individual entrusts himself to God and does not attempt the impossible, namely, to win salvation through his own uprightness. The law simply pointed out what is sinful (Rom. 3:20), whereas faith brings the power of the Spirit who sanctifies (Rom. 1:4; 8:11); faith thus gives salvation.

In obeying the law, the Israelite was seeking to satisfy his legitimate desire for a plenitude of life; the way of faith, however, leads to the salvation that God alone can give. Faith, moreover, gives a salvation that is something present now, yet also reserved for the future: "He confesses with his lips and so is saved" (Rom. 10:10), and when life is over and men are judged, no one who thus confessed his faith will be put to shame, but "every one who calls upon the name of the Lord will be saved."

The first reading, from Deuteronomy, connects the profession of faith (26:5-9) with a ritual in which the first fruits of the harvest are offered to the Lord (vv. 4, 10). The exegetes see in this passage the desire to transform the agrarian cults into the worship of Yahweh. The gifts of the earth thus become a present embodiment of salvation and show that God indeed intends to save his people, provided that they have trust in him. Evidently the first and second readings are linked together, with the second presenting the full Christian reality that is only distantly anticipated in the first.

In the Gospel of the temptation, the chief thing to be emphasized is trust in, and worship of, the one true God. The text provides us with another occasion to point out how one and the same text will be differently interpreted in different liturgies, depending on the other texts being read at the same time. The Gospel of the temptation is read on the first Sunday in all three cycles, but it calls for comment in each cycle from a viewpoint that is determined by the other two readings in the cycle.

Our transfigured bodies

Once again, the Gospel pericope for the second Sunday is the same as in the other two cycles, and once again our reading of it must take account of the two readings that accompany it.

The first reading tells us of Abraham's faith and the covenant (Gen. 15:5-12, 17-18). It recounts an awesome theophany in which the Lord makes a promise that is connected with a sacrificial rite. The first part of the account speaks of Abraham's faith in the Lord's promises; in the second part, immediately after the sacrifice and by way of recompense to Abraham for his faith, the Lord concludes his covenant. The narrative moves swiftly, and the elimination of some verses in the pericope as found in the liturgy makes the narrative even more succinct, perhaps even oversimplifies it a bit. We have the Lord's promise and Abraham's faith, and these are immediately followed by the fulfillment of the promise in the form of a covenant.

The responsorial psalm, Psalm 27, fits in nicely with the theophany in the reading: "Thy face, Lord, do I seek. Hide not thy face from me. Turn not thy servant away in anger. . . . I believe that I shall see the goodness of the Lord in the land of the living! Wait for the Lord; be strong, and let your heart take courage; yea, wait for the Lord!" (vv. 8-9, 13-14).

The first reading and the responsorial psalm indicate to us that obedience and unlimited trust provide the perspective in which we are to read the Gospel of the transfiguration. In Luke's version, as compared with those of Matthew and Mark, the account has a more pronounced paschal orientation. Not only does Christ appear in his glory, but Moses and Elias are present as witnesses to his Passion; they seem to be helping Jesus to face the trial that awaits him in Jerusalem. Christ's death is seen as a kind of baptism (his "departure"); in another context, the image of "baptism" for his Passion is accompanied by the image of the "cup," and the latter image recurs in Christ's words during the agony in the garden.

In chapter 24 of Luke's Gospel we find a typology of the paschal mystery: entry of Christ into the world, departure from this world, and entry into glory. This pattern is connected with Moses, and Jesus accomplishes in its perfect form the work that the Hebrew leader had done long before, since Jesus crosses the waters of death in order to save his people and lead them into the eternal kingdom of his Father. Jesus is thus the Moses of the new Exodus. He is also, however, the new Elias who has "come to cast fire upon the earth" (Luke 12:49).

As in the other accounts of the transfiguration, so in Luke's narrative the Father's voice tells us, in the presence of the Spirit, who Jesus is: "This is my Son, my Chosen." We have already pointed out the fullness of meaning attached to these words.

The reason, then, why Jesus is gloriously transfigured is his trustful, unconditional obedience to the Father's will. That obedience will motivate him in his passage through death to life. With him he will take all his followers, leading them along the way of salvation that culminates in glory.

In the second reading (Phil. 3:17–4:1), St. Paul develops the thought that all who are baptized will share in the glory of the transfigured Christ. He urges the Philippians to follow his own example and not let their hearts become attached to earthly things. They are already citizens of heaven. How, then, could they glory in what is really a cause for shame or make anything earthly the goal of their life?

The Christian is constantly confronted with choices he cannot evade. He must choose, and he must keep on choosing, since, though already a citizen of heaven, he still lives in that "form of a servant" which Christ himself assumed and in which he was humbled even to the point of dying (Phil. 2:6-11). But the day of the Lord's return will be the day when his fidelity will be rewarded: He will be transformed and become like the glorious Christ.

This, then, is the lesson of the second Sunday of Lent as it seeks to bring about our conversion: We must change our ways, we must choose and follow the Apostle, that is, in the last analysis we must follow Christ on his paschal journey so that with him we may finally rise transformed and glorious.

Third and Fourth Sundays of Lent, Cycle C
for years 1980, 1983, 1986, 1989, 1992

14. BE CONVERTED AND RECONCILED IN ORDER TO RISE NEW WITH CHRIST

Be converted or perish

The last three Sundays of Lent focus on conversion and on the new life of the convert. It is of some interest to observe how the first emphasis in the Lenten renewal is on conversion. The Gospel of the third Sunday is significant in this regard, as the problem of conversion is raised against the background of two somewhat unusual events: Pilate had some Galileans slaughtered while they were offering sacrifice, and in Siloam a falling tower killed eighteen people. Jesus asserts that these people were not greater sinners than the other inhabitants of Galilee or Jerusalem. He insists that conversion is an urgent need for all without exception: "Unless you repent you will all likewise perish" (Luke 13:5). At the same time, however, the Lord is patient as he waits for men to be converted.

God's patience is the subject of the second part of the pericope, the parable of the barren fig tree, in which the vinedresser says to the impatient landowner: "Let it [the fig tree] alone, sir, this year also, till I dig about it and put on manure. And if it bears fruit next year, well and good; but if not, you can cut it down" (vv. 8-9).

Let us analyze this passage a little more closely. To begin with, Jesus nowhere tells us that those who were victims of Pilate and of the falling tower were being punished for their sins. In fact, he tells us elsewhere that accidents of this kind are not always due to the victims' moral faults. Thus, in the case of the man born blind, Jesus says that his blindness was not due either to his own or his parents' sins

(John 9:3). Similarly, in today's Gospel he insists that the victims were no more sinful than their fellows who lived on.

Christ does, however, draw a practical lesson from the two events: "Unless you repent you will all likewise perish" (Luke 13:5). He rejects a certain idea of punishment in time and chastisement on earth, and sees in the events rather a warning about the punishment that will indeed come at the end of time. All of us are sinners and deserve to be rejected by God; therefore we must repent in anticipation of the judgment.

The second part of the pericope is especially interesting and has profound scriptural resonances. Israel is the Lord's vineyard (Is. 5:1-4; Jer. 2:21; Ezek. 17:6; 19:10-11; Ps. 80:9-17). When the vineyard fails and becomes barren, the avenging hand of God is felt (Is. 5:5-6; Jer. 5:10; 6:9; 12:10; Ezek. 15:6; 17:10; 19:12-14).

Nonetheless, toward sin and sinner God is patient in a way that deeply moves us and stimulates us not to procrastinate but to begin our conversion today and to put all our energies into it. In the last analysis, this patient mercy of God seems to be the most important point made in this passage from Luke's Gospel.

The first reading confirms this impression. Both the theophany in the form of fire and the conversation between the Lord thus present and Moses emphasize the Lord's boundless mercy: "I have seen the affliction of may people who are in Egypt . . . I know their sufferings, and I have come down to deliver them out of the hand of the Egyptians" (Exod. 3:7). So great is his compassion for his suffering people that he reveals himself once and for all, as the God of Abraham, the God of Isaac, and the God of Jacob; it is as such that he wishes to be celebrated for ever more. *That* is the lesson of this reading from the Book of Exodus.

The responsorial psalm, Psalm 103, picks up this last theme and sings of the tender love of this God for men: "The Lord is merciful and gracious, slow to anger and abounding in steadfast love" (Ps. 103:8).

The passage from St. Paul's First Letter to the Corinthians (10:1-6, 10-12) continues with the thought of what God did at the Exodus. Paul speaks of the journey through the desert and of the varied fates of those who journeyed. All indeed had crossed the Red Sea and had been united to Moses as though by a baptism in cloud and sea; all ate of the same spiritual food. Yet many of them died on the way; they perished in the desert because they were not pleasing to God.

This is a grim warning to each of us that we must not slip into the kind of sacramentalist mentality that excuses us from living in a spirit of fidelity and of respect for God's will. The really important thing to remember is that baptism in itself and alone is not enough — as such baptism does not prevent spiritual death; the baptized person must persevere in love and in obedience to God's holy will.

The return to the Father (Gospel, fourth Sunday)

We all know the story of the prodigal son that is told in today's Gospel from Luke (15:1-3, 11-32). We shall simply note two important points in the account. One is the movement of conversion that the prodigal son voices: "I will arise and go to my father, and I will say to him, 'Father, I have sinned against heaven and before you'" (v. 18). The other is the father's words to the older son: "This your brother was dead, and is alive" (v. 32).

At the end of the parable we are pervaded by the spirit of unrestrained paschal joy that finds expression in a banquet: "It was fitting to make merry and be glad, for this your brother was dead, and is alive; he was lost, and is found" (v. 32).

In this account the older brother evidently believes his father to be unjust, and he resents this. He has been faithful and observant; he has never neglected the smallest duty; he has been constantly at his father's side and has been scrupulous in helping him in his work. By thus giving us a picture of the elder brother as well as of the younger, the parable brings out the full character of God's mercy. He relies lovingly on the person who is faithful to him, but he cannot therefore be insensible of the person who strays, repents, and returns. Rather, his inner feelings burst forth and show us the infinite love God has for anyone who takes even a single step toward him. Not only does the Lord wait hopefully for this step, he even tries to get men to take it. Such is the full depth of God's tender love for the sinner.

The banquet in the Father's house

The first reading for this fourth Sunday shows the approach we are to take to the Gospel, for it is a reading about a banquet and a table to which sinners are invited (Jos. 5:9a, 10-12). What chiefly concerns the author of the passage is not so much the ritual followed in celebrating the Passover but the fact of entry into the promised land and of partaking of its food. (How can we fail, as we read, to think of the feast prepared for the prodigal son, a feast at which he will eat the food proper to his father's house?) The banquet Josue describes takes place at the end of the very difficult years in the desert and marks the beginning of a new way of life. The manna ceases to fall, for, while a nourishment, it was also a test, inasmuch as many died because they murmured as they ate, and refused to accept their circumstances as willed by God. Moreover, the manna pointed forward to the true food that Jesus alone will someday give.

It is, after all, only in Christ that we are truly reconciled to God. This is the theme of the second reading (2 Cor. 5:17-21). The reconciliation of all men in Christ is, St. Paul tells us, the basic purpose of the apostolic ministry. For as a result of Christ's death and resurrection, we are a new creation; the old order has passed away and a new order has already been born. God has reconciled us to himself through Christ. How poignantly relevant the urging of the Apostle is, today as in the past: "We beseech you on behalf of Christ, be reconciled to God!" (2 Cor. 5:20).

Do we perhaps answer him despairingly: "We would like

to be reconciled, but we feel incapable of it. We are so full of evil tendencies, so full of desires for this world and its pleasures that we cannot overcome them"? But Paul in turn replies: "For our sake he made him to be sin who knew no sin, so that in him we might become the righteousness of God" (2 Cor. 5:21). It is by the power of Christ who made our human nature his own that we can be reconciled. In fact, he has already reconciled us through his sacrifice; now we have the power to share in the holiness of God himself.

These are real possibilities for us, and our attitude must be one of desire to return to the Father and share in the banquet set for sinners, and, to this end, to be reconciled in Christ Jesus. Psalm 34, the responsorial psalm, becomes, in this context, a Eucharistic song, expressing the gratitude of all who experience God and know that he hears them as soon as they turn to him in their distress. In responding to the account of the Passover in the reading from the Book of Josue, the psalm also becomes the song of those who have been reconciled through Christ and have returned to their Father's house and who now, in the Eucharist (which is a sign of the definitive banquet at the end of time), share in a joyous feast to celebrate their homecoming.

Fifth Sunday of Lent, Cycle C

for years 1980, 1983, 1986, 1989, 1992

15. LIVE AGAIN AND REGAIN YOUR TRUE DIGNITY IN A NEW LIFE

Today's Gospel is a familiar one (John 8:1-11). At times it has been misinterpreted to mean that Christ is indulgent toward sins of the flesh. And yet the last words of the passage are clear enough: "Neither do I condemn you; go, and do not sin again" (v. 11). One of the suggested verses before the Gospel brings out the same point: "I do not wish the sinner to die, says the Lord, but to turn to me and live" (Ezek. 33:11). It would be a distortion, therefore, either to use the passage as a basis for moralizing or, on the other hand, to draw false inferences in favor of the weaknesses of the flesh.

The real meaning of the passage lies in quite another direction, for the point being made is that the Lord's mercy is inexhaustible and that he does not condemn men but wants them to live, though they must repent if they are to do so. As soon as man repents, God renews him and restores him to his true dignity. We can see this happening in the case of the adulterous woman. Once she has repented, she regains her dignity as a woman whom no one is now willing to condemn and who is determined henceforth to lead a new life.

The first reading (Is. 43:16-21) focuses on the same theme: "Remember not the former things, nor consider the things of old. Behold, I am doing a new thing; now it springs forth, do you not perceive it? . . . the people whom I formed for myself that they might declare my praise" (Is. 43:18-21). The Christian who has sinned but then repented has no past any longer. Once converted, he is a new man in a new world and is able to engage in the activity proper to the redeemed: the praise of God.

Our conversion and return to our dignity as sons of God is the greatest of God's "wonderful deeds." Thereby he leads us out of captivity, as he did his people of old. "The Lord has done great things for us," says Psalm 126 (v. 3), the responsorial psalm.

The hope of every Christian originates in the new life that is given him with the risen Christ. St. Paul, who experienced this new life, believed that the most important element in it is the knowledge of Christ (Phil. 3:8-14). There is only one goal worthy of the Christian's striving, he says, and that goal is to find Christ, in whom God acknowl-

edges us as upright. Our aim, then, must be to know Christ
through faith and to experience the power of his resurrection by sharing in his sufferings and by reproducing his
death in ourselves, in the hope of rising with him from the
dead. We must forget what lies behind and push forward so
as to obtain the prize to which God calls us on high in
Christ Jesus.

As soon as we seek Christ in faith, we who are sinners
regain our original dignity. All things become new for us,
and we come to know a God who, in his Son, summons us
to resurrection.

STRUCTURE OF THE FERIAS OF LENT

TABLE OF READINGS IN THE EUCHARISTIC LITURGY

Week of Ash Wednesday

A spiritual fast; interior conversion and sharing

Ash Wednesday	[1]	Interior conversion: Joel 2:12-18
	[2]	Now is the acceptable time: 2 Cor. 5:20–6:2
	[3]	Prayer and good works, in secret: Matthew 6:1-6, 16-18
Thursday	[4]	Choose the way of God: Deut. 30:15-20
	[5]	Lose your life to save it: Luke 9:22-25
Friday	[6]	Fasting means sharing: Is. 58:1-9a
	[7]	Fast when the Spouse is absent: Matthew 9:14-15
Saturday	[8]	Give your bread and live in the light: Is. 58:9-14
	[9]	The call of sinners to conversion: Luke 5:27-32

First Week of Lent
Love of neighbor and conversion

Monday	[10]	Justice to your neighbor: Lev. 19:1-2, 11-18

	[11]	What you do to one of my brothers . . . : Matthew 25:31-46
Tuesday	[12]	The word of God accomplishes the conversion he wills: Is. 55:10-11
	[13]	The Our Father: God's will be done; forgive us as we forgive others: Matthew 6:7-15
Wednesday	[14]	The sign of Jonah and the conversion of the Ninevites: Jonah 3:1-10
	[15]	The sign of the Son of Man: Luke 11:29-32
Thursday	[16]	The Lord is our sole help: Esther 14:1, 3-5, 12-15a
	[17]	Ask and you shall receive: Matthew 7:7-12
Friday	[18]	The Lord wants the sinner's conversion: Ezek. 18:21-28
	[19]	Conversion supposes reconciliation with our brother: Matthew 5:20-26
Saturday	[20]	Be a holy people for the Lord: Deut. 26:16-19
	[21]	Be perfect like your heavenly Father, and forgive: Matthew 5:43-48

Second Week
Forgiveness of sins (Monday, Tuesday, Saturday); Inwardness and true values (Thursday); Prediction of the Passion (Wednesday, Friday)

Monday	[22]	We have sinned: Dan. 9:4b-10
	[23]	Forgive, and you will be forgiven: Luke 6:36-38
Tuesday	[24]	Cease to do evil; become pure: Is. 1:10, 16-20
	[25]	Practice what you preach: Matthew 23:1-12
Wednesday	[26]	Strike down the prophet: Jer. 18:18-20
	[27]	Plotting Jesus' death: Matthew 20:17-28
Thursday	[28]	Trust in the Lord: Jer. 17:5-10
	[29]	Happiness now or in heaven? Luke 16:19-31
Friday	[30]	Joseph the dreamer: kill him! Gen. 37:3-4, 12-13a, 17b-28

[31] He is the heir: kill him! Matthew 21:33-43, 45-46

Saturday [32] Cast all our sins into the sea: Micah 7:14-15, 18-20

[33] Your brother was dead and has come back to life: Luke 15:1-3, 11-32

Third Week
Listen to the one Lord (Wednesday, Thursday, Friday); He saves all men (Monday); Forgive others (Tuesday); Interior worship (Saturday)

Monday [34] Naaman the Syrian is healed: 2 Kings 5:1-15a

[35] Jesus has been sent to all mankind: Luke 4:24-30

Tuesday [36] Receive us with humble and contrite hearts: Dan. 3:2, 11-20

[37] Forgive if you would be forgiven: Matthew 18:21-35

Wednesday [38] Keep the commandments: Deut. 4:1, 5-9

[39] The kingdom belongs to those who keep the commandments: Matthew 5:17-19

Thursday [40] They did not listen: Jer. 7:23-28

[41] With me or against me: Luke 11:14-23

Friday [42] God is the sole source of happiness: Osee 14:1-9

[43] The Lord is the only Lord; love him!: Mark 12:28b-34

Saturday [44] Love and not sacrifice: Osee 5:15c–6:6

[45] Interior worship: Luke 18:9-14

Fourth Week
Life through a new covenant (Monday, Tuesday, Wednesday); Unbelief and attempts to kill Christ (Thursday, Friday, Saturday)

Monday [46] A new earth and long life: Is. 65:17-21

[47] Go, your son lives: John 4:41-54

Tuesday [48] Saved by the water from the temple: Ezek. 47:1-9, 12

	[49]	The paralytic at the pool of Bethesda: John 5:1-3, 5-16
Wednesday	[50]	The Lord's love for his people: Is. 49:8-15
	[51]	The Son gives life to those he chooses: John 5:17-30
Thursday	[52]	Moses intercedes and allays the Lord's wrath: Exod. 32:7-14
	[53]	Moses will accuse the Jews because they did not listen to God's word: John 5:31-47
Friday	[54]	Condemn the just man to a shameful death: Wis. 2:1a, 12-22
	[55]	They sought to arrest Jesus: John 7:1-2, 10, 25-30
Saturday	[56]	Like a lamb led to slaughter: Jer. 11:18-20
	[57]	Arrest Jesus and condemn him: John 7:40-53

Fifth Week
The power of the Lord who by his death saves men and gathers them into unity

	[58]	Susanna falsely accused but rescued: Dan. 13:1-9, 15-17, 19-30, 33-62
Monday		
	[59]	The adulterous woman forgiven: John 8:1-11; or: Christ, the Light of the world: John 8:12-20
Tuesday	[60]	The serpent raised up and healing men: Num. 21:4-9
	[61]	The Son of Man lifted up on the Cross: John 8:21-30
Wednesday	[62]	The three young men saved from the fire: Dan. 3:14-20, 24-25, 28
	[63]	The truth will set you free: John 8:31-42
Thursday	[64]	Abraham receives the covenant and becomes the father of many peoples: Gen. 17:3-9
	[65]	Before Abraham was, I am; he who keeps my words will never die: John 8:51-59
Friday	[66]	Jeremias is persecuted but the Lord is with him: Jer. 20:10-13

[67] Jesus escapes from the hands of the Jews:
John 10:31-42

Saturday [68] I will make one nation of them: Ezek.
37:21-28

[69] Jesus must die in order to gather the
scattered children of God: John 11:45-57

16. THE MAIN THEMES OF THE LENTEN FERIAL CELEBRATIONS

It is not feasible for us to comment on each feria of Lent.
Nor would a commentary be very useful, since the choice of
readings and their meaning are often clear enough and
need no further explanation. More than that, a detailed
commentary might well make us lose sight of the essential
thing, which is the series of Sundays that provide the basic
framework of Lent. We shall therefore try rather to rein-
force what we have been saying about the Sundays by concentrating here on the main themes of the Lenten ferial
liturgies. In order not to overload our text with quotations,
we have assigned each reading in the foregoing list a
number in square brackets; in the next few pages we shall
use these numbers in referring to the readings.

Three major themes are developed in the ferial liturgies:
conversion and interior worship; forgiveness for ourselves
as conditioned by our forgiveness of others; renewal and
the gift of life through the Passion of Christ.

Conversion and interior worship

The readings on Ash Wednesday tell us the authentic
spirit that must characterize Lent: *Rend your hearts and not
your garments* [1]. We must struggle against the spirit of
evil (opening prayer for Ash Wednesday) and — to look at
the positive side — have a pure heart that has been renewed by the Lord (Psalm 51, responsorial psalm for Ash

Wednesday). The new optional formula for the imposition of ashes is meaningful in this context: "Turn away from sin and be faithful to the gospel" (Mark 1:15), as are the antiphons to be sung while the ashes are being imposed: "Come back to the Lord with all your heart . . ." (first antiphon), "Lord, take away our wickedness" (third antiphon), and "Let the priests and ministers of the Lord . . . say: Spare us, Lord; spare your people! . . ." (second antiphon). We must indeed be cleansed of our sins if we are to celebrate more effectively the Passion of Christ (prayer over the gifts, Ash Wednesday). But when we pray, it should be in secret, just as we should do our good works in secret [3].

The Lord desires the sinner's conversion [18]; he wants us to become a holy people [20] and to be perfect as he is perfect [21]. We must therefore cease doing evil and cleanse ourselves [24]; we must once again learn a proper scale of values [28]. All this has to be more than a mere abstraction; we must practice what we preach [25, 38–39]. Such a conversion supposes that we have listened to the word that effects whatever God wills [12]. If the Jews are to be accused by Moses at the judgment, it is because they have not listened to the word [53, 40].

The kind of conversion Christ preaches requires of us a deep inwardness: we must choose to follow God's way [4], be willing to lose our life in order to save it [5], be always attentive to God's will [13], and take advantage of the acceptable time [2]; in short, we must be either with Christ or against him [41]. The Lord is our only source of help [16] and of happiness [42]; he alone must be loved [43], and to him we must pray. What wins his good will toward us, however, is not outward rites but charity [44] and interior worship [45].

Such is the vision given us in the ferial liturgies of the conversion to which we are called [9].

Forgiveness for us conditioned by our forgiveness of others

Conversion on our part elicits forgiveness of our sins by God. But his forgiveness is also conditioned by the forgiveness we ourselves give to others.

It is worth our while to go through the list of readings and see what great emphasis is placed on our forgiveness of neighbor. Forgiveness, moreover, includes in this context our love of neighbor and our sharing with him.

From the very beginning of Lent, we are shown that fasting is a form of sharing [6]. Give your bread and live in the light — that is Isaiah's program for us [8]. The first week of Lent focuses almost exclusively on the fact that conversion necessarily involves our relations with our neighbor.

Love of neighbor consists first of all in being just toward him [10]. Justice is a first stage of love; this is so evident that it hardly seems to warrant mention. But experience of the world quickly shows us that justice to the neighbor is a far from easy thing and that men die and kill in the process of restoring or gaining justice. In fact, the whole drama of mankind is concentrated in the problem of justice to the neighbor.

What does "being just" mean? It is impossible for an un-enlightened person to be just, and a person cannot be enlightened until he has been forgiven by God. God's pardon, however, is obtained only by pardoning our fellow-man: "Forgive us our debts, as we also have forgiven our debtors" [13]. Every conversion supposes a reconciliation with our brothers [19], and we must forgive if we are to be forgiven [23, 37]. Conversion supposes that we see the Lord himself in our neighbor, so much so that what we do to our neighbor we do to God himself [11]. In this way we determine the measure of the pardon we ourselves will receive from God; the forgiveness of our own sins is conditioned by the forgiveness we bestow upon others, and our conversion is necessarily bound up with our generosity to others.

Such are the conditions we must fulfill if we are to be converted and have God forgive our sins. The conditions are simple enough but very difficult to put into practice.

Renewal and the gift of life through the Passion of Christ

Interior conversion and loving awareness of others are attitudes that lead to renewal and new life. Lent is the acceptable time for developing these attitudes [2]. In fact, we must say that for us Christians Lent is a sign we must obey if we are to be saved from destruction and that no other sign will be given to us [14, 15]. Lent is the time when we turn our attention more fully to the mystery of Christ, who gave himself that we might have life.

From the second week on, especially on Wednesdays and Fridays, the readings remind us of the opposition, to the point of death, that the Lord endured for our liberation. His words anger the Jews, and as they once persecuted Jeremias [26], so now they plot to kill Jesus [27]. They do not accept the Son whom the Father has sent: "Here comes this dreamer! Come now, let us kill him" [30]; "This one is the heir; come, let us kill him" [31]. The just man is threatened with a shameful death, and Jesus' enemies are constantly on the watch to get rid of him [54, 55]. When arrested and sentenced [57], he will be like a lamb led to slaughter [56]. And yet it is of his own free will that Jesus will hand himself over to the Jews when his "hour" has come. He is persecuted, but the Lord is with him [66], and he eludes the hands of the Jews [67] until such time as he decides to surrender to them.

During this period the whole history of salvation reaches its climax and center. Christ shows that he has been sent for the sake of all mankind [34, 35]. He gives signs that accredit him and through his miracles proclaims a new life [46]. He cures men of paralysis and thus prefigures the renewal effected by baptism [48, 49]. He brings the truth that frees men [63], and for the sake of that truth and for the liberation of the world every Christian must, like Christ, suffer even martyrdom [62]. The powers of evil seek to destroy the just man [58], but Jesus raises up the fallen and the scorned [59]. He gives life [47], and those who keep his word will never die [65]. Those who look upon him when he is lifted up on the Cross find everlasting life [60, 61], but the Son gives this life to whomever he wishes [51].

The entire work of salvation that is described in these readings leads to the restoration of the world that God had created in unity. The Lord wills to make his people a single nation [68], and Jesus responds to this divine will by dying so that the scattered children of God may be gathered and united [69].

This short synthesis may give the reader a first idea of the riches contained in the ferial lectionary. Our summary is elementary and incomplete, but it may at least serve to situate the various readings in a broader context and enable the reader to link them to each other, both within each celebration and from celebration to celebration. Use of the list we have given will help the reader find where he is, and give him a sense of direction so that he may fruitfully read and listen to the word of God.

The journey of the people of Israel

Meanwhile, in the ferial Office of Lent, the readings take us through the great moments of the history of Israel down to the great new Passover of Christ.

We shall not offer a commentary on these texts of the ferial Office. We shall, however, supply a list of the readings, along with titles that will enable the reader to follow the historical and spiritual journey of Israel. We make that journey our own during Lent; along with Israel, we go up to Jerusalem.

Those who do not possess the *Liturgy of the Hours* can use the table for selecting readings for communal celebrations or for private reading during Lent.

It will be clear from the list that in the Liturgy of the Hours the last week of Lent is entirely focused on Christ and his priestly action as being the final act in the history of salvation.

TABLE OF READINGS FOR FERIAS IN THE LITURGY OF THE HOURS

Week of Ash Wednesday

Ash Wednesday	The fast that pleases God: Is. 58:1-2
Thursday	Israel oppressed: Exod. 1:1-22
Friday	Birth and flight of Moses: Exod. 2:1-22; 18:4
Saturday	Call of Moses and revelation of the Lord's name: Exod. 3:1-20

First Week

Monday	Call of Moses: Exod. 6:2-13
Tuesday	First plague sent on Egypt: Exod. 6:29–7:25
Wednesday	Plague of darkness and warning of the death of the first-born: Exod. 10:21–11:10
Thursday	Passover and unleavened bread: Exod. 12:1-20
Friday	Death of the first-born: Exod. 12:21-36
Saturday	Departure of the Hebrews: Exod. 12:37-49; 13:11-16

Second Week

Monday	Crossing of the Red Sea: Exod. 14:10-31
Tuesday	The manna: Exod. 16:1-18, 35
Wednesday	The water from the rock at Horeb: Exod. 17:1-16
Thursday	Appointment of the judges: Exod. 18:13-27
Friday	Promise of the covenant; the Lord appears on Sinai: Exod. 19:1-19; 20:18-21

Saturday	The law is given on Sinai: Exod. 20:1-17

Third Week

Monday	The covenant is ratified on Sinai: Exod. 24:1-18
Tuesday	The golden calf: Exod. 32:1-20
Wednesday	Revelation of the Lord to Moses: Exod. 33:7-11, 18-23; 34:5-9, 29-35
Thursday	The Book of the Covenant: Exod. 34:10-28
Friday	The sanctuary and the ark: Exod. 35:30–36:1; 37:1-9
Saturday	The tabernacle and the cloud: Exod. 40:16-38

Fourth Week

Monday	The day of atonement: Lev. 16:2-28
Tuesday	Commandments concerning the neighbor: Lev. 19:1-18, 31-37
Wednesday	The spirit poured out on Joshua and the elders: Num. 11:4-6, 10-30
Thursday	Scouts sent into Canaan: Num. 12:16–13:3, 17-33
Friday	Murmuring of the people and intervention of Moses: Num. 14:1-25
Saturday	The waters of Meribah; the bronze serpent: Num. 20:1-13; 21:4-9

Fifth Week

Monday	Jesus, Author of salvation, like his brothers in every way: Heb. 2:5-18
Tuesday	Jesus, Apostle of our faith: Heb. 3:1-19
Wednesday	God's fidelity is our hope: Heb. 6:9-20
Thursday	Melchisedech, type of the perfect priest: Heb. 7:1-10
Friday	The eternal priesthood of Christ: Heb. 7:11-28
Saturday	The priesthood of Christ in the new covenant: Heb. 8:1-13

Palm Sunday, Monday, Tuesday, and
Wednesday of Holy Week

17. TOWARD MOUNT OLIVET

The celebration of these days in the past

Devotion to the paschal mystery is not optional, any more than its celebration is something exceptional in our liturgy. The paschal mystery rather exemplifies and prescribes the law that must govern our lives: the law of death and of life coming through and by means of death. So, too, the paschal mystery is really the very heart of the liturgy, and the entire liturgical year grows out of it.

The early generations of Christians were very conscious of the primordial place of the paschal mystery. They celebrated only the night of the "Pasch," which they understood as a "passage" through death to authentic life.

Even today the holy days are celebrated with great simplicity in some of the rites. In the Coptic Rite, for example, the celebration consists entirely of readings from the Old and New Testaments that enlighten us on the meaning of the paschal mystery, praise the Lord for it, render it present, and prepare the faithful for his return. This liturgy, with its monastic simplicity and essentially contemplative character, is especially notable during the Paschal Vigil, where, once again, it consists entirely of readings.

At Rome the focus of celebration was the Paschal Vigil that ended with the Eucharistic sacrifice and soon came to include the administration of baptism as well. This primitive nucleus was quickly expanded. In fifth-century Africa, when St. Augustine speaks of the paschal celebration, he calls it "the triduum of Christ crucified, buried, and risen," and is referring to Good Friday, Holy Saturday, and Easter

THE LAST DAYS OF LENT

READINGS IN THE EUCHARISTIC LITURGY

Palm Sunday

Procession   Blessed be he who comes in the name of the Lord! A: Matthew 21:1-11; B: Mark 11:1-10 *or* John 12:12-16; C: Luke 19:28-40

Mass   Is. 50:4-7, I gave my back to those who beat me; I am not disgraced

Phil. 2:6-11, Christ humbled himself, therefore God exalted him

Passion of our Lord Jesus Christ: A: Matthew 26:14–27:66; B: Mark 14:1–15:47; C: Luke 22:14–23:56

Monday   Is. 42:1-7, Here is my servant whom I uphold

John 12:1-11, Let her keep this perfume for the day of my burial

Tuesday   Is. 49:1-6, I will make my salvation reach to the ends of the earth

John 13:21-33, 33-38, One of you will betray me

Wednesday   Is. 50:4-9a, I did not cover my face against insults and spittle

Matthew 26:14-25, Woe to that man by whom the Son of Man is betrayed

READINGS IN THE LITURGY OF THE HOURS

Palm Sunday   We are sanctified through Christ's offering: Heb. 10:1-18

Monday   Perseverance in faith; waiting for God's judgment: Heb. 10:19-39

Tuesday   Let us go forth to the struggle with Christ as our Leader: Heb. 12:1-13

Wednesday   Let us ascend the mountain of the living God: Heb. 12:14-29

Thursday   Christ, our High Priest: Heb. 4:14–5:10

185

Sunday. The climax of the three days was the single Eucharistic celebration during the night between Saturday and Sunday.

At Jerusalem, however, where it was easier than elsewhere to follow the historical unfolding of the paschal mystery by visiting the holy places, the liturgy was already quite extensively developed. The travel diary of Egeria, a fourth-century widow, provides us with a detailed description of the Jerusalem liturgy, beginning with Palm Sunday.[160] The liturgy took the form of a deliberately accurate reconstruction of the final actions of Jesus' life; yet the liturgy celebrated the whole of the paschal mystery and did not break it up, even if each day was given over to one particular aspect of it.

In order to copy what was done at Jerusalem and to bring to life the details afforded by the evangelists, the Western liturgy expanded. A detailed celebration took up the whole of what we now call Holy Week, although the main concentration was on the last days of the week and on Easter Sunday.

The danger of such a detailed and anecdotal reconstruction of the sacred actions that make up the paschal mystery was that the faithful might break up the mystery into unconnected parts and might separate the celebration of Jesus' death too much from the celebration of his resurrection. The danger of fragmentation, of turning the whole into disparate aspects not seen in the context of the paschal mystery, was not always successfully avoided. In the Middle Ages, Holy Week was referred to as the "Week of Sorrow," thus emphasizing the suffering of Jesus and the loving compassion of Christians for him, but insufficiently adverting to the aspect of triumph and victory.

The tendency to an anecdotal reading of the Gospel had important consequences, some of which are still with us. Toward the middle or end of the seventh century, a commemoration of the Last Supper was introduced at Rome, where Holy Thursday had hitherto been chiefly the day for the reconciliation of penitents. This caused a displacement:

The paschal triduum now meant Holy Thursday, Good Friday, and Holy Saturday. We shall return to this later. The point to be made here is that this new triduum could turn the minds of the faithful from the full meaning of the paschal mystery, inasmuch as what we now call "the three holy days" do not perfectly coincide with what the Church of St. Augustine's time called the Holy Triduum. For Augustine, the three days were Friday, Saturday, and Sunday; for us they are Thursday, Friday, and Saturday.

The intention of people at that time was evidently to lend the liturgy a dramatic quality, but the quality was somewhat factitious; it could also be, and has in fact often been, misunderstood. The liturgy, after all, is not simply a play. We do not take part in the liturgy in order to recall past events in an atmosphere of spiritual emotion. We take part in it in order to celebrate a mystery that the liturgy itself renders present. The liturgical celebration makes present the spiritual efficacy of a moment that in its material, anecdotal form is historically past. The historical event was complete in itself. For this reason it does not have to be repeated; what we want is that it should be present to each moment of history as a source of value.

We must keep these basic considerations in mind, for they are essential to the celebration of Holy Week, and indeed to every liturgical celebration.

The messianic entry into Jerusalem

It was at Jerusalem, around the year 400, that an attempt was made to re-enact in all possible detail the Lord's entry into Jerusalem. As we noted above, from this Sunday on, Christians were very anxious to follow in the footsteps of Christ, incident by incident, through Holy Week.

Egeria the pilgrim describes the Palm Sunday procession as it was celebrated at Jerusalem toward the end of the fourth century:

> As the eleventh hour [five o'clock in the afternoon] draws near, that particular passage from Scripture is

read in which the children bearing palms and
branches came forth to meet the Lord, saying: *Blessed
is He who comes in the name of the Lord.* The bishop
and all the people rise immediately, and then
everyone walks down from the top of the Mount of
Olives, with the people preceding the bishop and responding continually with *Blessed is He who comes
in the name of the Lord* to the hymns and antiphons.
All the children who are present here, including those
who are not able to walk because they are too young
and therefore are carried on their parents' shoulders,
all of them bear branches, some carrying palms,
others, olive branches. And the bishop is led in the
same manner as the Lord once was led. From the top
of the mountain as far as the city, and from there
through the entire city as far as the Anastasis,
everyone accompanies the bishop the whole way on
foot, and this includes distinguished ladies and men
of consequence, reciting the responses all the while;
and they move very slowly so that the people will not
tire. By the time they arrive at the Anastasis, it is already evening. Once they have arrived there, even
though it is evening, vespers is celebrated; then a
prayer is said at the Cross and the people are dismissed.[161]

Egeria notes the presence of little children in the procession, whereas the evangelists say nothing about them. St.
Matthew does say that children, observing the wonders
Jesus had just accomplished, were shouting in the Temple
precincts, "Hosanna to the Son of David!" (21:15). Jesus
comments on their action by citing Psalm 8:2: "Out of the
mouth of babes and sucklings thou hast brought perfect
praise" (Matthew 21:16). At Jerusalem later on, the Palm
Sunday procession was turned into a kind of children's
feast. This may in turn have given rise to the antiphon "The
children of Jerusalem . . ." and the hymn "All Glory, Laud
and Honor," which are still used for the Palm Sunday

procession in the Roman liturgy; both of these speak of children praising Christ with hosannas.[162]

This kind of procession could not but be extremely successful and popular, so much so that in the East this Sunday concentrates entirely on the theme of Jesus' entry into Jerusalem, with both the Mass and the Office developing it fully. Naturally, dramatic touches were added to the celebration as time went on. Thus, while in Egypt the cross was carried in triumph on Palm Sunday, in Jerusalem the bishop representing Christ rode on an ass in the procession.[163]

As happened so often in the history of the liturgy, these customs passed from the East to Spain and Gaul. We should note that in Spain on this Sunday before Easter the *Ephpheta*, or rite of expulsion of the devil, took place in the morning, while the Mass contained the presentation of the Creed.[164] The *Liber ordinum* (beginning of the seventh century) gives us the readings for this Mass; only the Gospel deals with the entry of Jesus into Jerusalem. The *Liber ordinum* speaks of the procession with the palms, preceded by the blessing of the palms at the altar and the blessing of the people; there is, however, no description of the procession itself.[165]

In Gaul, Palm Sunday began to be celebrated toward the end of the seventh century. The liturgical books of the period describe a blessing of palms at the altar on Palm Sunday, but they say nothing about a procession. By the ninth century, however, the procession is clearly attested; it was for this that Theodulf of Orléans composed the hymn "All Glory, Laud, and Honor."

At Rome, meanwhile, the Passion narrative was read on Palm Sunday. The nineteen sermons of Pope St. Leo the Great on the Lord's Passion make it clear that in the Rome of his day attention was focused on the Passion. Seven of these homilies were given on the Sunday itself; the theme was then taken up again on Wednesday. At the end of his third sermon, St. Leo makes it clear that the reading of the Passion will begin anew on Wednesday.[166]

For the Romans, then, this Sunday before Easter is the "Sunday of the Lord's Passion." At the end of the seventh century, however, and during the eighth, we find the title "Palm Sunday" given to this day.[167] But it is only when the Romano-Germanic Pontifical (tenth century) reaches Rome in the eleventh century that the procession of the palms becomes a Roman custom.[168] The ceremony as described in this Pontifical is quite complex, being practically the same as what we used to have in the Roman Missal, before the reform of 1955, for the blessing and procession of palms. In other words, it was a kind of Fore-Mass with a reading of the Epistle and Gospel and several prayers for the blessing of the palms.[169] The procession proper came into use at Rome beginning in the twelfth century.

The Romano-Germanic Pontifical of the twelfth century describes the practice in Gaul or at Mainz at that time. While the churches of Rome were generally receptive to an elaborate blessing of palms and an elaborate procession, the papal church of the Lateran was not. The twelfth-century Pontifical shows that the papal liturgy of the palms was very modest. The Pope distributed the palms that were blessed in a chapel of his palace; then the papal retinue went to the Lateran Basilica for the celebration of Mass. Those in the procession carried palms in their hand and sang antiphons; the hymn "All Glory, Laud, and Honor" was sung before the closed door of the Lateran, and when it was opened, the procession entered singing the response "When the people heard that Jesus was entering Jerusalem. . . ."[170]

We can see, then, that Rome, or at least the papal liturgy, was reserved with regard to the procession of the palms. The reason is that at Rome there was a greater preoccupation with the Passion of Christ.[171]

The celebration today

The oldest Roman tradition makes the Sunday before Easter a day for commemorating the Passion of the Lord. In the second half of the seventh century, the name "Passion

Sunday" was transferred to the fifth Sunday of Lent, previously known as "Lazarus Sunday," and the sixth Sunday came to be called "Palm Sunday" in the seventh and eighth centuries. The recent reform has changed the first five Sundays of Lent once again into a continuous preparation for the paschal mystery of Christ's death and resurrection. The fifth Sunday is no longer "Passion Sunday" and has become again a Sunday that points ahead to the resurrection (Lazarus). Palm Sunday has become once again the Sunday of the Passion.

The tendency to extend a seasonal liturgy (that of the Passion, for example) back into the time preceding that season has affected the whole of Lent. Due to various influences, this penitential season became longer and longer, finally reaching back as far as Septuagesima Sunday, with Lent proper beginning on Ash Wednesday. The liturgical form has now imposed due limits on Lent. The reformers could have gone all the way and had Lent begin, as of old, on the first Sunday of Lent. The difficulty, however, was that everyone, even non-believers, had gotten used to Ash Wednesday as a day when all Christians acknowledged themselves to be sinners; it was no longer a day reserved for those obligated to public penance and public reconciliation.

The celebration of the liturgy of the palms has now been restored to a greater simplicity and can, moreover, be carried out in various ways, depending on available resources and the character of the place where the liturgy is being celebrated. The emphasis is on the messianic entry of the Lord into Jerusalem, and the blessing of the palms is quite secondary.

The custom of veiling the cross has now been suppressed (the origins of the custom were in any case obscure and debated). Since the thought of the Cross dominates the entire week, there is no longer any reason for veiling the cross.

Formerly the Passion of Christ was read on Palm Sunday and on Tuesday and Wednesday of Holy Week. Now it is read only on Palm Sunday (a different synoptic account in each year of the three-year cycle), while the account in St. John's Gospel is read every year on Good Friday.

We shall end our discussion of these first days of Holy Week with the penitential celebration on Holy Thursday (below, Chapter 19). The reconciliation of penitents, in fact, puts an end to Lent proper. The penitential fast ends on Thursday. The fast on Good Friday (the first day of the triduum of the dead, buried, and risen Christ) is actually a festive fast; it takes place within the paschal mystery, and the dominant mood is expectation of the Lord's glorious resurrection.

18. TOWARD THE GLORIOUS PASSION OF THE LORD

He who comes in the name of the Lord

As we have seen, the procession with palms was introduced in Rome at a relatively late date. Once it was introduced there, however, the folkloric spirit influenced it just as much as elsewhece. The amount of space that the Romano-Germanic Pontifical of the tenth century gives to the blessing and procession of the palms shows that the people of the day were enamored of these ceremonies, with their dramatic evocation of incidents in the Gospel.[172]

The people gather outside the city. There the priest blesses salt and water, as the *Hosanna* is intoned; the priest then reads a prayer. The Book of Exodus (15:27 and 16:1-10) is read, and the response "The princes of the peoples are gathered together . . ." is sung. The Gospel of the entry into Jerusalem is then proclaimed, either from Matthew 21:1-9 or Mark 11:1-10. The priest then blesses the branches, using any one of ten or so prayers, depending on whether the material is palms, boughs of trees, olive branches, etc. When olive branches are used, the blessing expands into a preface.

The palms are sprinkled and incensed, another prayer is said, the palms are distributed, and the procession begins. During the procession those present sing antiphons. When the procession reaches a place where a cross has been set up, the children approach it, spread their coats on the ground, prostrate themselves, and adore the cross, while the antiphon "The children of the Hebrews spread their cloaks . . ." is sung. Another group of children follows them and sings *Kyrie eleison*, while throwing palms down before the cross; they then prostrate themselves, while others sing, "The children of the Hebrews carried branches. . . ." At this point all sing the hymn to Christ the King, "All Glory, Laud and Honor," composed by Theodulf of Orléans. Psalm 147B (= Psalm 147:12-20), "Praise the Lord, O Jerusalem!", is then sung, and the faithful throw flowers and leaves. The bishop prostrates himself before the cross, then sings a prayer, and finally the procession moves on. When it reaches the gates of the city, the faithful sing *Kyrie eleison*, and the antiphon "As the Lord entered the holy city" is intoned. The procession is followed by Mass, during which the clergy and people hold the palms in their hand.

The whole ceremony was evidently conceived as an act of homage to Christ the King, one that we today might find a bit on the boisterous side. It might seem, too, that when this ceremony was introduced into the Roman liturgy, it would push into the background the theme of the glorious Passion of Christ. Yet that did not happen.

The reformed liturgy has not hesitated to highlight the procession in honor of Christ the King. The rite for blessing the palms has been much simplified, for the important thing is not the palms themselves but the procession in which the palms are carried. It is worth noting that the new liturgy has kept the custom of gathering for the procession outside the church, where this is feasible. As the faithful hold their palm branches, an antiphon strikes the keynote of the celebration that will follow: "Hosanna to the Son of David, the

King of Israel. Blessed is he who comes in the name of the Lord. Hosanna in the highest."

The priest then greets the people and gives a short introduction. After a prayer, the palm branches are sprinkled in silence. The Gospel of Jesus' entry into Jerusalem is then read. Then, to illustrate the Gospel, all present walk in procession to the church where Mass will be celebrated. During the procession an antiphon is sung: "The children of Jerusalem welcomed Christ the King. They carried olive branches . . . ," followed by Psalm 24. Thereupon another antiphon is sung: "The children of Jerusalem welcomed Christ the King. They spread their cloaks before him. . . ." followed by Psalm 47.

During the procession the following hymn in honor of Christ the King or another suitable hymn is sung:

> All glory, praise, and honor
> To you, Redeemer, King!
> To whom the lips of children
> Made glad hosannas ring. *Refrain*
>
> You are the King of Israel
> And David's royal Son,
> Who in the Lord's Name comest,
> The King and Blessed One.   *Refrain*
>
> The company of angels
> Are praising you on high;
> And mortal men and all things
> Created make reply.   *Refrain*
>
> The people of the Hebrews
> With palms before you went:
> Our praise and prayer and anthems
> Before you we present.   *Refrain*
>
> To you before your Passion
> They sang their hymns of praise:

To you, now high exalted,
Our melody we raise.   *Refrain*

As once you did accept their praise,
Accept the praise we bring,
You who rejoice in ev'ry good,
Our good and gracious King.   *Refrain*

In this procession we are to see much more than a mimetic reminder; we are to see the ascent of God's people, and our own ascent, with Jesus to the sacrifice. Moreover, although the procession recalls Christ's triumph at Jerusalem, it leads us here and now to the sacrifice of the Cross as rendered present in the sacrifice of the Mass that is soon to be celebrated. If we were to see in the procession only a crowd waving palms and singing joyous songs, we would miss its real significance in the Roman liturgy. That liturgy looks upon the procession not simply as a commemoration of Christ's entry into Jerusalem nor simply as a triumphal march, but as Christ's journey, together with his people, to Calvary and the great central act of redemption.

Palm Sunday, the first act of Holy Week, is perhaps the part of Holy Week that most sticks in the minds of simple people; sometimes there is even a certain amount of superstition mixed in with the celebration. Yet the rich content of the texts, and the frequent opportunities the pastor has of explaining them, can offset errors, and the faithful can be brought to a proper understanding of the paschal mystery that is now to be celebrated for us once again in a solemn manner.

The glorious Passion for the sake of the covenant

On Palm Sunday the account of the Passion is read, with the text taken from a different synoptic Gospel in each year of the three-year cycle.

Some exegetes stress that the Gospel of St. Matthew is to be read against the background of, and with reference to,

the story of Moses. They have found so many points of contact with the latter that they believe St. Matthew is deliberately presenting Jesus to us as the new Moses.[173] Now, it is
doubtless the case that the choice of St. Matthew's account
for Palm Sunday was not motivated by the parallel with
Moses and the desire to show Christ as the Man of the new
covenant or to bring out the close connection between
covenant and Passion. The liturgical reformers simply followed the traditional order of the four Gospels and had no
theological thesis in mind when they assigned Matthew
to Palm Sunday. We can nevertheless make use of the
Christ-Moses parallel.

The connection between Moses and Christ is already
present in the Gospel narrative of Christ's entry into
Jerusalem. The Midrash Rabbah (Great Midrash) on Qoheleth says: "As the first redeemer, so the last redeemer.
As it is said of the first redeemer: And Moses took his wife
and his sons and had them ride on an ass (Exod. 4:20), so
the last redeemer, for it is said: Lowly and riding on an ass
(Zech. 9:9)." [174]

It will be enough for our purpose here to cite the following passage that brings out the clear parallel drawn in Matthew's Gospel between Christ and Moses:

> Certain incidents in the Passion should be noted. We
> should mention first the few details given us concern-
> ing the betrayal by Judas. Matthew twice (26:14-16;
> 27:3-10) refers to Zechariah 11:11-13. The prophet
> had symbolically taken the place of Yahweh, the
> Shepherd of Israel (11:4) but when confronted with
> the bad will of the people, he broke off the covenant
> (11:10). The ruling class (the high priests) valued his
> efforts — and thus the pastoral action of Yahweh him-
> self — at thirty pieces of silver, which was the price of
> a slave (see Exod. 21:32).
>
> In Jesus this story finds its fulfillment, for he too,
> though he was the Shepherd of Israel, was valued at
> thirty pieces of silver. But Judas was stricken with

remorse and threw the coins into the sanctuary before going out and hanging himself (Matthew 27:5); the high priests then collected the blood-money (Matthew 27:6). The Passion of Christ, in which the blood so undervalued by the Jews was shed, put an end to the old covenant. . . .

We should also note the numerous references Psalm 22 in Matthew's account of the Passion (cf. 27:35, 39, 43, 46). The psalm ends with the promise that God's rule will extend to the entire universe, in consequence of the sufferings and preaching of the faithful Servant. The connection between the death of Jesus and the transition to a new covenant is brought out in many other ways too. Thus, Jesus is condemned to death and executed because he had predicted the coming of a new temple, which meant the end of the Sinai legislation concerning worship (Matthew 26:61; 27:40).[175]

The Church is well aware that she is the people of the new covenant. That is why she has us read from the Letter to the Philippians in the second reading for the Psalm Sunday Mass: "Have this mind among yourselves, which was in Christ Jesus, who, though he was in the form of God, did not count equality with God a thing to be grasped, but emptied himself, taking the form of a servant, being born in the likeness of men. And being found in human form he humbled himself and became obedient unto death, even death on a cross" (Phil. 2:5-8).

This vision of Christ's Passion, which will soon be rendered present anew in our midst, moves the Church deeply. For she knows that God has supremely exalted this Man who humbled himself in obedience to the point of dying on the Cross. God has given him the name that is above every name.

The acclamation before the Gospel repeats Philippians 2:8-9. This Christ is truly the Christ of the new covenant. In the acclamation, therefore, we greet this God who came and suffered in order to save us; who bowed in defeat, but in order to be triumphant; who died, but in order to give us eternal life. St. Leo the Great writes as follows in his eleventh sermon on the Passion: "What the false witnesses, bloodthirsty leaders, and wicked priests inflicted on the Lord Jesus Christ with the help of a cowardly procurator and an ignorant cohort is something every age must both detest and embrace. For the Cross of the Lord was not only cruel in the intention of the Jews, but admirable because of the power of the Crucified." [176]

The Church knows the price her Lord paid for the glory of the resurrection. In the first reading of the Palm Sunday Mass (Is. 50:4-7), she shows us the Christ who did not defend himself against the insults of men. The response to this reading is from Psalm 22 and shows us still another aspect of Christ's suffering as he cries out on the Cross: "My God, my God, why have you abandoned me?"

How fitting, then, that the Christian should sing, as he approaches the Communion table, the words: "Father, if this cup may not pass, but I must drink it, then your will be done" (Matthew 26:42). For to drink the blood of the new covenant is to accept the Lord's Passion in a fully real and concrete way so that we may also share his triumph with him.

The Passion according to St. Matthew implicitly compares the mystery of the new covenant and of Christ, its Leader, with the old covenant that Moses had concluded. St. Mark, for his part, tells the story of the Passion in a very concrete manner and in a spirit of tragic realism. The Christian feels overwhelmed by the suffering Christ, who remains silent throughout and dies alone and abandoned by the Father. At this moment every Christian, indeed every human being, becomes aware that in his own earthly life he must meet the same fate: like the Son of Man, he too must go up from Galilee to Jerusalem, ascend the cross, and go down into death. It is the penitential journey that fallen man must make, but Christ determined to make it for us all. He made the journey, but it led him to resurrection and to glory at the Father's side. He thus became our Way that leads to salvation and life. His suffering won the forgiveness of our sins, and he showed us the way we must travel in imitation of him in order to make that forgiveness our own.

St. Luke, in his account of the Passion, emphasizes the Cross as a cause of conversion. He has no hesitation about departing from the Marcan scheme. When, for example, he introduces Simon of Cyrene and the women whom Jesus meets along the way of the Cross and the other women whom we find on Calvary, he does so because he wants witnesses to the events, but much more because he wants the Christian to become more intimately associated with the Cross of Christ. Simon carries the Cross after Jesus, and every Christian should want to do the same. Luke mentions several groups of nameless devout women: those who weep for Jesus along the way to Calvary (Luke 23:27) and those who had followed Jesus during his ministry and now stand at a distance watching everything (Luke 23:49).

As for the power of the Cross, Luke notes that "all the multitudes who assembled to see the sight, when they saw what had taken place, returned home beating their breasts" (Luke 23:48). One of the two criminals crucified with Jesus repents and is saved: "Truly, I say to you, today you will be with me in Paradise" (Luke 23:43). When Jesus dies, the centurion is struck by the accompanying phenomena and says: "Certainly this man was innocent" (Luke 23:47).

We may sum up our observations on the various accounts of the Passion by saying that St. Matthew presents Christ as seen in the light of faith and in his relation to the Church; St. Mark emphasizes the revolution produced by the events involving Jesus and his disciples; and St. Luke insists on the bond that links the disciples as followers of Jesus and his Cross.

The first of the readings at Mass is from the third of the Servant Songs of Isaiah (50:4-7). the words are those of the Servant who listens to the word morning after morning, and does not rebel against it but opens his heart to it. Hearing the word means accepting events as they come. Therefore the Servant submits to being struck on his back and cheek, and to having his beard pulled. He does not protect his face against insult and spittle. How can we help seeing in this poem the very story of the Lord's Passion? But God comes to the aid of his obedient Servant and does not let him end in disgrace.

Psalm 22, chosen as the responsaory psalm for this Sunday, was on Christ's lips as he hung on the Cross: "My God, my God, why have you abandoned me?" The New Testament rightly saw in it the psalm that was supremely transformed by Christ's application of it to himself. The Christian community realized how closely the psalmist's prayer corresponded to what Jesus suffered, and the evangelists made use of the correspondence.

What does Christ's Passion mean for us? It must be admitted that in reflecting on it devout Christians have often had eyes exclusively for Christ's sufferings. It is true enough, of course, that the prophecies describe Christ as a man of sorrows. It is also undoubtedly very important not to forget that Christ endured suffering and opposition from the world and that he was a suffering witness and martyr. His purpose, after all, in suffering and dying was to establish the reign of God among liberated human beings and to bring into the kingdom a race all of whose wretchedness he had shared, except the wretchedness of sin.

If, however, we look only at the painful side, we shall not understand the Passion. The danger here is to have eyes only for details and incidents; it is a danger that the Good Friday liturgy has managed to overcome in the Roman Rite. Surely it is a striking fact that the evangelists, being witnesses also of the resurrection, cannot present the Passion to us in terms solely of suffering. They see and understand the Passion in the light of the glorious vision of the risen Christ whom they had seen ascend into glory. Their outlook is summed up for us in the words of the Acts of the Apostles: "God has made both Lord and Christ, this Jesus whom you crucified" (2:36).

The best means of avoding a one-sided emphasis on suffering in our approach to the Passion is given us in the second reading for Palm Sunday. In it St. Paul tells the Philippians of the self-humbling of Christ, who adopted the rank of a slave, became like other men, and carried obedience to the length of dying on a cross. But Paul immediately adds: "Therefore God has highly exalted him" (Phil. 2:9). In consequence, at his name all beings in heaven and earth bend their knee, and every tongue proclaims that Jesus is Lord, to the glory of God the Father.

The Palm Sunday liturgy thus gives a complete and rounded theological vision of the mystery of Christ. It tells that this mystery is not a mystery of death alone but a mystery of life that triumphs over death. This vision is important for a proper conception of the spiritual life.

The day of Jesus' glorious death is coming

The liturgical celebrations of Monday, Tuesday, and Wednesday continue to show Christ to us as the obedient, suffering Servant, but also as the Servant who dies only to be victorious in the end.

On Monday, Tuesday, and Wednesday, the first reading is one of the first three Servant songs (Is. 42:1-7; 49:1-6; 50:4-9a). All three show a close connection between the Servant's sufferings and experience of abandonment, and what happens to Christ. The Christian community understandably had a high regard for these poems.

Each of the poems, however, offers its own particular insight. On Monday we see Christ as the chosen Servant on whom the Lord makes his Spirit rest (Is. 42:1-7). The Servvant's characteristics are carefully described: He will not quench the smoldering wick; he will establish justice in the land, so that the coastlands will wait for his teaching. The Lord has made of him a covenant of the people and a light for the nations. Moreover, as a sign that the kingdom is now present, he will open the eyes of the blind, bring prisoners from their cells, and those who live in darkness from their dungeons. The responsorial psalm for this reading, Psalm

27, applies the theme of light to this Servant who need not fear even if the wicked come at him, because the Lord is his light and salvation and his life's refuge.

The second poem (Is. 49:1-6), which is read on Tuesday, hails the appointment of the Servant by God: "You are my servant, Israel, in whom I will be glorified" (Is. 49:3). The poem also continues a theme of the first song: "It is too light a thing that you should be my servant . . . ; I will give you as a light to the nations, that my salvation may reach to the end of the earth" (v. 6). The responsory psalm, Psalm 71, reasserts the confidence of the Servant, whose God is rock and fortress, a God who in his fidelity hears and saves.

The third poem (Is. 50:4-9a) is read on Wednesday. This is the supreme poem of the Passion, in the sense that it describes Christ's suffering in such detail. The responsory psalm, Psalm 69, speaks of the Christ who is insulted and whose face is covered with shame, but who endures it all in order to praise God. His food is bitter, vinegar is his drink, but the Lord hears his prayer.

The Gospel pericopes for these first three days of Holy Week are a preparation for the death of Jesus. The first tells of his embalmment in the well-known story from John 12:1-11. John tells us how during a meal in the home of Lazarus, the latter's sister Mary anoints the feet of Jesus with perfume. John also reports Judas's criticism; more than that, he emphasizes it and lays bare its motivation. Judas did not suddenly turn into a traitor on this day; there had been a long preparation for the final act, which was but the end result of a deliberately adopted attitude.

Judas's words provide Christ with an opportunity to foretell his own death. The fact that the meal is being taken in Lazarus's home permits John to speak of the attitude of the Jews toward Lazarus. The raising of Lazarus had stupefied the Jews. It was impossible to deny the power Christ had shown in raising this man from the dead, and impossible also not to ask some earthshaking questions about the event. Was not the raising of a dead man a sign that the coming kingdom and the coming Messiah were already present? The raising of Lazarus was a prediction that Jesus too would be raised up. The Jews therefore decided to put to death not only Jesus but Lazarus as well.

The Gospel for Tuesday (John 13:21-33, 36-38) foretells betrayal — in fact, a twofold betrayal: not only the treachery of Judas but the inexplicable weakness of Peter: "Truly, truly, I say to you, the cock will not crow till you have denied me three times" (v. 38). We should not overlook how this passage links the Supper, the treachery of Judas, and the glorification predicted by Christ (the glorification of both the Son of Man and the Father). Here is summed up the whole meaning of Calvary, but also the whole meaning of the Supper that makes Calvary present for the glorification of Father and Son. The passage shows clearly the perspective of the glorious Passion; the sufferings of Christ bring glory to the Father and to himself.

The Gospel for Wednesday is from St. Matthew (26:14-25). The theme is the same as in Tuesday's Gospel, but there is a greater emphasis on the treachery and the curse it brings upon the betrayer.

The prayers of these three days focus on the imitation of Christ in our lives. The Passion of Christ that we celebrate should be a source of strength for us (opening prayer, Monday); it should be a wellspring of forgiveness (opening prayer, Tuesday); and it will rescue us from Satan's power and lead us to share in the resurrection (opening prayer, Wednesday).

19. RECONCILIATION

The term "public penance" has frequently led to two misunderstandings. First of all, despite what people may think, public confession of sins has never been the rule in the Church; sins were confessed privately to the bishop, and this confession was always obligatory. History does indeed record examples of public confession, but such confessions were entirely a matter of personal initiative, special signs of profound repentance; they were not an obligatory part of the ancient penitential discipline.

Secondly, we should not think that alongside this "public" penance there existed another kind of sacramental penance that was private. Except in Ireland from the seventh century on, there was no private, repeated sacramental penance in the Church before the ninth century. Confession was private, but the only penance was public (the reason for it being known to the confessor alone). The distinction between sins in terms of relative seriousness arose less from an analysis of the sin in itself than from the way it was expiated. A sin was serious or mortal when it required canonical penance, a penance that presupposed the intervention of the Church in the process of reconciliation. A sin was venial or light when it could be expiated by private mortifications.[177]

From the end of the first century on, a kind of penitential discipline can be seen taking shape. The person who sinned seriously was, above all else, deprived of the Eucharist. The leaders of the community determined the extent of this ex-communication.[178] In the third century, penitential practice became more specific due to social changes. The reconciliation of sinners who were guilty of adultery, fornication, or, above all, apostasy led to controversies that in turn caused the gradual elaboration of a penitential doctrine.

Tertullian (d. 220) exercised a major influence in the controversies. In his treatise on penance[179] he provides a fairly detailed description of the penitential customs of his day. In order to win the forgiveness of serious sins, a person had to spend a period in rather harsh expiation. A confession of sins and a total interior conversion were presupposed; the inner conversion included sorrow and the resolution to amend one's life. The confession itself was not public, but the outward penitential practices required let everyone know that the person was indeed a sinner. Penitents prayed, prostrate and with ashes on their heads, first outside the church, then within it, for a period determined by the bishop, down to the day of reconciliation. This public penance could not be repeated — an extremely harsh practice that lasted until the seventh century. The penitent who sinned again was left to the mercy of God; the Church did not intervene a second time to reconcile him.

We observe a decline in the ancient penitential practice from the fourth to the sixth centuries. Yet the ancient discipline which decreed that serious sin required ecclesiastical penance remained in force. The difficulty arose with the principles for classifying the sins that required such penance, as distinct from sins that could be expiated by good works.

In the seventh and eighth centuries, people hardly ever sought reconciliation until they were dying. Canonical penance had become too severe for these later generations and no longer had any place in the life of Christians. In the seventh century, therefore, the Celts and Anglo-Saxons started something new: a kind of penance that could be repeated. Beginning in the eighth century we find in use a book of penances that a priest or bishop could consult in assigning a predetermined penance for various sins. In this new situation the working principle was that serious but private sins were expiated according to a list in the book of penances; public serious sins still required public penance. In fact, public sinners were also subject to imprisonment.

The Gelasian Sacramentary contains a ritual for reconciliation, and some of its prayers are very beautiful. In brief outline, the ceremonies connected with reconciliation were as follows. On Ash Wednesday, before Mass, the bishop received the penitents and gave them the sackcloth they were to wear; after a series of prayers, the penitents were expelled from the church and locked up until Holy Thursday.[180] On Holy Thursday they were released and came to the church, where they prostrated themselves at the door. The deacon then asked the bishop to reconcile them. The bishop exhorted the penitents and then spoke the very beautiful prayers of reconciliation.[181]

In the tenth century (950), the Romano-Germanic Pontifical took over the Gelasian ritual and made it more showy and expansive.[182] Later on, at the end of the thirteenth century, William Durand, bishop of Mende, composed a Pontifical containing a ritual of reconciliation that has come down to us only slightly modified in later Pontificals.[183] It was this ritual that the modern Pontifical still preserved down to the post-Vatican II reform. The following is a description of the ceremony along with the prayers in it.[184]

The reconciliation of penitents takes place on Holy Thursday. At the beginning of Lent the Church has segregated the penitents from the rest of the community and assigned them a solemn penance. Now, on the day of reconciliation, the bishop comes, surrounded by his clergy, and prostrates himself at the faldstool before the altar, while the Litany of the Saints is sung. Meanwhile, the penitents, barefooted, are kneeling at the door of the church, carrying unlit candles in their hands.

When the invocation "All you holy patriarchs and prophets, pray for us" has been sung and the choir has repeated it, there is a pause. The bishop then sends out to the penitents two subdeacons, who carry lighted candles and sing, "As I live, says the Lord, I want the sinner not to die but to be converted and live." When the antiphon is finished, they extinguish their candles and return to their place as the litany continues.

When the invocation "All you holy martyrs, pray for us" has been sung and the choir has repeated it, there is another pause, and the bishop once again sends out to the penitents two subdeacons with lighted candles. The subdeacons stand at the door of the church and sing the antiphon "The Lord says: Do penance, for the kingdom of God is at hand." They extinguish their candles, and the penitents return to their former position. The litany then continues down to "Lamb of God" (exclusively).

The bishop now sends out to the penitents a single elderly deacon holding a tall lighted candle. He stands at the door of the church and sings the antiphon "Lift up your heads, for your redemption is at hand." The penitents then light their candles from the deacon's, and the deacon returns with his candle still lit. The "Lamb of God" and other invocations are then sung to the end of the litany.

The bishop stands up; the clergy and ministers also stand and process before the bishop with cross, censer, and candles, and the whole cortege leaves the choir. A kind of throne has been set up at the center of the church; the clergy line up along both sides of the nave, facing the door. Then the archdeacon, at the threshold, says aloud, in a reading tone, to the penitents standing before the door: "Be silent and listen attentively." Then, turning to the bishop, he says, still in a reading tone:

> Venerable Pontiff, the acceptable time is at hand, the day of God's mercy and man's salvation, when death is destroyed and eternal life begins; the day when new shoots are to be planted in the vineyard of the Lord of Hosts so that the ancient curse may be removed. For, although there is no moment when God's goodness and love are absent, now in his mercy his forgiveness of sins is more abundant, and he more effectively raises up those who are reborn through grace. Now our community is increased by the reborn, our numbers augmented by those returning. The waters cleanse and so do tears; therefore we rejoice at those who are first called, and our joy is great when sinners are forgiven. Your servants have fallen into various sins through neglect of the heavenly commandments and through transgression of approved ways. Now, humbled and prostrate before you, they cry out to you with the prophet, "Like our fathers we have sinned, we have acted wickedly; have mercy on us, Lord, have mercy on us!"
>
> Not in vain have they heard the words of the Gospel, "Blessed are those who mourn, for they shall be comforted." As Scripture bids them, they have eaten the bread of sorrow and dampened their pillow with tears; they have afflicted their hearts with grief, their

bodies with fasting, so that they might regain their lost health of soul. Penance is the extraordinary remedy that is useful to each individual and helpful to the community.

The bishop with his ministers now goes to the door of the church (the choir of priests stay where they are). Standing in the doorway, the bishop addresses the penitents in a brief exhortation on God's mercy and his promise of forgiveness; he tells them how they will soon be brought back into the Church and how they must live therein. Then he sings the antiphon "Come, come, come, children, listen to me and I will teach you the fear of the Lord." Then the deacon takes his place beside the penitents and says in their name, "Let us kneel," and "Let us arise." The bishop sings the same antiphon three times in all, the deacon following it each time with "Let us kneel" and "Let us arise."

The bishop enters the church and stands at a suitable distance from the door. The archdeacon intones an antiphon, and the choir finishes it: "Look to him, and be radiant; so your faces shall never be ashamed," and adds Psalm 33(34), "I will bless the Lord at all times."

The penitents meanwhile enter the church and kneel before the bishop; they remain there until the psalm and antiphon are finished. The archdeacon then says in a reading tone:

Bishop and successor of the apostles, restore to these people what was corrupted under the devil's influence. With the help of your prayers and through the grace of divine reconciliation, draw them close to God so that while earlier they displeased him by their perverse actions, they may now happily please him in the land of the living, once he who caused their death has been overcome.

The bishop asks the archdeacon: "Do you believe them worthy of reconciliation?" The archdeacon replies: "I know and attest that they are worthy." Another deacon then says to the penitents, "Arise." They stand up, and the bishop takes the hand of one of them, while all the others link hands to form a chain.

The archdeacon says in a loud voice: "I know my iniquities. ℟.: And my sins are always before me. ℣.: Turn your gaze from my sins. ℟.: And wipe away all my iniquities. ℣.: Give me again the joy of your salvation. ℟.: And strengthen in me your spirit that makes me holy."

The bishop then intones an antiphon, which is taken up by the choir: "I tell you, the angels of God rejoice over a single sinner who repents." Now he draws the person whose hand he is holding (and he in turn the others) and leads him to the throne that is set up at the center of the church. There he stops, and turning to the penitents, who kneel down, begins the antiphon "My son, you should rejoice because your brother was dead and is alive again, was lost and has been found."

He then prays: "May the almighty and eternal God absolve you from every bond of sin so that you may have eternal life and live: through Jesus Christ our Lord. . . ." Then, joining his hands at his breast, he continues in a lower tone:

> It is truly right . . . to praise you, Lord, through Jesus Christ, your Son, whom you, almighty Father, willed should be born in a mysterious way so that he might pay the debt Adam owed to you, eternal Father, and that he might destroy our death by his own, bear our wounds in his own body, and wash away our stains with his blood. Thus we who had been laid low by the hatred of the ancient enemy might be raised up by your Son's mercy. Through him, Lord, we humbly ask and beseech you to hear our prayers for the sins of others, since we cannot adequately petition you for our own. Therefore, most merciful Lord, in your wonted kindness call back to yourself these servants of yours whom sin has separated from you. You did not scorn the guilty Ahab when he humbled himself, but remitted the punishment he deserved. You ac-

cepted Peter's tears and afterwards gave him the keys of the heavenly kingdom. When the thief confessed his guilt, you promised him the rewards of the kingdom. Therefore, merciful Lord, accept these men and women for whom we pray, and restore them to the bosom of the Church so that the enemy may not triumph over them. Let your Son, who is equal to you, reconcile them to you, cleanse them of all their sins, admit them to his holy Supper, and so strengthen them with his Flesh and Blood that he may lead them into the heavenly kingdom when this present life has run its course: Jesus Christ, your Son and our Lord.

When the preface is finished, the bishop prostrates himself at his place, the ministers on the carpet, the clergy and people on the floor, while the cantor begins the antiphon, and the choir finishes it and adds the psalms. "Create a clean heart in me, O God, and renew within me a right spirit." The psalms are Psalms 50, 55, and 56.

The bishop now stands and turns to the penitents, praying: "Lord, have mercy on us. Christ, have mercy on us. Lord, have mercy. Our Father. . . ." Then, after the introductory versicles, he says a series of prayers:

Let us pray. Hear our prayers, Lord, and in your mercy listen to me, though I am the first to need your forgiveness, for through no merits of my own but solely through your grace I have been appointed minister of this reconciliation. Grant me confidence in carrying out your work, and do you, through my ministry, accomplish your loving will. Through Jesus Christ. . . .

Let us pray. Lord, grant that these servants of yours may produce worthy fruits of repentance so that after departing through sin from the purity of your Church, they may be forgiven and restored. Through Jesus Christ . . .

Let us pray. Lord, I implore you, by the mercy proper to your Majesty and your Name, that you would pardon these your servants who confess their sins and misdeeds, and that you would release them from the bonds of their past sins. You carried the lost sheep back to the fold on your shoulder; you were pleased by the tax collector's confession and listened to his prayer. Lord, do you also have mercy on these servants of yours and in your goodness hear their prayers so that they may continue to weep and confess their sins, and may quickly experience your mercy. Then, given access again to your holy altar, they may be renewed in hope of eternal glory in heaven: you who live and reign. . . .

Let us pray. Lord, in your goodness you created mankind and in your mercy you created it anew. When man was cast forth from eternal life by the trickery of Satan, you redeemed him with the blood of your only Son. Give life now to these servants of yours, whom you do not wish to see dead. You let them go when they strayed; take them back now that they have changed their ways. Let their tearful sighs move you to mercy, Lord; heal their wounds, reach out your saving hand to them as they lie downcast, lest your Church be deprived of any part of its Body and your flock suffer any loss, and lest the enemy boast of a loss to your family or the second death take possession of those who had been reborn in the bath of salvation. To you, then, Lord, do we humbly pour out our prayers and tears. Spare those who confess to you, and grant that they may weep for their sins during this mortal life so that on the day of fearful judgment they may not receive the sentence of eternal damnation nor experience the terrible darkness and the whistling flames. Let them turn from error to the true path. Let them be wounded no more but retain forever in its fullness the gift of your grace and the renewal your mercy brings: through Jesus Christ. . . .

Let us pray. Kind and merciful God, in your great goodness you wipe away the sins of the repentant and forgive their past misdeeds. Look now upon these servants of yours and hear their prayer as they ask with sincere hearts for the forgiveness of all their sins. Loving Father, make new in them what their earth-bound weakness has corrupted or Satan's trickery has profaned. Restore them through complete forgiveness to the unity of your Church's Body. Have mercy, Lord, on their groans; have mercy on their tears. Admit to the sacrament of reconciliation these servants who trust only in your mercy: through Jesus Christ. . . .

Let us pray. We humbly implore your divine Majesty, almighty, ever-living God, to bestow the grace of forgiveness on these servants, who are worn out from long and difficult penance. Let them put on the wedding garment and be admitted once again to the royal table from which they were excluded for their sins: through Jesus Christ. . . .

[Absolution] Let us pray. May our Lord Jesus Christ, who wiped away the sins of the whole world by handing himself over and shedding his pure blood, and who said to his disciples: "Whatever you shall bind on earth will be bound also in heaven, and whatever you loose on earth will be loosed also in heaven," and who willed that I, unworthy and sinful though I am, should be one of these disciples and his minister — may he, through the intercession of Mary the Mother of God, St. Michael the Archangel, St. Peter the Apostle, who received the power to bind and loose, and all the saints, absolve you, by the power of his sacred blood that was shed for the forgiveness of sins, and through my ministry, from all your sins of negligent thought, word, and action, and may he lead you, freed from the bonds of your sins, to the kingdom of heaven: through the same Jesus Christ. . . .

Then the Bishop sprinkles the penitents with holy water

and incenses them, saying: "Rise up, sleeper! Rise from the dead, and Christ will enlighten you!"

Finally, he gives them such indulgences as he chooses. Then, with hands raised and extended over them, he says: "By the prayers and merits of Blessed Mary ever Virgin, St. Michael the Archangel, St. John the Baptist, the holy apostles Peter and Paul, and all the saints, may almighty God have mercy on you, forgive you your sins, and bring you to everlasting life. ℟. Amen.

"May the almighty and merciful Lord grant you pardon, absolution, and remission of all your sins. ℟. Amen."

At the end he blesses them: "May almighty God bless you, the Father and the Son and the Holy Spirit. ℟. Amen."

This ritual of reconciliation is unknown to most Christians, and yet it can help us to grasp what the sacrament of penance really is. As a way of pulling together the elements of the ceremony, we need only sum up the rich insights provided by the prayers.

The bishop prays for himself as minister of this sacrament, being fully aware that he who acts as God's instrument is himself a sinner and that he is subject to weakness like the others whose misdeeds he forgives (first in the final series of prayers). The second prayer is more general in character, asking for the restoration to the Church of those whose sins had excluded them from the company of the faithful. The confession of sin leads to pardon, and pardon in turn gives the sinner access to the holy altar and allows him to hope for eternal glory in heaven (third prayer).

Forgiveness, then, is life-giving. The Lord has not in fact abandoned sinners even for a moment. The Church is not to be deprived of one of her members, nor is the second death to lay hold of those who have been reborn. Confession, followed by forgiveness that is intended to be definitive, rescues the sinner from a final condemnation (fourth prayer). This pardon will make the sinner once again fully a member of the ecclesial body (fifth prayer). He will don again the wedding garment and be readmitted to the royal table from which he had been excluded (sixth prayer).

Notable throughout is the emphasis on the community aspect of reconciliation. Sin is an attack on the flock of Christ; reconciliation, on the contrary, means growth for the Church. Penance is seen as closely connected with the paschal mystery of death and resurrection, light and life. The prayers, scriptural in their inspiration, also point out the parallelism between baptism and penance. The role of bishop or priest is carefully indicated, especially that of the bishop, who stands for Christ and the apostles and who in the name of the Lord welcomes the sinner back after first urging him to return to the Church. Above all, penance allows the forgiven sinner to take his place once more at the Eucharistic banquet, in which the Body of Christ renews and restores him and gives him once again the pledge of eternal life.

A careful and meditative reading of this ceremony (once we prescind from the secondary bits of the theatrical that it picked up over the centuries) would enable many Christians of our day to acquire a more accurate understanding of penance. The ceremony could also serve as the basis for penance services of a kind that might well fill in for the former Holy Thursday usage. Such services would bring out the fact that confession of sins and absolution from them restore the person to his old state as one newly born again or else establish him more firmly in it if it had not been entirely lost. We would realize more fully that the new birth of baptism gives us the right to sit at the common table of the Eucharistic banquet, and that absolution restores us to our full place in the people of God. These truths are essential elements in the paschal mystery as applied to us, and they were brought home to Christians in an especially striking way in the ancient Holy Thursday ritual of reconciliation.

It is because of Christ's death and triumph over death that we can constantly renew the new covenant with the Father, through the Son. Because of Christ's pasch, we can, at the climactic moment of the Paschal Vigil, eat the Bread and drink the Blood of the new and eternal covenant. Not only does the sacrament of penance derive its efficacy from the blood of the Lord; it also gives us renewed access to the Eucharistic table, where the feast of victory and resurrection is celebrated. Penance is thus closely connected with the painful yet triumphant paschal mystery; it is indissolubly linked to baptism and the Eucharist; it renews the Christian people and strengthens the structure of God's people as realized in the Church.

Penance, then, is to be seen first and foremost as bound up with the presence of the risen Christ. All the actions that make up the sacrament of penance have as their focal point the Christ who "always lives to make intercession" for us (Heb. 7:25), the Christ who is always present with, and praying for, his Church. The repentant Christian stands before the Christ who is at the Father's right hand. It is in his presence that Christians should speak of sin and repentance, and it is in his presence that the Lenten liturgy speaks of it. The sinner must undergo a conversion, that is, he must "lose his self-centeredness and [must] focus on God in Jesus Christ. Conversion is man's entrance into the mystery of Christ's death and Resurrection, because it is God in Jesus Christ who enables him to repent, to reunite with Him, to surrender himself and to plunge anew into eternal life." [185]

All genuine repentance implies an intense desire to enter into a full and unreserved dialogue with God. This dialogue once involved God and Christ; now it involves God and the Church, with each Christian sharing in the dialogue in and through the Church. The penitential outlook, then, is not solely an entering into oneself; it also supposes another speaker, someone who listens, answers, and forgives. The repentant sinner engages in a dialogue. The dialogue in turns helps him face the struggle that characterizes the whole period between the resurrection of Christ, in whom we are certain that salvation has been won for us once and for all, and the return of Christ, when the salvation thus won will become definitively ours.

"You know what hour it is," says St. Paul (Rom. 13:11).

We have been saved in hope; we have the root of salvation in us through baptism into the death of Christ; but we still live in a period of conflict. The whole of the Lenten liturgy insists on this last fact and endeavors to help us understand it more fully. The activity of repentance is, however, also linked in the liturgy with the eschatological period and the promised return of Christ that is the foundation of our hope for salvation. We should recall here how the entire fourth week of Lent looks forward to the return of Christ and to the heavenly Jerusalem. In her expressions of repentance, the Church always looks to this return of the Lord and to the coming of the new Jerusalem.

It is against this eschatological background that we can discern the real mind of the Church concerning penance, as reflected in the seasonal liturgy of Lent.

Repentance always takes place in the Church and with reference to the risen Christ seated at the Father's right hand and present here and now with his Church. The penitent stands before this Christ, but he does so in the Church and in the consciousness of Christ's infinite power of intercession. The aim of the penitent is to turn away from sin, to struggle with it, and to be converted. The Good Shepherd cannot resist the sinner's sincere and humble faith, and he grants his forgiveness. Penance is not a static thing but an onward journey toward the heavenly Jerusalem, where the penitent will be transformed by the glory of the risen Christ.

In his commentary on the Gospel of the widow of Naim, St. Ambrose writes:

> Even if there be serious sin that you cannot wash away yourself by tears of repentance, let Mother Church weep for you, for she intercedes for each individual like a widowed mother for her only son. . . . Let this devoted mother mourn, then, and let the crowd stand by. . . . Presently you will rise up from the dead; presently you will be liberated from the tomb.[186]

It is possible to use at least some of the texts from this Holy Thursday ritual of reconciliation by taking their themes and adapting them to our mentality. In any case, it seemed important, at the end of our reflections on Lent, to show how the Church saw the sacrament of penance as the climax of the season's asceticism in its various aspects.

20. THE ONGOING RENEWAL OF CREATION

The chrism of salvation

It seems that in Gaul, until the end of the seventh century, the blessing of the holy oils took place during Lent rather than on Holy Thursday. The blessing appears in the Gelasian Sacramentary toward the end of the seventh century, but the section in which it appears was redacted in Gaul.[187] Yet, despite the clear influence of Gallican custom, the blessing of the holy oils and of chrism is originally Roman.

From the theological point of view, the blessing of the holy oils and the consecration of the chrism can be linked to the Eucharist. This interesting theology, which makes all the sacraments depend on the Eucharist, cannot however be regarded as the reason why the blessing of the oils and chrism was put on Holy Thursday. It seems rather that the the reason was purely practical: the oils and chrism would be needed for baptism and confirmation during the Paschal Vigil; therefore there had to be a ceremony of blessing.

The reform of 1955 restored the Chrism Mass. The origin of the various formularies that make it up is not clear. Some scholars claim the prayers cannot have originated in Rome;[188] others maintain that some at least may have been Roman.[189] Moreover, the Chrism Mass originally had no liturgy of the word, but the reason for this is again not clear. Perhaps the liturgy of reconciliation preceded this Eucharistic celebration and took the place of the liturgy of the word. Perhaps what we have is a vestige of the ancient discipline according to which there was neither a liturgy of the word nor a Eucharistic liturgy on Thursdays; when, finally, the Eucharist began to be celebrated on Holy Thursday, no one thought of beginning it with a liturgy of the word.

Before the reform of 1955 the blessing of the oils and the consecration of the chrism took place apart from Mass.

The reform initiated by the Second Vatican Council puts the blessing of oils and consecration of chrism before the offertory and after the renewal by priests of their commitment to service. Here we glimpse a novelty introduced in the present reform: The blessing of oils and consecration of chrism are an occasion for bringing all the clergy together with their bishop and for introducing into the ceremony a renewal of priestly promises. The Eucharistic celebration in the evening will again highlight the unity of the priesthood.

The new Chrism Mass emphasizes this "feast of priesthood" element; the texts selected for the readings bring out the traits a man should have who has been chosen to exercise priestly functions. The texts are easily grasped, and in addition we have met some of them already.

The first reading is from Isaiah (61:1-3a, 6a, 8b-9). The theme is familiar and quite suited to the present celebration as now conceived: "The Spirit of the Lord God is upon me, because the Lord has anointed me to bring good tidings to the afflicted . . . to give them . . . the oil of gladness." The Gospel pericope fits in perfectly with this first reading, because in it Christ reads this very passage from Isaiah in the synagogue at Capharnaum and claims that it refers to himself (Luke 4:16-21). The responsory psalm, Psalm 89, sings of the anointing of David, God's servant. The second reading, from the Apocalypse of St. John (1:5-8), is the one most explicitly focused on the object of the celebration: Christ has "made us a kingdom, priests to his God and Father."

The renewal of priestly promises provides an opportunity for recalling the theology of priesthood. Ordination was accepted out of love for Christ and in order to serve the Church. Priests are stewards of the mysteries of God and exercise their stewardship by preaching the word and celebrating the Eucharist and other sacraments. The bishop's office is that of the apostles; amid priests and faithful he holds the place of Christ, who is Priest, Good Shepherd, Teacher, and Servant of all.

When it is time to bless the oils and chrism, the bishop blesses the oil of the sick, then the oil of catechumens, and finally consecrates the chrism.

Sacred signs

The blessings of creatures that are to serve man in a new way for the glory of God are a manifestation of the fact that Christ's work in this world has been effective. God is constantly acting through elements made for man; through them he is accomplishing the salvation, not of our soul alone, but of soul and body together, of the whole human person. Our entire being is gradually being transformed and re-created according to the image God dreamed of when he first created the world. We are becoming once again the kings of the created world. We are once again becoming prophets and priests, spreading the Good News of Christ's death and resurrection throughout a world that is still undergoing its reconstruction, still acquiring its true meaning. Because of the death and resurrection of Christ, these created elements can now be a means of communicating to us the grace of the Holy Spirit, whom the heavenly Christ is constantly sending to us.

We are now caught up into the mighty action of the Three Persons: the Father who created us and loved us enough to send his Son to us; the Son whose brothers we now are, because we are adopted sons of his Father; and the Spirit

who is sent to us by the Son and constantly makes us grow
into a more perfect likeness to the Father. Not we alone,
but the whole of creation is being reformed and brought to
fulfillment; the holy oils manifest the extent to which this
reformation has already succeeded. Creatures now serve
God's glory by contributing to the life of man and to his
transformation into a king who is invited to sit at the banquet table on the last day.

All this is possible because of Christ's sacrifice. Subhuman creatures have had their original power restored to
them, and they now act upon our bodies that have been
corrupted by sin and have become the dwelling place of
evil powers bent on destroying the body's true being.
These creatures, by the power that the Spirit communicates
to them, act upon our persons, and we gradually recover our
true powers; we see that we can become masters of ourselves and regain the balance that should be ours. We are
healed and capable of living in God.

Our soul and body are not two separate, isolated spheres.
Our body became mortal because our soul was fatally
wounded by sin. The sacrament of chrism consolidates the
union and unity of soul and body. In this sacrament a
created substance becomes capable once again, through the
power of the Spirit, of exercising its true role, which is to
serve man, and to do so by touching him and healing him in
body and soul. More accurately, it is by touching the soul
through the body that it heals the soul and thereby the body
as well.

We should reread the texts for the blessing of the oils.
They are rich in content and can bring home to us a truth
that is a source of intense joy: the truth, the certainty, that
salvation is ours even now.

21. LENT IN THE LITURGIES
OF THE PAST

In accordance with our usual plan, we shall here look briefly at the Lenten liturgy as we find it in the early Roman liturgy and in some of the non-Roman liturgies. We emphasize again that our purpose is neither idle curiosity nor the study of the past for its own sake, but to indicate texts that may prove helpful and for the knowledge of other mentalities.

1. Lent in the Roman Tradition

We have chosen to reproduce in the Table only the most characteristic lists; to give a list for all the divergent lectionaries would occupy far too much space and would not be in keeping with our purpose here.

As the list makes clear, a well-established tradition was reflected in these various lectionaries. The older books show the absence of a Thursday liturgy, which began to be celebrated only in the eighth century. These older books likewise show no liturgy for the second Sunday of Lent; the reason for this is that the Ember Day Mass was celebrated during the night between Saturday and Sunday, and consequently there was no further celebration on Sunday.

We can see that the Gospel pericopes found in the Roman Missal that was in use until recently were already present in the Würzburg Evangeliary and passed from there to the Murbach Lectionary and the Roman Missal of 1570. By the time of the Würzburg Evangeliary (ca. 645), the celebration of the scrutinies had already been shifted to weekdays.

	Würzburg Epistolary[190]	Würzburg Evangeliary[191]	Murbach Lectionary[192]	Roman Missal of 1570
Ash Wednesday	Joel 2:12-13	Matthew 6:16-21	Joel 2:12-13 Matthew 6:16-21	Joel 2:12-19 Matthew 6:16-21
Thursday			Is. 38:1-6	Is. 38:1-6
			Matthew 8:5-13	Matthew 8:5-13
Friday	Is. 58:1-9	Matthew 5:43-6:4	Is. 58:1-9 Matthew 5:43-6:4	Is. 58:1-9 Matthew 5:43-6:4
Saturday			Is. 59:9-14 Mark 6:47-56	Is. 58:9-14 Mark 6:47-56
First Week Sunday	2 Cor. 6:1-10	Matthew 4:1-11	2 Cor. 6:1-10 Matthew 4:1-11	2 Cor. 6:1-10 Matthew 4:1-11
Monday	Ezek. 34:11-16	Matthew 25:37-46	Ezek. 34:11-16 Matthew 25:37-46	Ezek. 34:11-16 Matthew 25:31-46
Tuesday	Is. 55:6-11	Matthew 21:10-17	Is. 55:6-11 Matthew 21:10-17	Is. 55:6-11 Matthew 21:10-17
Wednesday (Ember Day)	Exod. 24:12-18 1 Kings 19:3-8	Matthew 12:18-50	Exod. 24:12-18 1 Kings 19:3-8 Matthew 12:18-50	Exod. 24:12-18 1 Kings 19:3-8 Matthew 12:18-50

Thursday			Ezek. 18:1-9 John 8:31-47	Ezek. 18:1-9 John 8:31-47
Friday (Ember Day)	Ezek. 15:20-28	John 5:1-15	Ezek. 18:20-28 John 5:1-15	Ezek. 18:20-28 John 5:1-15
Saturday (Ember Day)		Matthew 17:1-9	Matthew 17:1-9	Deut. 26:12-19 Deut. 11:22-25 Sir. 36:1-10 Dan. 3:47-51 1 Thess. 5:14-23 Matthew 17:1-9
Second Week Sunday	1 Thess. 4:1-7		1 Thess. 4:1-7 Mark 1:40-45	1 Thess. 4:1-7 Matthew 17:1-9
Monday	Dan. 9:15-19	John 8:21-29	Dan. 9:15-19 John 8:21-29	Dan. 9:15-19 John 8:21-29
Tuesday	1 Kings 17:8-16	Matthew 23:1-12	1 Kings 17:8-16 Matthew 23:1-12	1 Kings 17:8-16 Matthew 23:1-12
Wednesday	Est. 13:9-17	Matthew 20:17-28	Est. 13:8-17 Matthew 20:17-28	Est. 13:8-11, 15-17 Matthew 20:17-28
Thursday			Jer. 17:5-10 John 5:30-47	Jer. 17:5-10 Luke 16:19-31
Friday	Gen. 37:6-22	Matthew 21:33-46	Gen. 37:6-22 Matthew 21:33-46	Gen. 37:6-22 Matthew 21:33-46
Saturday	Gen. 27:6-39	Luke 15:11-32	Gen. 27:6-39 Luke 15:11-32	Gen. 27:6-40 Luke 15:11-32

Third Week Sunday	Eph. 5:1-9	Luke 11:14-28	Eph. 5:1-9 Luke 11:14-28	Eph. 5:1-9 Luke 11:14-28
Monday	2 Kings 5:1-15	Luke 4:23-30	2 Kings 5:1-15 Luke 4:23-30	2 Kings 5:1-15 Luke 4:23-20
Tuesday	2 Kings 4:1-7	Matthew 18:15-22	2 Kings 4:1-7 Matthew 18:15-22	2 Kings 4:1-7 Matthew 18:15-22
Wednesday	Exod. 20:12-24	Matthew 15:1-20	Exod. 20:12-24 Matthew 15:1-20	Exod. 20:12-24 Matthew 15:1-20
Thursday			Jer. 7:1-7 John 6:27-35	Jer. 7:1-7 John 6:27-35
Friday	Num. 20:1-13	John 4:6-42	Num. 20:1-13 John 4:6-42	Num. 20:1-3, 6-13 John 4:5-42
Saturday	Dan. 13:1-62	John 8:1-11	Dan. 13:1-62 John 8:1-11	Dan. 13:1-9, 15-17 John 8:1-11
Fourth Week Sunday	Gal. 4:22-31	John 6:1-15	Gal. 4:22-31 John 6:1-15	Gal. 4:22-31 John 6:1-15
Monday	1 Kings 3:16-28	John 2:13-25	1 Kings 3:16-28 John 2:13-25	1 Kings 3:16-28 John 2:13-25
Tuesday	Exod. 32:7-14	John 7:14-31	Exod. 32:7-14 John 7:14-31	Exod. 32:7-14 John 7:14-31

Wednesday	Ezek. 36:23-28 Is. 1:16-19	John 9:1-38	Ezek. 36:23-28 Is. 1:16-39 John 9:1-30	Ezek. 36:23-28 Is. 1:16-19 John 9:1-38
Thursday			2 Kings 4:25-38 John 5:17-39	2 Kings 4:25-38 Luke 17:11-16
Friday	1 Kings 17:17-24	John 11:1-45	1 Kings 17:17-24 John 11:1-45	1 Kings 17:17-24 John 11:1-45
Saturday	Is. 49:8-15 Is. 55:1-11	John 8:12-20	Is. 49:8-15 Is. 5:1-11 John 8:12-20	Is. 49:8-15 John 8:46-59
Fifth Week Sunday	Heb. 9:11-15	John 8:46-59	Heb. 9:11-15 John 8:46-59	Heb. 9:11-15 John 8:46-59
Monday	Jonah 3:1-10	John 7:32-39	Jonah 3:1-10 John 7:32-39	Jonah 3:1-10 John 7:32-39
Tuesday	Dan. 14:27-42	John 7:1-13	Dan. 14:27-42 John 7:1-13	Dan. 14:27-42 John 7:1-13
Wednesday	Lev. 19:11-19	John 10:22-38	Lev. 19:11-19 John 10:23-38	Lev. 19:1-2, 11-19, 25 John 10:22-38
Thursday			Dan. 3:34-45 John 7:40-53	Dan. 3:25, 34-45 Luke 7:36-50
Friday	Jer. 17:13-18	John 11:17-54	Jer. 17:13-18 John 11:17-54	Ler. 17:13-18 John 11:47-54

Saturday	Phil. 2:5-11			Jer. 18:18-23 John 6:53-71	Jer. 18:18-23 John 12:10-36
Holy Week Palm Sunday		Matthew 26:2-27:66		Phil. 2:5-11 Matthew 26:2-27:66	Matthew 21:1-9 Phil. 2:5-11 Matthew 26:26-27:60
Monday	Is. 50:5-10		John 12:1-36	Is. 50:5-10 Zech. 11:12-13, 10-11a; 13:6-9 John 12:1-23	Is. 50:5-10 John 12:1-9
Tuesday	Jer. 11:18-20 Wis. 2:12-22		John 13:1-32	Jer. 11:18-20 Wis. 2:12-22 John 12:24-43	Jer. 11:18-20 Mark 14:32-15:46
Wednesday	Is. 62:11-63:7 Is. 53:1-12	Luke 22:1-23:53		Is. 62:11-63:7 Is. 53:1-12 Luke 22:1-23:53	Is. 62:11-63:7 Is. 53:1-12 Luke 22:39-23:53

	Northern Italy Aquileia Evangeliary [193]	Southern Italy Beneventan Liturgy [194]
First Sunday	Matthew 4:1-11. Temptation of Christ	
Second Sunday	Luke 12:32-34. Sell your possessions, give alms, be ready	John 4:5-42. The Samaritan woman
Third Sunday	John 8:12-59. Jesus, Light of the world; before Abraham	John 8:12-59
Fourth Sunday	John 9:1. The man born blind	John 9:1-38
Fifth Sunday	John 11:1. Raising of Lazarus	John 11:1-45

2. Lent Elsewhere in Italy

Other Italian traditions show different readings that had probably been used at Rome before the time of the Würzburg Lectionary and Evangeliary. We shall pause for a moment only on two sections of the country and limit our examples to the Sundays (see chart, page 227).

It should be noted that in the Beneventan liturgy, the Gospel of the Samaritan woman is read on the second Sunday, while on the third the Gospel is the rather long passage on Jesus as the Light of the world who is before Abraham was. The introduction of the Ember Days, however, doubtless caused the Gospel of the second Sunday to be suppressed, since the Ember Day liturgy was celebrated during Saturday night, and the Sunday had no liturgy of its own.

3. Lent at Milan

The only witnesses to the Ambrosian liturgy that we shall call upon here are the Sacramentary of Bergamo[195] and the Ambrosian Missal.[196] Once again, we shall limit ourselves to the Sundays. For the most part, the Bergamo Sacramentary repeats the readings used in the earlier liturgical books of the Milanese rite.

Readings

	Sacramentary of Bergamo	Ambrosian Missal
First Sunday		Is. 57:21–58:12
	2 Cor. 6:1-10	2 Cor. 6:1-10
	Matthew 4:1-11. Temptation of Christ	Matthew 4:1-11
Second Sunday		Exod. 20:1-24 1:15-23
	Eph. 1:15-23	Eph. 1:15-23
	John 4:5-42. Samaritan woman	John 4:5-42
		John 4:5-42

Third Sunday	1 Thess. 2:20–3:8	1 Thess. 2:20–3:8
		Exod. 34:1-10
	John 8:31-59. Jesus and Abraham	John 8:31-59
Fourth Sunday		Exod. 34:23–35:1
	1 Thess. 4:1-12	1 Thess. 4:1-11
	John 9:1-38. Man born blind	John 9:1-38
Fifth Sunday		Exod. 14:15-31
	Eph. 5:15-22	Eph. 5:15-22
	John 11:1-45. Lazarus	John 11:1-45
Palm Sunday		Is. 53:1-12
	2 Thess. 2:15–3:5	2 Thess. 2:14–3:5
	John 11:55–12:11. Anointing at Bethany	John 11:55–12:11

Prayers

The Milanese liturgy offers us some fine prefaces. Here is the one in the Bergamo Sacramentary for the first Sunday of Lent:

> Through Christ our Lord, who nourishes the faith, deepens the hope, and intensifies the love of those who fast. For he is the true and life-giving Bread, being the substance of eternity and the food of virtue. Your Word, through whom all things were made, is the Bread not only of human souls but of the very angels themselves. Sustained by this Bread, your servant Moses, when about to receive the Law, fasted forty days and nights, abstaining from earthly food so that he might be better able to taste your sweetness. That is why he did not feel bodily hunger, but forgot about material food. The sight of your glory enlightened him, and under the influence of the Spirit of God your word nourished him. You never cease to give us this same Bread, Jesus Christ, and you exhort us to hunger for it constantly.[197]

Each day of Lent has its own special preface, and it is often quite rich in content. Let us look at the preface for the second Sunday, a day on which, in this liturgy, the Gospel of the Samaritan woman was read: "Through Christ our Lord, who in order to help us grasp the mystery of his humility, sat wearied by the well. There he who had bestowed faith on the Samaritan woman asked her for a drink of water."[198]

The preface for Tuesday of the third week reads as follows: "You do not want souls to perish, nor do you always pass judgment straightway on sinners and their misdeeds, but you move them to repentance and wait for them. Turn away from us the wrath we deserve, and pour out upon us the mercy we ask. May we be purified by the holy fast and joined to the assembly of your chosen ones."[199]

4. Lent in Gaul

For the Gallican tradition our Table lists the collections whose data is the most valuable to us. We have not listed the Lectionary of Luxeuil because its data are too sparse; the lectionary is fragmentary and gives only a few pericopes. The same holds for the Wolfenbüttel palimpsest, which gives the readings only for the first Sunday and four weekdays.

To be noted especially is the originality of a number of choices in these lectionaries from Merovingian Gaul. The variety is most interesting. On the other hand, the connection of these readings with the Lenten season is not always evident at first sight. Not to be overlooked is the reading from the discourse on the bread of life (John 6) in the Evangeliary of Trier.

5. Lent in Spain

Readings

The liturgical books provide abundant information on the readings in the Lenten liturgy of Spain. For the most part, the lectionaries copy and repeat one another. Nonetheless, for the sake of the reader who has no access to these sources, we list the readings from several of the lectionaries, just as we did above for the early Roman liturgy. We list only the readings for the Sundays.

Other manuscripts, such as the *Liber commicus* of Carcassone (800) or the Madrid Bible (9th–10th centuries), list the readings only for weekdays.

Prayers

The *Liber mozarabicus sacramentorum* is very rich in prayers for Lent.[205] As is usual in this liturgy, the formularies are quite lengthy; they are also full of images and endeavor to give a current application to the events related in the Gospel of the day.

The Sunday Masses are as follows: second Sunday, Mass of the Samaritan woman; third Sunday, Mass of the man born blind (but the title reads: "Mass to be said on the second Sunday of Lent"); fourth Sunday, Mass of mid-Lent (twentieth day of Lent); fifth Sunday, Mass of Lazarus.[210] The following are some examples of the prayers in the Spanish Lenten liturgy.

> Therefore, though wearied in the flesh, he did not let us grow weak in his weakness. For his very weakness is stronger than men. Consequently, when he came in lowliness to rescue the world from the power of darkness, he sat and thirsted and asked for water. He was humbled in his flesh when he sat at the well and conversed with the woman. He thirsted for water and asked her to believe. But he himself created in this woman the faith he sought and asked for. When his disciples returned, he said of that faith: "I have food to eat of which you do not know." He who had already bestowed upon her the gift of faith asked her for a drink; he who was burning her in the flame of love for him asked her for the cup that would slake his thirst.[211]

	Bobbio Epistolary[200]	Bobbio Missal[201]	Sélestat Lectionary[202] I	Sélestat Lectionary[202] II	Evangeliary of St. Kilian[203]	Evangeliary of Trier[204]
First Sunday	2 Cor. 6:2-10 2 Cor. 12:12	1 Kings 19:3-15 2 Cor. 6:2-10 Matthew 6:1-8 Matthew 4:1-11		1 Cor. 2:11-14 2 Cor. 6:2-10	Matthew 7:12 Luke 15:20	Matthew 6:1-8
Second Sunday	Eph. 4:23	Luke 15:11-24	Prov. 3:19-34	1 Thess. 3:6-8	Luke 15:11-32	Luke 15:11-32
Third Sunday	Col. 2:4	John 6:28-54	Is. 58:1-8		John 8:12-54	John 6:30
Fourth Sunday	Gal. 1:4		Zech. 8:19-23		Luke 20:1-19	John 6:71
Fifth Sunday	Rom. 6:17		Jer. 18:13-23			John 11:47
Palm Sunday	Rom. 13:12	Is. 57:1-4, 13 1 Peter 2:21-25 John 12:1-16	Zech. 9:7-17		John 11:47-12:8	John 12:1-50 John 17:1-26

	Toledo Missal[206]	Toledo Lectionary[207]	Silos Lectionary[208]	San Millan Lectionary[209]
First Sunday	Prov. 1:23-32 John 4:5-42	1 Kings 19:3-15 2 Cor. 6:2-10 Matthew 4:1-11	1 Kings 19:3-15 2 Cor. 6:2-10 Matthew 4:1-11	1 Kings 19:3-15 2 Cor. 6:2-10 Matthew 4:1-11
Second Sunday	Prov. 14:33-15:8 Gen. 41:1-45 James 2:14-23 John 9:1-36	Osee 14:2-10 Dan. 2 James 2:21-3:13 1 Peter 3:5-9 John 6:28-40 John 4:5-42	Osee 14:2-10 Dan. 2 James 2:21-3:13 1 Peter 3:5-9 John 6:28-35 John 4:5-42	Osee 14:2-10 Dan. 2 James 2:21-3:13 1 Peter 3:5-9 John 6:28-35 John 4:5-42
Third Sunday	(Num. 13:3-14:24) Prov. 20:7-28 Num. 22:2-23:11 1 Peter 1:1-2 John 11:1-53	Dan. 4 1 John 1:5-2:2 John 9:1-38	Dan. 4 1 John 1:6-9 John 9:1-38	Dan. 4 1 John 1:5-9 John 9:1-38
Fourth Sunday	 Sir. 14:11-22 1 Kings 1:1-21 2 Peter 1:1-12 John 7:2-15		Dan. 13:1-64 James 4:1-16 John 8:15-20 Dan. 10:1-11:2 James 3:14-18 John 7:14-20	Dan. 13:1-65 James 4:1-16 John 8:15-20 Dan. 10:1-11:2; 12:1-13 James 3:14-18 John 7:14-20

Fifth Sunday	1 Kings 26:1-25 Sir. 47:24-30, 21-23 1 John 1:1-8 John 10:1-17		Lev. 23:5-8, 23-28, 39-41 1 John 5:16-20 John 11:1-52	Lev. 23:5-8, 23-28, 39-41 1 John 5:16-20 John 11:1-52
Palm Sunday	John 11:55-12:13	Exod. 19:4-5 + Deut. 5:32-33 + 6:2-3 + 10:17-21 + 11:16-22 + 30:3-5 + 28:10-11 1 John 2:9-17 John 11:55-12:13	Is. 49:22-26 1 Peter 1:25-2:10 Mark 7:31-37	Is. 49:22-26 1 Peter 1:25-2:10 Mark 7:31-37

Here is another example of liturgical theology, this time in relation to the man born blind:

> He [Christ] dispelled the world's darkness by the light of faith in himself and turned those who were prisoners by sentence of the law into children of grace. He came to judge the world so that the blind might see and the seeing might become blind; that those who admit they are in darkness might receive the eternal light and emerge from the darkness of sin, while those who boasted that by their merits they possessed the light of justice might find themselves in darkness, being puffed up with pride and trusting in their own righteousness. They did not seek the Physician who could heal them.[212]

On "Lazarus Sunday," an "After the Sanctus" prayer says:

> His grace freed us from the burden of the law and made us adopted sons. When he came to raise Lazarus, he cried out, "Take away the stone," so that the weight of damnation might be removed from this man who already stank from the dreadful action of the grave. "Take from him," Jesus said, "the weight of the law which has forced him down into death so that the grace of my voice may come to his aid." For it is a grace of God when we hear his voice and, with Lazarus, follow Christ by walking in right paths.[213]

These texts, the flavor of which is so difficult to capture in translation, show us how the Eucharistic liturgy in Spain attempted to "sacramentalize" the readings in the liturgy of the word. Indeed, it is one of the characteristics of this liturgy that throughout the Mass it continues to develop the main theme in the celebration of the word. It does this at times in ways that are not always adapted to our modern mentality, but the Spanish liturgy nonetheless remains a rich source of "sacramentalist" meditation on the word of God.

The Lenten season proves to be an inexhaustible source from which each of us can draw what he needs. We have seen that, far from being a somber period of negative asceticism, it is rather a starting point for the development in which man rises above himself and contributes to the authentic reconstruction of a world whose values can certainly be useful if approached in a prudent, balanced way. Living through these weeks in depth can help the Christian toward the unconditional that is the goal of his life. The true Christian attitude is not one of contempt for men and material things; the Christian is rather one who loves human beings and material things, but allows none of them to be his master. When the liturgy is fervently celebrated, it helps us to develop such an attitude.

March 19

ST. JOSEPH, HUSBAND OF MARY

This feast was introduced into the calendar at a relatively late date. The proclamation of the gospel had always, of course, reminded Christians of this Saint and offered him to them for their veneration. The Eastern Rites made frequent mention of him in their chants. In the West, there is evidence of a spontaneous cultus as early as the seventh century, but there was no organized veneration until about the twelfth century. The reader will recall that Pope John XXIII introduced the name of Joseph into the Roman Canon.

Readings

Joseph did as the angel has commanded him (Matthew 1:16, 18-21, 24)

The first part of the passage consists of the mention made of Joseph in the genealogy of Jesus. The text then passes immediately to the miraculous conception of Jesus and to the quandary in which Joseph was placed by Mary's condition. The angel explains the mystery to him in a dream. Joseph is thus the first after Mary to receive word from God of the coming and proximate birth of the Messiah, a child who will be named Jesus, that is, "The Lord saves." The Gospel shows that Joseph does not hesitate, once the angel has informed him of the true state of affairs. With a restraint we may find surprising, the evangelist says simply that "when Joseph woke from sleep, he did as the angel of the Lord commanded him."

Luke 2:41-51 (alternate Gospel)
Your father and I have been looking for you anxiously
(see Vol. 1, p. 245)

2 Sam. 7:4-5a, 12-14a, 16
    Joseph, descendant of David; Jesus, Son of David (see
    Vol. 1, p. 152)
Rom. 4:13, 16-18, 22
    The faith of Abraham, father of believers (see Vol. 4,
    p. 81)

In celebrating this feast, the Church wants to exalt the
servant who is faithful in doing God's will. Abraham is the
great Old Testament type of such obedience, and Jesus is
its perfect fulfillment. The new and eternal covenant was
made possible, in part, because Joseph too obeyed so fully
and devoutly, just as the old covenant was made possible
by Abraham's obedience.

The opening prayer of the Mass underscores Joseph's
role: to his care God entrusted the mystery of salvation. The
prayer over the offerings reminds us of Joseph's complete
dedication to the service of God's Son, who had been born
of Mary. The preface of St. Joseph likewise praises Joseph
as the wise and faithful servant whom God had put in
charge of the Holy Family and who watched like a father
over God's Son.

March 25

THE ANNUNCIATION

Mention of this feast occurs first in an evangeliary of the
seventh century. An inscription found in the ruins of an ancient basilica at Nazareth may contain the words *Ave Maria*,
but this does not allow us to assert that as early as the fourth
century there was a church dedicated to the Annunciation
or a feast celebrating this mystery. Only in the seventh century do we find sure evidence in East and West of a feast of
the Annunciation.

Readings

Luke 1:26-38
He will be called Son of the Most High (see Vol. 1, p. 154)

Is. 7:10-14
Behold, a virgin shall conceive (see Vol. 1, p. 157)

Heb. 10:4-10
I have come to do thy will, O God (see Vol. 1, p. 225)

The preface for this feast as well as the presidential prayers speak of the Annunciation as the fulfillment of God's promise (the preface) and emphasize the two natures of Christ.

The feast is in fact a repetition of what has already been celebrated during Advent. It is understandable, however, that the expansion of the Christmas cycle should have led to a desire for a special celebration of this moment in the coming of the Word.

NOTES

[1] C. Charlier, editorial in *Bible et vie chrétienne*, no. 4 (December–February, 1953–54), pp. 3–4.

[2] C. Duquoc, "Acte créateur et humanité de Dieu," *Lumière et vie*, no. 48 (June–August, 1960), p. 88.

[3] Pseudo-Chrysostom, *In Pascha sermones* 2 (*PG* 59:725), quoted by H. de Lubac, *Catholicism*, trans. L. C. Sheppard (New York, 1950), p. 4. The first chapter of de Lubac's book offers numerous citations from the Fathers that make the same point.

[4] See A.-M. Dubarle, *The Biblical Doctrine of Original Sin*, trans. A. M. Stewart (New York, 1965).

[5] J. Guillet, *Themes of the Bible*, trans. A. J. LaMothe, Jr. (Notre Dame, 1960), p. 99.

[6] *Odes of Solomon*, ch. 12; French translation in J. Labourt, "Les Odes de Solomon," *Revue biblique* 7 (1910), p. 493.

[7] See J. Jeremias, "Adam," *TDNT* 1:141–43.

[8] *Quaestiones ex utroque [Testamento] mixtim* 70: *De ieiunio* (*PL* 35:2364).

[9] *Sermo* 206, 2–3 (*PL* 38:1041–42).

[10] *Sermo* 207, 3 (*PL* 38:1044).

[11] *Ibid.*

[12] *Sermo* 39, 6 (*SC* 49bis:77; *CCL* 138A:220).

[13] *Sermo* 40, 5 (*SC* 49bis:91; *CCL* 138A:231).

[14] *Sermo* 41, 3 (*SC* 49bis:99; *CCL* 138A:237).

[15] *Sermo* 43, 4 (*SC* 49bis:127; *CCL* 138A:256).

[16] *Sermo* 47, 3 (*SC* 49bis:169; *CCL* 138A:277).

[17] *Sermo* 48, 4 (*SC* 49bis:179; *CCL* 138A:283).

[18] *Sermo* 49, 5 (*SC* 49bis:191; *CCL* 138A:290).

[19] *Sermo* 50, 3 (*SC* 49bis:201; *CCL* 138A:294).

[20] *Sermo* 211, 1 (*PL* 38:1054).

[21] *Sermo* 211, 2 (*PL* 38:1055).

[22] *Sermo* 208, 2 (*PL* 38:1045).

[23] *Sermo* 205, 3 (*PL* 38:1040).

[24] *Sermo* 39, 6 (*SC* 49bis:77; *CCL* 138A:221).

[25] *Sermo* 41, 3 (*SC* 49bis:97; *CCL* 138A:235).

[26] *Sermo* 43, 4 (*SC* 49bis:127; *CCL* 138A:256).

[27] *Sermo* 48, 5 (*SC* 49bis:179; *CCL* 138A:283).

[28] *Sermo* 49, 6 (*SC* 49bis:193; *CCL* 138A:290).

[29] *Sermo* 40, 4 (*SC* 49bis:87; *CCL* 138A:228).

[30] *Sermo* 42, 2 (*SC* 49bis:103; *CCL* 138A:240).

[31] *Adversus ebriosos et de resurrectione sermo* (*PG* 50:433).

[32] *Sermo* 44, 2 (*SC* 49bis:133; *CCL* 138A:259).

[33] *Sermo* 43, 3 (*SC* 49bis:123; *CCL* 138A:254).

[34] *Sermo* 50, 3 (*SC* 49bis:199; *CCL* 138A:294).

[35] *In Genesim homiliae* 1, 4 (*PG* 53:25).

[36] *Quaestiones ex utroque* [*Testamento*] *mixtim* 70: *De ieiunio* (*PL* 35:2364).

[37] *Sermo* 207, 2 (*PL* 38:1043).

[38] *Sermo* 47, 1 (*SC* 49bis:161; *CCL* 138A:279).

[39] *Sermo* 41, 2 (*SC* 49bis:95; *CCL* 138A:234).

[40] *Sermo* 210, 10–11 (*PL* 38:1052–53).

[41] St. Leo the Great, *Sermo* 49, 3 (*SC* 49bis:187; *CCL* 138A:287).

[42] St. Leo the Great, *Sermo* 48, 1 (*SC* 49bis:173; *CCL* 138A:280).

[43] *St. Benedict's Rule for Monasteries*, trans. L. J. Doyle (Collegeville, Minn., 1948), pp. 65–66.

[44] "Tamen quia paucorum est ista virtus." Cf. St. Leo, *Sermo* 42: "Sed quia haec fortitudo paucorum est" (*SC* 49bis:102; *CCL* 138A:238).

[45] "Omnes pariter et neglegentias aliorum temporum his sanctis diebus diluere." Cf. St. Leo, *Sermo* 39: "Omnes praeteritae desidiae castigantur, omnes neglegentiae diluuntur" (*SC* 49bis:68; *CCL* 138A:214).

[46] "Ergo his diebus augeamus nobis aliquid solito penso servitutis." Cf. St. Leo, *Sermo* 40: "Omnem observantiam nostram ratio istorum dierum poscat augeri," and again: "Ad mensuram consuetudinis nostrae necessariis aliquid addamus augmentis" (*SC* 49bis:78; *CCL* 138A:223).

[47] L. C. Mohlberg (ed.), *Liber sacramentorum romanae aeclesiae ordinis anni circuli (Sacramentarium Gelasianum)* (Rerum ecclesiasticarum documenta, Series maior: Fontes 4; Rome, 1960), no. 53. (Henceforth: Gel. with number of text, e.g., Gel. 53).

[48] See Tertullian, *De praescriptione haereticorum* 1, 3 (*CCL* 1:187).

[49] See *La Tradition Apostolique de saint Hippolyte: Essai de reconstitution*, ed. B. Botte (Liturgiewissenschaftliche Quellen und Forschungen 39; Münster, 1963), chaps. 15–20 (pp. 33–59).

[50] G. Hudon, *La perfection chrétienne d'après les sermons de saint Léon* (Lex orandi 26; Paris, 1959), p. 253. Vatican II's *Dogmatic Constitution on the Church* speaks of the Church as a "sacrament."

Lent used to begin, for the entire Church, on the first Sunday of Lent. This is why on the Wednesday of Quinquagesima (Ash Wednesday), when the fast of public penitents began, the prayer over the gifts in the Gelasian Sacramentary asks that God prepare the faithful "to celebrate the imminent beginning of the holy sacrament [sc., of Lent]" ("venerabilis sacramenti venturum celebramus exordium": Gel. 91).

[51] Gel. 91.

[52] Gel. 104.

[53] Gel. 235.

[54] Opening prayer, Saturday of third week; cf. Gel. 99.

[55] Prayer over the gifts, Thursday of second week.

[56] Opening prayer, Friday of first week.

[57] Opening prayer, Ash Wednesday.

[58] Gel. 138: "Da nobis observantiam, domine, legitimam devotione perfectam."

[59] Gel. 245: "Prosequere, quaesumus, omnipotens deus, ieiuniorum sacra mysteria."

[60] "Annua nobis est, dilectissimi, ieiuniorum celebranda festivitas," in L. C. Mohlberg (ed.), *Sacramentarium Veronense* (Rerum ecclesiasticarum documenta, Series maior: Fontes 1; Rome, 1960), no. 860. (Henceforth: Ver. with number of text, e.g., Ver. 860).

[61] Ver. 209.

[62] This Gospel pericope is read on the first Sunday of Lent, the day that originally signaled the beginning of the Lenten season.

[63] This prayer is from the Verona Sacramentary (no. 207), where it served as the opening prayer for Ember Wednesday after Pentecost.

[64] Ver. 894.

[65] Ver. 927: "Ad hostes nostros, domine, superandos praesta quaesumus ut auxilium tuum ieiuniis tibi placitis et bonis operibus impetremus."

[66] Ver. 864, prayer over the gifts on Ember Saturday in September: ". . . sed cum in ipsis nostris observationibus a noxiis et illicitis non vacamus, non hoc te ieiunium delegisse prophetica voce testaris quoniam non solum prodesse non poterit castigatio corporalis si spiritus noster nefandis cogitationibus implicetur sed hoc constat esse deterius si etiam terrena conditione mitigata mens ab iniquitatibus non quiescit."

[67] H. Küng, *The Council, Reform, and Reunion*, trans. C. Hastings (New York, 1961), pp. 31–32.

[68] The Latin text is from Gel. 104.

[69] Ver. 1313: "Quoniam . . . per observantiae competentis obsequium de perceptis grati numeribus de percipiendis efficimur gratiores."

[70] Ver. 229: ". . . post illos enim laetitiae dies quos in honorem Domini a mortuis resurgentis et in coelos ascendentis exigimus postque perceptum Sancti Spiritus donum necessarie nobis haec ieiunia sancta provisa sunt ut pura conversatione viventibus quae divinitus ecclesiae sunt collata permaneant."

[71] Opening prayer, Monday of first week; cf. Gel. 1170.

[72] Prayer over the gifts, fifth Sunday; cf. Gel. 255.

[73] Gel. 210: "Deus, qui nos formam humilitatis ieiunando et orando Unigeniti tui Domini nostri imitatione docuisti. . . ."

[74] Gel. 178.

[75] See the opening prayer, Ash Wednesday; cf. Gel. 654.

[76] Opening prayer, Monday of second week. A literal translation of the Latin brings out the point more clearly: "God, who bade us chastise our bodies so that our souls might be healed . . ." ("Deus, qui ob animarum medelam castigare precepisti . . ."); cf. Gel. 173.

[77] Prayer over the gifts, Monday of fifth week.

[78] See the opening prayer, Friday of fifth week.

[79] See the prayer over the gifts, Thursday of fifth week.

[80] See the first prayer for the blessing of the ashes: "May they [all who receive these ashes] keep this lenten season in preparation for the joy of Easter." A more literal translation of the Latin would be somewhat fuller: ". . . so that by keeping the Lenten observance they may come with purified minds to celebrate the paschal mystery of your Son" ("ut, quadragesimalem observantiam prosequentes, ad Filii tui paschale mysterium celebrandum purificatis mentibus pervenire mereantur").

[81] Prayer after Communion, Friday of first week. A more literal translation: "Purify us of all that is old, stale, and worn-out in us and lead us to participation in the mystery of salvation" ("a vetustate purgatos, in mysterii salutaris faciat transire consortium").

[82] Cf. Gel. 377.

[83] Cf. Gel. 257.

[84] Prayer after Communion, Tuesday of fourth week, according to the Latin text (which is derived from Gel. 488 or 1225).

[85] The Latin text, literally translated, reads: "May this offering, Lord, purify us of our sins and sanctify the bodies and souls of your faithful so that they may celebrate the paschal feast" ("Haec hostia, Domine, quaesumus, emundet nostra delicta, et ad celebranda festa paschalia fidelium tuorum corpora mentesque sanctificet"). The official English translation reduces the text to: "Lord, make us holy. May this eucharist take away our sins that we may be prepared to celebrate the resurrection."

[86] Gel. 1204.

[87] Gel. 251.

[88] Gel. 129. The adverb "already" implies what would be made more explicit in a literal translation of the Latin text: "God . . . you already give us, even while we are still on earth, a share in heavenly blessings."

[89] An *Ordo* is a document showing in detail the rubrics to be followed in a celebration; as such it is an essential complement to the Sacramentary, which normally contains only the prayers the celebrant needs to say. *Ordo XI* dates from the second half of the

seventh century and evidently is closely related to the Gelasian Sacramentary. It has been edited by M. Andrieu in his *Les Ordines Romani du Haut Moyen Age 2* (Spicilegium Sacrum Lovaniense 23; Louvain, 1948), pp. 380–447. See A. Chavasse, "La discipline romaine des scrutins," *Recherches de science religieuse* 48 (1960), pp. 225–40.

[90] In Luke 10:17-20 we are told of the disciples' amazement at seeing the demons subject to them in the name of Christ.

[91] "You are of your father the devil" (John 8:44).

[92] *Enarrationes in Psalmos* 60, 3 (*CCL* 39:766).

[93] J. Mouroux, *The Meaning of Man*, trans. A. H. G. Downes (New York, 1948), p. 141.

[94] *Breviarium in Psalmos* (*PL* 26:1163).

[95] *De mysteriis* 7, 34 (*SC* 25bis:174).

[96] *Sermo de Transfiguratione* 3 (*SC* 74:17-18; *CCL* 138A:299).

[97] Gel. 286.

[98] For the ritual, see *Rite of Christian Initiation of Adults* (Washington, D.C., 1974).

[99] *Ibid..*, no. 82.

[100] *Ibid.*, no. 83.

[101] *Ibid.*, no. 87. Cf. Gel. 286. [The Latin text in the *Ordo initiationis christianae adultorum* has "gloriae tuae rudimenta," which is here translated as "your initial teachings." Mohlberg's critical edition has "magnitudinis gloriae rudimenta" (i.e., without "tuae"), which Nocent interprets above (see text corresponding to footnote 97) as meaning "the beginning of his (the catechumen's) future great glory." — Tr.]

[102] *Ibid.*

[103] *Ibid.*, no. 95; cf. Gel. 285.

[104] *Ibid.*

[105] *Ibid.*, no. 149; cf. Gel. 287.

[106] *Ibid.*

[107] *Adversus eos qui differunt baptismum oratio* (*PG* 46:417), trans. in J. Daniélou, *The Bible and the Liturgy* (Notre Dame, 1956), p. 22.

[108] *Egeria: Diary of a Pilgrimage*, trans. G. E. Gingras (Ancient Christian Writers 38; New York, 1970), p. 123.

[109] *Homilia in dictum Pauli: Nolo vos ignorare* 4 (*PG* 51:248–49).

[110] *De sacramentis* V, 3 (*SC* 25bis:120–22); cf. *De mysteriis* 8, 48 (*SC* 25bis:183).

[111] *Tractatus in Evangelium Ioannis* 26, 12 (*CCL* 36:265).

[112] *Epist.* 63, 8 (*CSEL* 3:706–7), in J. Daniélou, *From Shadows to Reality: Studies in the Biblical Typology of the Fathers*, trans. W. Hibberd (Westminster, Md., 1960), p. 195.

[113] *Tractatus in Evangelium Ioannis* 15, 6 (*CCL* 36:152).

[114] *Ibid.*, 26, 12 (*CCL* 36:265).

115 See M.-E. Boismard, "Water," in X. Léon-Dufour (ed.), *Dictionary of Biblical Theology*, trans. under the direction of P. J. Cahill (New York, 1967), p. 567.

116 *Rite of Christian Initiation of Adults*, no. 377. In the Latin *Ordo initiationis christianae adultorum*, the prayer is taken directly from the Gelasian Sacramentary (no. 193). It reads, in translation: "Lord, grant that these chosen ones may advance worthily and wisely to the celebration of your praises so that by your glorious power they may be re-established in the pristine dignity they lost through original sin" ("Da, quaesumus, Domine, electis nostris digne atque sapienter ad confessionem tuae laudis accedere, ut dignitate pristina, quam originali transgressione perdiderunt, per tuam gloriam reformentur"); cf. *Ordo*, no. 377.

117 Gel. 291. Text and translation in *Collectio Rituum*, ed. W. J. Schmitz (Milwaukee, 1964), p. 85.

118 Gel. 292; translated in Schmitz, *op. cit.*, p. 87.

119 Gel. 293; translated in Schmitz, *op. cit.*, pp. 103–5.

120 Gel. 298; translated in Schmitz, *op. cit.*, pp. 119–21.

121 *Rite of Christian Initiation of Adults*, no. 164.

122 The Latin original of these prayers is taken over from Gel. 194–98; see *Ordo initiationis christianae adultorum*, no. 377. The English version in the *Rite of Christian Initiation of Adults* is an adaptation of the Latin prayers.

The Gelasian Sacramentary adds an *Oratio super populum* (no. 199): "Lord, your holy family humbly awaits the gift of your mercy. Grant that they may receive from your generous hand what at your bidding they desire."

123 At this point, in the Gelasian Sacramentary (no. 197), though not in the *Ordo* or the *Rite*, it is explicitly stated that the names of the candidates are to be read out. The prayer then continues: "Lord, we ask you to bestow the gift of your Spirit on those who are to be made new in the baptismal font, and thus to prepare them for the full effect of your sacraments."

124 *De sacramentis* III, 12–15 (*SC* 25bis:98–100).

125 *Tractatus in Evangelium Ioannis* 44, 2 (*CCL* 36:382).

126 *Ibid.*, 34, 9 (*CCL* 36:315–16).

127 Gel. 294; translated in Schmitz, *Collectio Rituum* (1964), pp. 93–95, with the same second exorcism for women, pp. 111–13.

128 Gel. 295.

129 *Rite of Christian Initiation of Adults*, no. 171.

130 *Tractatus in Evangelium Ioannis* 49, 12 (*CCL* 36:426).

131 A. Rose, "Les grands évangiles baptismaux du carême romain," *Questions liturgiques et paroissiales* 43 (1962), p. 15.

132 Quoted in Rose, *loc. cit.*, p. 16.

133 *Tractatus in Evangelium Ioannis* 49, 5–6 (*CCL* 36:422).

134 *Commentaria in Ezechielem* 37, 14 (*CCL* 75:515).

[135] *Rite of Christian Initiation of Adults*, no. 178.

[136] Gel. 310.

[137] Gel. 315–18.

[138] Gel. 319–28.

[139] *Rite of Christian Initiation of Adults*, no. 187. The prayer is based on Gel. 298.

[140] See A. Chavasse, "La discipline romaine des scrutins," *Recherches de science religieuse* 48 (1960), pp. 237–38.

[141] *Rite of Christian Initiation of Adults*, no. 192.

[142] Gel. 299–309.

[143] On the Deluge, see J. Daniélou, *The Bible and the Liturgy*, ch. 4: "The Types of Baptism: Creation and the Deluge" (pp. 70–85); *From Shadows to Reality*, Bk. 2, ch. 1: "The Flood, Baptism, and Judgment in Holy Scripture" (pp. 69–84).

[144] Daniélou, *From Shadows to Reality*, p. 82.

[145] *Dialogus cum Tryphone* 138, 1–2 (*PG* 6:793).

[146] *De baptismo* 8 (*SC* 35:77–78).

[147] *Constitutiones Apostolicae* II, 14, 19. The work dates from the second half of the fourth century.

[148] *De Noe et arca* (*CSEL* 22:413–97; *PL* 14:361–416).

[149] *De sacramentis* is a collection of notes taken by a stenographer during Ambrose's catechetical sermons to the newly baptized. *De mysteriis* was written by the Saint himself.

[150] See *De sacramentis* I, 6, 23 (*SC* 25bis:72).

[151] *Ibid.*, III, 1, 1 (*SC* 25bis:75).

[152] *De mysteriis* 10–11 (*SC* 25bis:160–62).

[153] *Commentaria in Evangelium secundum Matthaeum* XV, 23 (*PG* 13:1322).

[154] *De peccatorum meritis et remissione* II, 7, 10, quoted in Mouroux, *The Meaning of Man*, p. 294, n. 142.

[155] *De vita Moysis* (*PG* 44:327).

[156] *De sacramentis* IV, 6, 27 (*SC* 25bis:116).

[157] The text as we have it is the subject of debate among scholars today. See N. Lohfink, "Les dix commandements dans le Sinaï," in his *Sciences bibliques en marche: Un exégète fait le point* (Paris, 1969), pp. 114–27. [This is a translation by H. Savon of Lohfink's *Bibelauslegung im Wandel: Ein Exeget ortet seine Wissenschaft* (Frankfurt, 1967).]

[158] *Homiliae in Exodum* 8, 1 (*PG* 12:350; *SC* 16:184–85).

[159] See C. H. Dodd, *The Interpretation of the Fourth Gospel* (Cambridge, 1953).

[160] See *Egeria: Diary of a Pilgrimage* (ch. 6, n. 19, above).

[161] *Ibid.*, ch. 31, pp. 104–5. The procession starts at Mount Olivet and moves through Jerusalem to the Anastasis, or rotunda church containing the Holy Sepulcher.

162 See J. Ziegler, "Die *Peregrinatio Etheriae* und die hl. Scrift," *Biblica* 12 (1931), pp. 188–89.

163 See A. Baumstark, *Comparative Liturgy*, rev. B. Botte and trans. F. L. Cross (London, 1958), p. 149.

164 On Lent in Spain, see p. 230.

165 See M. Férotin, *Le Liber Ordinum en usage dans l'Eglise Wisogothique et Mozarabe d'Espagne du cinquième au onzième siècle* (Monumenta Ecclesiae Liturgica 5; Paris, 1904), cols. 178–84.

166 *Sermo* 54, 5 (*SC* 74:35; *CCL* 138A:322).

167 The title is found in, e.g., the Gregorian Sacramentary; see J. Deshusses (ed.), *Le sacramentaire grégorien* (Spicilegium Friburgense 16; Fribourg, 1971), n. 312.

168 The Romano-Germanic Pontifical is a collection compiled at Sankt Alban in Mainz in the tenth century. Several individuals seem to have collaborated in the work. The Pontifical has been edited by C. Vogel: *Le Pontifical romano-germanique de dixième siècle* (2 vols.; Studi e testi 226–27; Vatican City, 1963).

169 See Vogel, *op. cit.*, 2:40–54.

170 See M. Andrieu, *Le Pontifical romain au Moyen Age* 1: *Le Pontifical romain du XII*e *siècle* (Studi e testi 86; Vatican City, 1938), pp. 210–14.

171 On all these usages and on the history of Palm Sunday, see H.A.P. Schmidt, *Hebdomada Sancta* (2 vols.; Rome, 1956–57), with an abundant bibliography. See also A.-G. Martimort (ed.), *L'Eglise en prière: Introduction à la liturgie* (Paris, 1961), pp. 711–13. We have frequently had recourse here to the excellent article of P. Jounel, "Le dimanche des Rameaux," *La Maison-Dieu*, no. 68 (1961), pp. 45–63.

172 For the history of the procession, see N. Maurice-Denis Boulet, "Le dimanche des Rameaux," *La Maison-Dieu*, no. 41 (1955), pp. 16–33; H. J. Gräf, *Palmenweihe und Palmenprozession in der lateinischen Liturgie* (Veröffentlichungen des Priesterseminars St. Augustin, Sieberg, 5; Kaldenkirchen, 1959). The *Ordinarium* of the Hospice of St.-Jacques at Melun (13th cent.), for example, gives a detailed description of the procession, which started outside the city gates (Bibliothèque Nationale, Paris, Latin MS. 1206). And see U. Chevalier, *Sacramentaire et martyrologie de l'Abbaye Saint-Remy de Reims* (Paris, 1900), pp. 270–79.

173 See, for example, R. Bloch, "Quelques aspects de la figure de Moïse dans la tradition rabbinique," *Moïse, l'homme de l'Alliance* (Tournai-Paris, 1955), quoted by J. Lécuyer, *Le sacrifice de la Nouvelle Alliance* (Lyons, 1962), p. 98.

174 Qoheleth Rabbah 1, 28 on Qoh. 1:9, quoted in J. Jeremias, "Mōusēs," *TDNT* 4:860.

175 Lécuyer, *op. cit.*, pp. 103–4.

[176] *Sermo* 62, 5 (*SC* 74:77; *CCL* 138A:380–81).

[177] See C. Vogel, "Sin and Penance," in J. Delhaye *et al.*, *Pastoral Treatment of Sin*, trans. C. Schaldenbrand, F. O'Sullivan, and E. Desmarchelier (New York, 1968), pp. 178–79.

[178] St. Polycarp, *Letter to the Philippians* 6, 1 (*PG* 5:1010).

[179] *De paenitentia* 9 (*SC* 35:78).

[180] Gel. 78–83.

[181] Gel. 349–74.

[182] See Vogel, *Le Pontifical romano-germanique du dixième siècle* 2:59–67.

[183] M. Andrieu, *Le Pontifical romain au Moyen-Age* 3: *Le Pontifical de Guillaume Durand* (Studi e testi 88; Vatican City, 1940), pp. 560–69.

[184] The ceremonial presciptions are shortened and paraphrased in our account; the various texts are translated in full.

[185] J. Mouroux, *The Mystery of Time: A Theological Inquiry*, trans. J. Drury (New York, 1964), pp. 254–55.

[186] *Expositio Evangelii secundum Lucam* V, 92 (*SC* 45:216; *CCL* 14:164).

[187] See A. Chavasse, *Etude sur l'onction des infirmes dans l'Eglise latine du IIIe au XIe siècle* 1: *Du IIIe siècle à la réforme carolingienne* (Lyons, 1942); Schmidt, *Hebdomada Sancta* 2:727–28.

[188] See, for example, Schmidt, *op. cit.*, 2:738, 734–36.

[189] See, for example, A. Chavasse, "A Rome, le jeudi saint au VIIe siècle d'après un vieil Ordo romain," *Revue d'histoire ecclésiastique* 50 (1955), pp. 21–35; idem, *Le sacramentaire gélasien: Vaticanus Reginensis* 316: *Sacramentaire presbytéral en usage dans les titres romain au viie siècle* (Tournai, 1958), pp. 126–37. The two opposed views on the origin of the prayers are related to the positions taken on the origin and use of the Gelasian Sacramentary. Chavasse regards it as a book composed at Rome for use in the presbyteral churches of the city; Schmidt considers it to be a compilation of various Roman *libelli* which made their way to Gaul in the sixth century and to which Gallican and other formularies were added.

[190] The Würzburg Epistolary (ca. 560–90), ed G. Morin, "Le plus ancien lectionnaire de l'Eglise Romaine," *Revue bénédictine* 27 (1910), pp. 41–74. For its history, see C. Vogel, *Introduction aux sources de l'histoire du culte chrétien au Moyen Age* (Biblioteca degli "Studi Medievali" 1; Spoleto, n.d. [1965]), pp. 309–10, 313–14, 321–25.

[191] The Würzburg Evangeliary (ca. 645), a pure Roman document; see Vogel, *op. cit.*, pp. 313–14.

[192] The Murbach Lectionary, composed at Murbach, France, toward the end of the eighth century; it was later followed at Rome,

and the Missal of Pius V (1570) makes extensive use of it. Edition: A. Wilmart, "Le Comes de Murbach," *Revue bénédictine* 30 (1913), pp. 23–69. See Vogel, *op. cit.*, pp. 318–19.

[193] The Evangeliary of Aquileia (8th cent.); see Vogel, *op. cit.*, p. 298.

[194] Liturgy of Benevento, as reflected in the Comes of Naples; see Vogel, *op. cit.*, p. 306.

[195] A. Paredi (ed.), *Sacramentarium Bergomense* (Monumenta Bergomensia 6; Bergamo, 1962); see Vogel, *op. cit.*, pp. 301–2.

[196] M. Ceriani (ed.), *Missale Ambrosianum Vetus* (Monumenta Sacra et Profana 8; Milan, 1912); see Vogel, *loc. cit.*

[197] "Per Christum Dominum nostrum. In qua ieiunantium fides alitur, spes provehitur, caritas roburatur. Ipse enim panis verus et vivus, qui est substantia aeternitatis, esca virtutis. Verbum enim tuum, per quod facta sunt omnia, non solum humanarum mentium sed ipsorum quoque panis est angelorum. Huius panis alimento Moyses famulus tuus quadraginta diebus ac noctibus legem suscipiens ieiunavit et a carnalibus cibis, ut suavitatis capacior esset abstinuit. Unde nec famem corporis sensit et terrenarum oblitus escarum est. Quia illum et gloriae tuae clarificabat aspectus et influente spiritu Dei sermo pascebat. Hunc panem etiam nobis ministrare non desinas, quem ut indeficienter esuriamus hortaris Iesum Christum" (*Sacramentarium Bergomense*, p. 100).

[198] "Per Christum Dominum nostrum, qui ad insinuandum humilitatis suae mysterium fatigatus resedit ad puteum et a muliere samaritana aquae sibi petiit porrigi potum qui in ea creaverat fidei donum" (*Sacramentarium Bergomense*, p. 110).

[199] "Qui peccantium non vis animas perire sed culpas et peccantes non semper continuo iudicas sed ad poenitentiam provocatos expectas. Averte quaesumus a nobis quam meremur iram et quam optamus super nos effunde clementiam. Ut sacro purificati ieiunio electorum tuorum adscisci mereamur collegio" (*Sacramentarium Bergomense*, p. 123).

[200] Bobbio Epistolary. A Vatican manuscript from northern Italy (6th–7th cent.) gives a marginal list (8th cent.) of readings from Paul for Advent to Holy Saturday; the list is called the "Bobbio List" or "Bobbio Epistolary." See Vogel, *op. cit.*, pp. 292–93.

[201] Bobbio Missal: eighth century, preserved at Paris. Edition: E. J. Lowe and J. W. Legg, *The Bobbio Missal* 1: *Facsimile*; 2: *Text* (Henry Bradshaw Society 53 and 58; London, 1917, 1920). See Vogel, *op. cit.*, p. 293.

[202] Sélestat Lectionary, in two states. I = a Merovingian lectionary (ca. 700) from northern Italy; partial edition in G. Morin, "Un lectionnaire mérovingien de Sélestat avec fragments du texte occidental des Actes," *Revue bénédictine* 25 (1908), pp. 161–66, reprinted in *Etudes, Textes, Documents* 1 (Maredsous, 1913), pp.

404-56. The readings given run from Advent to Good Friday; see Vogel, *op. cit.*, p. 292. II = a fragment of a lectionary from Sélestat (also ca. 700 and from northern Italy), giving readings from Advent to the second Sunday of Lent; see Morin, *art. cit.*, p. 166; Vogel, *loc. cit.*

203 Evangeliary of St. Kilian. Marginal notes (7th and 9th cent.) in a text of the four Gospels; edited by G. Morin, *Revue bénédictine* 28 (1911), pp. 328-30. See P. Salmon, "Les système des lectures liturgiques contenues dans les notes marginales du ms. M. p. th. Q. Ia de Wurzbourg," *Revue bénédictine* 61 (1951), pp. 38-53; 62 (1952), pp. 294-96; Vogel, *op. cit.*, p. 294.

204 Evangeliary of Trier. 125 marginal notes (8th cent.) in an eighth-century manuscript; see Vogel, *op. cit.*, p. 295.

205 M. Férotin (ed.), *Le Liber mozarabicus sacramentorum et les manuscrits arabes* (Monumenta Ecclesiae Liturgica 6; Paris, 1912).

206 Toledo Missal. Really a lectionary (or more exactly a *Liber commicus*) from the ninth to tenth centuries; see Vogel, *op. cit.*, p. 303.

207 Toledo Lectionary. A fragmentary manuscript from the end of the ninth century; see Vogel, *op. cit.*

208 Silos Lectionary. From before 1041/1067, Abbey of Silos; see Vogel, *op. cit.*, p. 302.

209 San Millàn Lectionary. Written in 1073 for the Church of San Millàn; see Vogel, *op. cit.*, p. 304.

210 *Liber mozarabicus sacramentorum*, pp. 166-212.

211 "Ideo igitur, etsi fatigatus ille in carne, non tamen nos sinit infirmari in sua infirmitate. Nam quod infirmum est illius fortius est hominibus: ideoque per humilitatem veniens eripere mundum a potestate tenebrarum, sedit et sitivit quando aquam petivit. Ille enim humiliatus in carne, quando sedens ad puteum loquebatur cum muliere. Sitivit aquam, et exegit fidem ab ea. In ea quippe muliere fidem quam quasivit quamque petiit, exegit: atque venientibus dicit de ea discipulis: "Ego cibum habeo manducare quem vos nescitis." Ille iam qui in ea creaverat fidei donum, ipse poscebat aquae sibi ab ea porrigi potum: quique eam dilectionis suae flamma cremabat, ipse ab ea poculum quo refrigeraretur sitien postulabat" (*Liber mozarabicus sacramentorum*, p. 168).

212 "Qui illuminatione suae fidei tenebras expulit mundi et fecit illos esse gratiae qui tenebantur sub legis iusta damnatione. Qui ita in iudicium in hunc mundum venit ut non videntes viderent, et videntes caeci essent; qualiter et ii qui in se tenebras confitentur errorum perciperent lumen aeternum, per quod carerent tenebris delictorum; et ii qui de meritis suis arroganter lumen in semetipsos habere se iustitiae estimabant, in se ipsos merito tenebrescent, qui elati superbia sua et de iustitia confisi propria; ad sanandum

Medicum non quaerebant" (*Liber mozarabicus sacramentorum*, pp. 180–81).

[213] "Cuius nos gratia liberavit a pondere legis, et fecit filios suae adoptionis. Qui ad suscitandum veniens Lazarum, "Tollite lapidem," clamabat, ut pressuram auferret ab eo damnationis, quem iam fetidum reddiderat horrenda actio supulchralis. Tollite, Iesus ait, ab eo pondus legis, quod eum deprimit in morte; ut succurrat illi gratia vocis meae. Gratia quippe Dei est cum vocem eius audivimus, ut cum Lazaro rectis Iesum gressibus adsequamur" (*Liber mozarabicus sacramentorum*, pp. 210–11).

ABBREVIATIONS

AAS	*Acta Apostolicae Sedis*
CCL	*Corpus Christianorum, Series Latina.* Turnhout, 1953–.
CL	*Constitution on the Sacred Liturgy*
CSEL	*Corpus Scriptorum Ecclesiasticorum Latinorum.* Vienna, 1866–
Flannery	*Vatican Council II: The Conciliar and Post Conciliar Documents,* Austin Flannery, O.P., General Editor. Collegeville, Minn., 1975
LH	*Liturgy of the Hours*
PG	*Patrologia Graeca,* ed. J. P. Migne. Paris, 1857–66
PL	*Patrologia Latina,* ed. J. P. Migne. Paris, 1844–64
SC	*Sources Chrétiennes.* Paris, 1942–
TPS	*The Pope Speaks.* Washington, 1954–
TDNT	*Theological Dictionary of the New Testament.* Grand Rapids, 1964–74